With Robert Lowell
and His Circle

KATHLEEN

SPIVACK

With Robert Lowell
& *His Circle*

SYLVIA PLATH,

ANNE SEXTON,

ELIZABETH BISHOP,

STANLEY KUNITZ,

AND OTHERS

Northeastern University Press
Boston

NORTHEASTERN UNIVERSITY PRESS
An imprint of University Press of New England
www.upne.com
© 2012 Kathleen Spivack
All rights reserved
Manufactured in the United States of America
Designed by Eric M. Brooks
Typeset in Arno Pro by A. W. Bennett, Inc.

University Press of New England is a member of the
Green Press Initiative. The paper used in this book meets
their minimum requirement for recycled paper.

For permission to reproduce any of the material in this
book, contact Permissions, University Press of New England,
One Court Street, Suite 250, Lebanon NH 03766; or visit
www.upne.com

Library of Congress Cataloging-in-Publication Data
Spivack, Kathleen.
With Robert Lowell and his circle: Sylvia Plath, Anne Sexton,
Elizabeth Bishop, Stanley Kunitz, and others / Kathleen Spivack.
    p.   cm.
Includes bibliographical references.
ISBN 978-1-55553-788-3 (pbk.: alk. paper)—
ISBN 978-1-55553-765-4 (ebook: alk. paper)
1. Spivack, Kathleen. 2. Poets, American—20th century—
Biography. 3. American poetry—Massachusetts—Boston—
History and criticism. I. Title.
PS3569.P56Z46   2012
811'.54—dc23
[B]   2012027775

5 4 3 2 1

TO PETER DRUCKER & DORIS DRUCKER,
whose talents, courage, resourcefulness, love of life,
strong opinions!, zest for ideas, hard work, originality,
gutsy spirits, gifts of surprise, fun, family, friendship,
and relationship inspired us and forever shaped our
lives. Thank you.

Contents

Acknowledgments

Thank You

To the writers cited in this book, first of all: their words, their
generosity, the journey, the adventure!

To modern American poetry experts: Laura Jehn Menides, Steven
Gould Axelrod, Thomas Travisano, Alice Quinn, Carolyn French,
and to my editor, Richard Pult.

To the Robert Lowell, Elizabeth Bishop, and Stanley Kunitz
Societies. To Lois Ames.

To the journals and magazines that published parts of this work
when it was still in progress.

To the MacDowell Colony, Yaddo, Ragdale, Dorset House. To
Elizabeth Morse, Marilyn Rinzler.

To Kathryn Deputat, Connie Brown, Anne Hoffman, Bridget Nault,
and Lisa Tandy.

In the Boston area, to Louisa Solano, Ifeanyi and Carol Menkiti, the
Grolier Poetry Bookshop, The Bagel Bards.

To Elena Dodd, Marlaina Nugent, Meredeth Turshen, Kate Frank,
Abigail Adler, Judith Steinbergh. Also to Tony Priano, Barbara
Waldorf.

In France, to Jacques Pothier, Odile Hellier, Claire Bruyere, George
and Sylvia Whitman, Dominique Masson, Laurence Fosse,
Virginia Larner, Rosalie Footnick, Tama Carroll, Adrian Leeds,
Patricia LaPlante Collins, David Barnes, Colin Dixon, Paul Volsik,
and special thanks to Jean-Pierre Ledoux. Also to the Village
Voice Bookshop and to Shakespeare and Company.

To Robert and Gail Melson, Cecilia Wolloch, Hazel Rowley,
Anya Achtenberg, Diana Norma Szokolai, Barry and Lorrie
Goldensohn, Paula Phipps, Nadia Stevens, Margot Berdeshevsky,
Rosary O'Neill, Doug Holder, Sam Cornish, Harris Gardner,
Elizabeth Doran, Lee Bartell, Karen Sharpe, Ruth Hanham, Sajed
and Rosie Kamal, Steve Glines, Hannelore Hahn, Phil Helfaer.

With special thanks to the writers who lived this Lowell-Bishop
time, many of whom have written their own works about the
experience. Thank you for generously sharing your insights

Acknowledgments

through essays, personal letters, poems, and interviews: James
Atlas, Judith Baumel, Frank Bidart, Caroline Blackwood, William
Corbett, Jonathan Galassi, Grey Gowrie, Elizabeth Hardwick,
Alice Ryerson Hayes, Fanny Howe, Donald Junkins, Robert
Pinsky, Roger Rosenblatt, Stephen Sandy, Lloyd Schwartz, Anne
Sexton, Richard Tillinghast, Helen Vendler, Andrei Voznesensky,
Alan Williamson.

To Vincent Drucker, Cecily Drucker, Joan Drucker Winstein, Bruce
Winstein. To Mayer Spivack, Nova Spivack, Marin Spivack, who
unify this narrative.

To Joseph Murray, creator of beauty and peace. Thank you for
believing in and encouraging this project.

To the Reader

I might have called this book *Labor of Love*. For that is what it has been: a labor of love. I first started to write down some of my memories about Robert Lowell and his circle during a period when my oldest child, then fourteen years old, was in a children's hospital.

There was a preliminary list of topics I wanted to write about, episodic and sometimes simultaneous, like memory itself. I wrote in the brief interludes that were available to me at that time: in the hospital family waiting areas where, afraid and alone, I passed the days and nights. Whenever I had a moment, I scribbled down memories of happier days.

I had been with Robert Lowell since 1959. My long-term intimate friendship with Robert Lowell and other poets of his time, those happy totally absorbing hours, seemed the furthest thing that I could think of from what I was living then. I had been privileged to be a witness to deeply committed poets and to how they approached their work. Trying to remember as much as I could, I realized I had to choose to write about only what I knew, what I had actually observed and lived with the writers. Much has been written about the poets. But I had occupied a unique vantage point. In my mind, I took the photographs.

Later, putting together this book, or rather, trying to choose what was most important, made me smile, especially when I thought of what I was leaving out! I worked on the book for years. An urgency drove me, kept me working, writing, revising. I wanted to give the flavor of the times, the experience, put it down exactly as I had seen it: before I died — and history and memory died with me. The project found me: insisted. It would not let me go.

I am older now than were the poets in this book and have had plenty of time to reflect on my experiences and what they meant. Meanwhile, the young poets who lived with me in the book and the times went on to realize their early promise. Subsequent scholarly and revelatory work that has come out continues to inform our understanding.

To the Reader

Often, as I was writing and revising this book about Robert Lowell and the poets around him, I felt impatient. It was taking so much time. I wanted to get back to what I thought of as "my *real* work": my own creative writing. Then I realized that this book had become a part of my "real work": living, loving, writing it down — and trying to make sense of it all.

With Robert Lowell
and His Circle

Introduction

In January 1959 I came to Boston on an undergraduate fellowship to study with poet Robert Lowell as an alternative to my senior year at college. That single act changed my life. I worked with Robert Lowell both privately, in tutorial at his house on Marlborough Street, and in a class with others who were in the first bloom of their careers. As my poems and friendships with these poets set their roots, I continued to work with and to be associated with him until his death in 1977. At the time of this writing, I am one of the very few writers still around from that period.

He gave me formal letters of introduction to Sylvia Plath, Anne Sexton, Adrienne Rich, and other older women poets of the time. He introduced me to Bill Alfred and Stanley Kunitz, as well as to the British poets Jonathan Griffin and Basil Bunting. These became deep poetic friendships. I met Elizabeth Bishop through him.

He asked me to come to his house on Marlborough Street two or three times a week, during which occasions he would read poems aloud to me, and "we" — I would not have dared say a word — would discuss them. Afterwards there were long teatimes at the Lowells' house. Lowell became *in loco parentis* for me in many ways. I spent a lot of time there and also used the Lowells' home as my fake mailing address when I was living with my boyfriend, whom I later married. Lowell was my friend and champion in all this, took me and my husband under his wing, and went to see my parents, who opposed the marriage. We developed a lifelong friendship.

My parents, Peter and Doris Drucker, were refugee intellectuals who had come to the States in 1938. They had friends from every stage of their travels. Many were old-style European intellectuals also — mathematicians, musicians, scientists, artists, economists — who had found a foothold in English-speaking countries.

We four children lived a family-centered life in an enclosed and protected world. It was easy and comfortable for me to be with my parents' friends, eminent though they may have been to outsiders. Many of them also had children our ages. I made friends easily, even from the age of three, and have kept my close friends all my life while making new ones too. "Friend" is a special word, much misused, but if you read this, you will understand the depth of that word and concept.

When I ask myself, writing from this vantage point, how it was that I was able to feel so comfortable and at home with Robert Lowell and the other poets at such a young age, it was probably my experience within the family, our confidence in friendship that made it possible and easy. I might have been timid at first with some of these poets and their hospitality, but I never questioned my place in it, my own personal goodwill and kindness, and the reciprocal nature I brought to these relationships. I loved good conversation but was comfortable with silence too. Like my mother, I liked to cook and invite people. Friendship and social ease were in my nature, or perhaps a gift at my birth from some fantasy fairy godmother. "Kathleen will get along with everybody. . . . She'll always feel at home." I never questioned it. "Friendship" was a Drucker family trait (along with bad knees), and I had inherited both. I was in a direct genetic line, it seemed from my father, but also from my paternal grandfather.

In tutorial sessions Lowell talked to me about issues both personal and professional. I came alive poetically, and flowered in this unique circumstance. I found myself able to laugh and talk freely with him. My private friendship with the man and the more public persona were two different things. When Lowell moved to New York, and then was offered a job at Harvard, he'd ask me to sit in while he personally chose the students for his classes, spend afternoons in long postmortems of the classes, and sometimes go out with him and his friends in the evenings. Later, when Elizabeth Bishop came to Harvard, Lowell introduced me and asked me to look out for her, since she didn't know many people in the area. I visited her a couple of times a week, played Ping-Pong, had long lunches, and spent late afternoons there too. She introduced me to Octavio Paz and his wife, and I played tennis with Paz's wife, Marie-Jo.

Lowell was then married to Elizabeth Hardwick. Later he married Caroline Blackwood, with much public airing of guilt and recrimination. This added a new facet, as Caroline was somewhat near my age. It took a new turn. Our two youngest children, Marin Spivack and Robert Sheridan Lowell, were born at more or less the same time. When Lowell and Caroline were in Boston during his later years at Harvard, our two families got together in the afternoons with the children, in Brookline or my house in Watertown, so that was another surprising and domestic part of the friendship entirely. I never expected to be part of a young children's "playgroup" with "Mr. Lowell." But Lowell at that point did not know many other friends with young children; he had passed through that stage once already long ago.

Often I was invited to the Lowell household on Sunday mornings when they were in residence in the Boston area. (This took place over the almost twenty years I knew him.) Blissful Sunday mornings! We would all lounge around near or on the bed; I would think "Tamed by Miltown . . .";[1] and Lowell would drink quantities of thick milk straight from the carton and take Antabuse, a drug that was supposed to make you nauseous if you drank alcohol with it. And then he would drink alcohol. He would read poetry aloud to whoever happened to be the current wife and to me, and discourse on it. "Discussions" of poetry with Cal, as his close friends called him, were rather one-sided; his questions were rhetorical, and often too brilliant for me to have anything to add or ask. By unspoken agreement we were allowed to say yes and no and *How brilliant Cal, I never knew that,* but he did all the reading aloud and investigating.

Lowell encouraged an unusually large number of poets: his contemporaries as well as younger students. He was committed to his students' development and shared his poetry journey with them. The loyalty he inspired and the impact of his life and work on students and friends can be seen in the picture of American literature today. Nearly all of Robert Lowell's friends, wives, and students were writers. Obsessed, he conveyed a sense of the central importance of poetry, and alternately scolded, prodded, encouraged, ignored, protected, and pitted his students and friends against each other to ensure their development. Writers flocked from all over to work with him.

It was not so much what he said about someone's work that made an impact, but rather what he showed in his approach to the literature of the past, as well as his compulsive attention to his own multiple drafts and revisions. Although my friendship with him covers only one period in his life — Robert Lowell in his middle and late years in Boston — it is important to look at how Lowell communicated his zest for poetry.

To a young woman arriving in Boston from the Midwest, some of the social aura surrounding Lowell was overwhelming. For the most part, our friendship existed outside of that ambience. I enjoyed his poetry, good conversation, and laughter. During the course of almost twenty years together, our intimacy, which had been there from the beginning, grew. We had long walks and late afternoon tea and private moments. We shared a belief that poetry was the central thing in life. Like other writers, I was struck by the penetrating power of his mind. But there were darker glints to the man, too, and I have tried to voice my impressions of these.

During this period the social context surrounding women writers changed. I came to know the women poets I met through Robert Lowell, and observed with a special keenness those gifted women writers older than myself: Sylvia Plath, Anne Sexton, Maxine Kumin (who was Anne Sexton's friend), Adrienne Rich, and Elizabeth Bishop. The term "role model" had not entered the vernacular, but I was nevertheless interested. I saw these women's gifts and wondered how and where the parts of my own life passions would arrange themselves. Although I felt the difficulties of being both a woman and a writer, I was younger and bridged a new historical reality. The "women's movement" was beginning, and the recognition of women as serious writers was becoming possible. One did not have to be labeled "crazy" in order to write. Women could be heard.

For some of the women poets, this validation came too late. Many of the poets of Lowell's era, the men as well as the women, ended their lives in suicide and/or madness. It is encouraging to note that this has been less true for successive generations of poets.

Robert Lowell, singular among poetry teachers of his day, supported and furthered the careers of all who studied with him and was unique in validating women writers. I was fortunate to be among this group. He was a part of major decisions in terms of my work. He knew my marriage, knew my family and children, as well as my poetry. And such friendship was reciprocal. I became more aware of issues having to do with poetic survival, and especially of survival, or the obverse — the lack of it — among women poets.

It was a pivotal moment for American poetry, a convergence of political and personal history. The idea of what could be said in a poem was changing. I saw gifted poets, of my generation and older, engaged together in the work of making poems. Discussing poems. Rewriting. And under Lowell's wing, a protégé, I was able both to participate in and to observe the process.

During this period, the country rocketed abruptly from the late '50s through the upheavals of the '60s and '70s, the Cold War, civil rights and other liberation movements, and the Vietnam War. Literature — especially on the East and West Coasts — was infused with these events. But doom and gloom were not the prevailing atmosphere; could not be. The "post-modern period" — so dubbed — was not the ponderous literary moment one reads about in books.

Writing and reading poetry were fascinating, fun! It was a source of passionate interest, an endless mystery to puzzle out, like pure mathematics. One couldn't wait to wake up, get to one of Lowell's classes, and see what would happen next. It was theater: there was always something to learn. Meanwhile, we were writing, rewriting, talking about it, and reading too.

This memoir is an attempt to look at Lowell's strengths as poet and teacher, as well as at some of the outstanding poetic personalities surrounding him. Its focus is, one hopes, to catch the spirit in which poetry is written and, as Lowell showed, is transmitted, and taught. It is also an attempt to recreate a time and a place, a kind of Golden Age of contemporary American poetry that has proved formative for so many writers now prominent in American letters today.

This book is in no way to be taken as a biography of Lowell, nor of the other poets within its pages. It is a personal memoir, a subjective recounting of an important historical and literary period and some of the people in it. It is a story about two people, a student and a teacher, about their long-term relationship, and about the meaning of poetry in their lives.

Although this book is mostly about Robert Lowell and the other poets I admired so much, in it lives the author as well: a young woman, at first a student, sometimes confident and often overwhelmed, actor and observer; struggling, writing, and moving toward her own realization as a person and poet.

Long afternoons engaged in conversations, long silences too. Our "real lives" were a backdrop to this shared companionship. Through the lifelong act of looking at poems together came inquiry and tenderness and listening. There was humor, revelation, sympathy of mind, and understanding. And there was to be, already written into this period, of course, as in any story of unconscious and unfolding happiness, the deep contralto undercurrents: *love,* and her twin sister, *loss.*

The "Family"

I was the oldest of four children. Our parents came to the United States in 1938. My father was Peter Drucker, the economist. He had left Vienna, gone to work at a newspaper in Frankfurt, and was forced to leave in 1933. He first went to England. My mother, Doris Schmitz, had met my father briefly while she was studying international law at the University of Frankfurt, where he was a teaching assistant. She went on to work at the Hague for the League of Nations in international law. She also left and went to London when Hitler came to power. There, to their surprise, they re-met each other on the up and down escalators in Harrods department store. My grandmother massively disapproved, but they lived together anyway. My mother has written about this in her own memoir, *Invent Radium or I'll Pull Your Hair.*[2]

Peter and Doris stayed and worked in London. Eventually our father was sent to America to write a series of newspaper articles on U.S. attitudes preceding entry into World War II. At that time my parents decided to marry, and they sold their wedding gift, a complete set of the *Encyclopædia Britannica,* to pay my mother's shipboard passage. That is how they arrived in New York. They already knew they would not go back.

I was born soon after, family lore had it, on a fire engine during the hurricane of '38. Struggling with joblessness, after managing to get much of the "family" out of Europe, my parents settled in Vermont. My father had been offered a modest, not quite full-time faculty position at Bennington College, teaching comparative religion. My paternal grandparents lived with us much of this time until my grandfather also got a university position. He ended his days at the University of California in Berkeley. My mother took care of her parents, whom she managed to get out of Germany. They were living sometimes with us and sometimes in England. Nevertheless, we lost family in the extermination camps of Europe. Our parents never spoke of this in front of us, not once.

Our mother kept the family going; she managed our victory garden, sewed all our clothes, cooked and canned and bottled, baked bread, and made maple syrup from the Vermont trees. At one point, she made sauerkraut. The barrels where the cabbage was fermenting exploded, and for months we were picking cabbage shreds out of the nearby apple orchard. In the midst of this she managed to get a master's degree in physics. She continued to work and follow her intellectual interests, and showed us that it was normal for women to have both a career and a family without seeming conflict. She also took time to encourage my creative interests. She was the person I most admired.

The parents embraced America — with its tolerance and freedom. They gave us Anglophone names. They fell in love with baseball, though it was my mother who tried to get my brother and myself interested in pitching, catching, and batting.

My brother Vincent was my best friend. We were terrified of sports that involved things being thrown in our direction, and ran away from the ball! Patiently, "Fa," who couldn't even see a flying object, he was so nearsighted, tried to play "catcher." Baseball was the national sport, our parents insisted. They wanted us to fit in. They put up a basketball net. But they also sat with us for hours over homework or as we practiced our music. They were, and still are, the most amazing people I have ever met.

It was a refugee story. They would shelter their children. Now piecing together a life, they were hopeful. My parents had no self-pity, ever. They helped countless others escape from Europe. My father was very involved with the International Rescue Committee and also with Care, two organizations that helped refugees. We overheard a lot about DP camps too.

Peter Drucker, who seemed mild at home, was a powerful force: on the one hand an authoritarian, on the other a pussycat. My mother was strong on the authoritarian side, but with a wonderful eye for human interest and detail and humor. They approached life with enthusiasm.

My father had written several books already, both in Germany and in England, about history and political theory. The Druckers were curious and interested in everything. They took their children everywhere to see this country. We went to Washington, DC, and observed government in action. We climbed the Green Mountains, the White Mountains, and the Rocky Mountains in Colorado too. We went to New York to see art and stood at the opera. We had a chronic case of "museum feet." But *they* were tireless.

Our father made sure we saw industrial America. We traveled with him to the Pittsburgh steel mills and to the assembly line at the Ford Motor Company. At Ford he witnessed "automation" and starting investigating and writing about the practical issues of management. Suddenly his work caught on. Before we knew it, our modest, curious, fun-loving father became an "icon." This was hard on the family, as we unexpectedly had to cope with outsiders' views of the "public" person, while our private "Fa" continued to behave like the person we knew. In the later part of his life, Peter Drucker became fed up with what he termed corporate greed. He decided to devote his work to advising nonprofit organizations. Having moved to Claremont College, he taught management there, but also, his passion, Japanese art.

Our parents had a graciousness that extended to friends. They entertained a lot: students, colleagues, and other associates. Yet we were a close family unit, spending our evenings at home doing our homework, reading, or playing chess. We put on plays and puppet shows (my mother made all the puppets, the costumes, the little theater, everything). We played music. With the other few faculty kids around us, my brother and I were an irrepressible duo, lugging our younger sisters with us.

After my father died, we "sibs" and my mother were reminiscing. My sisters thought we should discuss any remaining "issues" we might have. This was hard, because whenever we remembered Peter Drucker it was with some funny little vignette or incident. We basically drew a blank — until my youngest sister, Joan, confessed "an issue." She complained that all one summer, she had been forced to stand at attention while we played "Coronation." I had been much taken with "Lilibet," now Queen Elizabeth II, and the grandeur of the event. We played and replayed the event obsessively. I, of course, was "Lilibet." My brother played the role of Archbishop of Canterbury. This meant that he got to wear our father's dressing gown, to "crown me" (over and over) and then, to the amusement of all of us, had to scuttle out backwards on all fours. My sister, Cecily, with curly blonde hair, was "Margaret." But Joan, being the youngest, had to be "A Page." Her role: to stand at attention all summer long holding a butter knife — nothing sharp! — while the rest of us swanned about being royalty.

I was already writing, and putting on more elaborate musicals and plays with my siblings and friends. The family encouraged all this even though my mother tried hard to steer us into math and science, her specialties. The "family" had prepared me for eccentricity, ease, and humor. But I had a special emotional closeness with my father.

In the early years of his coming to this country, "Fa" had had lots of time to spend with me, his oldest child — he was trying to find work, but as a

Doris and Peter Drucker.

refugee it was difficult — and so he spent hours with me, reading aloud, discussing books, and generally enjoying time together. By the age of three I knew I would be a writer. I wanted to live forever in the world of books. This was my pattern with him life long. He was my closest person, and also the person I had to rebel against the most to become myself.

In the evenings, as the privileged "oldest" I often lay on the bed with my mother and father, everyone with his or her nose in a book, or my father reading aloud to us. So the pattern, continued with Lowell (and Elizabeth Hardwick or Caroline Blackwood), was totally familiar. I adored my father, fought like mad to have a separate identity, and to this day treasure him as my soul mate.

Our parents had high expectations for us. And although my father wasn't so famous when I was growing up, his later fame cast a shadow, especially on the younger children. But even then, teachers reproved us when we didn't do well, and I deliberately flunked subjects like economics in college.

Outside of the family, or so it seemed to me then, I had no confidence. I was shy, tongue-tied, terrified of making a wrong decision or of being late to something. We couldn't take a bus or train without our father giving us elaborate directions and then meeting us at the station. The family joke was that he was always three hours early, for fear of missing a plane or train. His favorite reading was actually airplane timetables! We teased him about it. Peter Drucker made all the important decisions for me. He was also the one who comforted me through little crises.

Even up to his last years, whenever one of his daughters felt depressed — or even if we didn't — we liked to go and sit on his lap while he patted us rather abstractly and muttered "there there" in his heavy Viennese accent. We confessed to each other that as he grew older we tried to not put our entire weight on his feeble little knees. But we felt soothed by his voice, even if he could no longer really hear ours.

As a child, I brought my homework into his study where he was writing. Lying on my stomach on the scratchy rug, I pored over my schoolbooks. At one point, I had become entranced with medieval costumes and especially what the men wore — i.e., those mysterious tights and codpieces! My term project for my seventh-grade social studies class was called "Costumes through the Ages." Mostly it involved drawing pictures of lords and ladies in fancy dress. But my drawings got worse and worse, and I soon got tired of all those codpieces and bustles. With good humor, "Fa" left his typewriter, got down on the floor with tracing paper and books and helped me finish the project. He typed it too, somewhere in between grading papers and writing his articles and the newest book.

The next year I chose something more serious, "Common Diseases of Mankind." I wanted to impress my biology teacher. But reading the *Merck Manual*, my one research source for this paper, made me so sick that I had to stop. "In your own words, Kathleen," my father admonished. He sat at his typewriter waiting to take dictation. I lay on his scruffy rough study rug clutching my head and stomach, and tried to paraphrase the contents of the book, wondering how to use my own words on a disease like "The Black Plague." I suffered every symptom in the book in the course of doing the paper. My father laughed.

When I had to decide which college to attend — Oberlin or Swarthmore — it was a major crisis. My father "didn't know!" Making my own decisions was a revelation for me.

Much as I adored him, I needed to get away from home. I couldn't wait to change my name from Drucker, so that no one could accuse me of "using his influence" to succeed. And I chose to become a writer, the "least competitive" occupation. (Or so I thought — *dream on dream on*!) And poetry especially was a code-language, which no one in the "family" would really understand, especially in English. Poetry was discovery, it was sanctioned betrayal: the real "toads in imaginary gardens." It concealed, in elegant form, a world of turbulent emotions. Secretive, I hid myself in music and in books, with friends and with my boyfriends, whose chief merit often lay in the fact that they had "never heard of my father." As a result of my father's growing reputation, and all the hangers-on, the "Drucker-Fuckers," as I termed them, I wanted to live as privately as possible.

During a later identity crisis I joked with my future husband, Mayer Spivack, that he should change his name to "Raul de Montmorency"; it sounded much more noble, I thought. We laughed about it. "Spivack," why, that had almost the same clunky sound as the name "Drucker." It was not at all poetic. I was reading all about Rilke and a fascinating woman, Lou Andreas-Salome. She had been analyzed by Freud. Then I realized that "Drucker" meant "printer, or book maker," and "Spivack" meant "singer of songs." What great names for a poet-to-be! For a short while I put my full name on the manuscripts and on our mailbox too; "Kathleen Romola Drucker-Spivack." It sounded, I thought, appropriately Germanic and important. I loved that hyphen! But the name was too long to fit on the mailbox.

Nevertheless, owing to my father's scope and intellectual vision, as well as his warmth and love, I was very comfortable with "genius" and had a deep appreciation for it. In the public sphere, my father had a brilliance of mind and an ability to synthesize historical and political events with his current observations of what was happening. His writing and speeches were clear, direct, pragmatic, and to the point. He said things that made one laugh; they were so true and clear and funny. Lowell was more obscure in his thinking, each moment layered with depth of history and poems that had "gone before." Both men had such a breadth of mind that it made one hang on every word. I was familiar with this scope, and appreciated listening without feeling I had to have an answering or equivalent intellect. But it was my appreciation, recognition, enjoyment, if you will, of how they worked and thought, plus my ease of being with them, that created the bond. It was possible for me to talk with them about almost anything. Time together was enjoyable, funny, stimulating. I was confident of their tenderness and love for me, and accepted being over my head in their subjects of study.

The relationship with my father, with all the ups and downs and closeness and struggle for independence had also prepared me for being with Lowell, and others — a cross between a "favorite daughter" and a "Viennese lady," with all the *schlag* ("whipped cream") and rebellious streak that goes with the stereotype. Sometimes I was unable to cope with the Great Man moods, the egotism that came with their public selves and fame, their devouring narcissism. At those times I disappeared, as during Lowell's manic periods.

Later, to my father on one of our many walks and talks together, I joked that my role in life was that of "Cordelia" to two mad kings! But — and this was a big difference — Peter Drucker was eminently sane. He laughed, of course, and I loved to make him laugh. So did we all; humor was our family's way of coping with almost everything.

Oberlin and Boston, 1958–1959

I came to Boston in the middle of my senior year to study with Robert Lowell on a Gage Foundation fellowship from Oberlin College, where I had written for the undergraduate newspaper and also edited the literary magazine. I also wrote a series for the *Cleveland Plain Dealer*. The metropolitan newspaper had hired me to write some columns from the vantage point of a college student.

My little column, "Notes of a College Student," largely consisted in holding up my end of a never-ending and feverish political exchange with my father, the writer Peter Drucker. The column was always due in on a Tuesday morning, and each Sunday night I called my father from the only telephone available in my dorm, at the Bell Desk, with the entire dorm listening in — or trying not to. My father was hopelessly conservative, I felt.

"But Fa, Fa I have writer's block," I wailed. Then the *cri de coeur*: "You just don't *understand!*" That was the worst thing then: "writer's block." Overtones of Freud! At that, Peter Drucker, the Official Great Advice Giver, sprang into action and began to pontificate. He couldn't resist helping a Lost Cause. His daughter. This usually made me so irritated that the rebuttals sprang to mind. "You just don't understand!" I cried again, after noting down everything he had said. I rushed to my room. And wrote my answer to him — the exact opposite of his advice and good sense — in a white heat of passion and righteousness. "Notes of a College Student" flew off my fingers, off the beloved Olympia typewriter I had bought myself with the first money I ever earned as a dog washer, wrestling large, smelly mutts twice my size into a bathtub and picking off the ticks and fleas that floated to the water's surface.

At the end of the year at Oberlin my columns had won the prestigious Gage Fellowship for "original views." I still credit it to my father, and I might well have written "Seth (Peter) Speaks" ("*And Kathleen argues!*") as well as the abbreviations "op. cit." and "ibid." throughout. My advisor thought I should use this money to study with a poet — any poet — in the United States. John Gardner had spent a semester at Oberlin, and I had studied fiction writing with him. This was in the late fifties, before the advent of the "creative writing programs" that later swept the country, producing a plethora of factory-made poets and poems. So there were not many possibilities: a few poets, forgotten, desperate, living on the edge of poverty and/or madness, scattered in remote parts of the country, scraping a little living from farming, mostly, and like Robert Frost, hoping to be published in England first. The "academic poet" hardly existed. I had been running a little writing class, also as part of my Oberlin College scholarship.

At that time in the universities one could not even get a degree in American literature; it had to be in *British* literature — everyone knew we Americans didn't have a real literature of our own after all: one survey course, a brief passage through Emerson, Thoreau — that was it. Hawthorne was too "risqué." Emily Dickinson got a brief mention, but only because she was religious.

Oberlin College, founded by missionaries, prided itself on being the "first institution of higher learning in the United States to admit blacks and women," and therefore liberal. The Underground Railway ran right through the little town of Oberlin, Ohio, a green leafy village square with a bandstand, surrounded by cornfields. The college required compulsory daily chapel attendance, pious Protestant prayers, forbade interracial dating, and insisted on the kind of strict supervision of students that cried out for rebellion at every turn. In addition, the town was the bastion of the Woman's Christian Temperance Union, and its one "jukebox joint" served only "near beer," a bitter, nearly non-alcoholic morass.

At the time I received the news of my scholarship, Allen Ginsberg was in San Francisco. I was ready to leave Oberlin, to shed its prayers and rules, to fling myself at his feet the very next day. For I was wild to go to San Francisco, that city of sin and sex and topless bars and filthy "pads." Although I had always, up until that point, wanted desperately to be "bohemian" in Paris, I would settle for being "beat" on the West Coast instead. Suddenly I wanted to go and sleep on a mattress on a floor with a bearded totally unkempt raving drug addict poet and read my poetry in topless bars. The beatniks believed in "free love." So did I! I was tired of being well brought up, the secretly-bound-for-rebellion Drucker daughter, a good girl and a good student. Inside me lived a raging soul. I was ready for 1968! But it was only 1958: a few years too early — and Oberlin was not.

Ostensibly for my last year of study at Oberlin, the fellowship was changed to allow me to study writing with a poet "acceptable to the Oberlin English Department." The chairman of the department, Professor Andrew Bongiorno, commented, "Man is a social animal," as he set about signing the necessary papers for me to leave Oberlin. It was arranged that I take that year away — handing in the first draft of my honors thesis before I went — and return in June to take final honors exams and graduate with my class. The thesis, on Andrew Marvell's "Thoughts in a Garden," was already too much written about, but with the help of friends I was able to construct something barely acceptable. "Metaphysics" and the "seventeenth century" were English department catchwords then, and the pressure to write something original about the lines "Ripe apples drop about my head . . ." was high.[3] There was no way Oberlin would give me credit for a senior year of studying with Allen Ginsberg, whose morals were considered questionable. "Modern poetry" at Oberlin had stopped at Thomas Hardy.

Reluctantly, oh very reluctantly, I was forced to look around for another sin city and for another, "more acceptable" poet to whom I could apprentice myself. I went to my second choice: Boston. Ranked lower as a sin city, Boston happened to house Robert Lowell, a poet I had heard of, but whose work I could not understand at all. Lowell had published *The Mills of the Kavanaughs* and *Lord Weary's Castle,* which seemed thick, clotted, and obscure. But Lowell was affiliated with Boston University, and the Oberlin English Department found him acceptable.

Lowell agreed to take me on. He seemed the poetic descendant of Emily Dickinson, Emerson, Wallace Stevens, closely linked to Pound and Eliot, of the "we came over on the *Mayflower*" Boston Brahmin family. His poetry had the proper religious allusions. It was formal and scholarly, and looked to Europe for its references. Best of all, few people could understand Lowell. Who could argue with that choice? Ginsberg had been understood only too well. At that time I had never actually read a word of Robert Lowell's poetry, and neither had my professors, but Oberlin agreed to let me go to Boston and study with Lowell anyway. And Lowell agreed to be my teacher. That apprenticeship was to become the formative influence of my life. It turned out to be an extremely lucky choice. Lowell was to help the careers of every poet who worked with him, and his friends and peers as well.

Lowell and Ginsberg were united against the war in Vietnam, and both men wrote about that moment. To hear them both on stage as, for instance, in Carnegie Hall in the seventies before Lowell's death, was one of the great poetic moments.

I hastily turned in a version of my thesis on Marvell's poem, which was typed by friends, in order to get out of Oberlin in time for the term at Boston University. "What wondrous life in this I lead . . ."[4] A classmate went with me to the train station in Cleveland, and as he said goodbye confessed with shame that he was "an invert." I did not understand what he meant.

My professor of Russian literature took a highly romantic view of my leaving college. "Farewell, little Katya," he cried. "You are leaving us, leaving on the Great Railroad Train of Art." He was a small, square, excitable man: the last person I saw as the train pulled out of the station.

Early Days in Boston

First Impressions, January 1959

My mother helped me find a place to stay in Cambridge: a rooming house on Chauncy Street, run by Mr. and Mrs. Paddy Ryan. Mrs. Ryan was a large bustling person, Paddy a small skinny fellow, much henpecked. Mrs. Ryan had a firm bosom and corseted hips, and let my mother and me know that she would tolerate no "hanky-panky" in her house. The shades were constantly drawn in the parlor, there were lace curtains (my mother nudged me), and I would later suspect Mrs. Ryan of steaming open my mail. My room was at the top of the house. Appropriately a garret, I took it. The room was small and dark, with sloping ceilings and a hot plate. (The Chauncy Street house was later torn down.)

It was winter, the streets of Cambridge filled with dirty slush. My mother was dubious. So was I. What kind of an adventure was I embarking upon? Coming to Boston was uncertain, and a bit gloomy. My mother did not say anything, but I sensed her sympathy. I had not yet met Robert Lowell, and had only an assurance to go on.

My mother took me downtown and bought me a proper winter coat. As usual in emotional situations, a paralyzing indecision attacked me, and I couldn't decide which coat to get. I felt we would never get out of Filene's department store, as I tried on coat after coat and felt more and more hopeless. My mother managed to find a Viennese pastry shop in Cambridge, The Window Shoppe, and consoled me with sacher torte before she left me and drove home. As she left me at Chauncy Street, I longed to throw myself after her, howling, "Don't go!"

At the time of this writing, my multi-talented mother, Doris Drucker, at one hundred years old, is still one of the sharpest people I know. She's seen me through all the ups and downs of the writing process. I still call her to share news of any poetry triumph, just as I did in grade school. I love to hear the stories of her past, part of which is my past too. While my father wrote about social and economic events, my mother has always had a great eye for human interest. We always wonder how she managed to keep her own career going, support my father and his career — which was more than a full-time job — and oversee four children while keeping her own identity.

In Cambridge I experienced such loneliness that it was practically a sickness. One could die of this, I thought. I had never lived in a city before, and this was the first time I had ever lived by myself. I came from a large family, had lived in cooperatives in college, and had always been surrounded by friends. Now I stared out of the small windows of my attic room, watching the old people picking their way down the treacherous sidewalks. Never had I seen such poverty and sadness, I felt, projecting my own despair. Also, I had never had to cook and eat entirely alone. It was easy to feel dismal. I was too shy to talk to my housemates and was intimidated by Mrs. Ryan's elbows and insolent stare.

First Meeting with Robert Lowell

Boston University, 1959

"How are you?" my parents shouted when I telephoned them from the downstairs front hall. I replied to them with false cheer. "Fine!" I still had not yet met Robert Lowell, although I had been telephoning his offices at Boston University for days. Lowell was having a series of breakdowns at the time, it later turned out.

I had already declared to one and all at Oberlin that I was going to work with him, and my senior year's credit and graduation were dependent upon that happening. I was beginning to feel more and more desperate. I considered writing my English advisor, the kind Mr. Bongiorno, who had arranged this adventure for me. I continued to telephone Boston University, but no one there had any knowledge of my coming from Oberlin, and Mr. Lowell — they were so chirpingly sorry to inform me — was not available.

"He's scheduled to come in today," said the secretary Harriet Lane one gray day. "Perhaps if you get here early he might be willing to speak to you." With elaborate directions, I managed to get myself through the burrows of Boston and out to the university.

Robert Lowell had no recollection of having agreed to work with me when I arrived at his office. "Who are you?" he queried mildly. He was eating his lunch, and looking abstracted. I had arrived in a rainstorm, in blue jeans and boots. "I never take anyone under thirty," he countered coldly. He didn't remember getting my letter, or the arrangement with Oberlin. I was stunned. As I stood in the crowded office, wet and depressed, not knowing quite how to handle his amnesia, Lowell took pity on me. "Would you like part of this sandwich?" he offered.

We sat in silence for a while. The sandwich stuck in my mouth. I tried not to swallow loudly. I watched my final term at Oberlin slide away from me, but felt helpless to deal with it. I stood up, dispiritedly, to leave. "No. No, wait," he said. He hunched forward, watching me, and I caught a playful, somewhat malicious glint behind the thick spectacles. He was not done with amusing himself, half cruelly at my expense, yet genuinely absent-minded.

Lamely, Lowell offered an "Oh yes, I do seem to remember something." He seemed gloomily resigned. There was more silence; he looked into space. I wanted to disappear but could barely manage to hide my frightfully large boots under my chair. Rain dripped from my clothes into a puddle. The gloom was palpable. Later I was to associate that gloom with Robert Lowell: he never turned on lights in his classrooms and was oblivious to the darkness that pervaded Boston much of the year.

We sat together then, in a surprisingly comfortable silence, both of us sunk into a sort of familiar depression. I didn't yet know the man, who, although nervous, seemed at ease beneath this surface tremor. His large bulk, the head bent in thought, the tapered fingers; all this I saw instantly, or rather felt. But while he appeared to be lost in a forgetful funk, he was also furtively watching me as closely as I him. He had a strong physical presence, a strong will and focus, and an intensity of mind. He had a playful side too, I saw immediately; he liked to tease. He was waiting to see how I would react. Although totally intimidated, I also wanted to laugh. We both seemed, at that moment, to accept that there would be a relationship between us. It was instantly perceived, yet it would last a lifetime. A foreshadowing, although such a moment is hard to express, a little waiting-it-out duel, so full of possibility. And warning too.

At the end of what seemed an eternity, but was probably only three-quarters of an hour, Lowell grudgingly suggested that since I was here in Boston, I might as well audit his class at Boston University. And I might as well, additionally, come to his house on Marlborough Street one afternoon a week or more for individual tutoring and stay for tea. "Whom have you read?" he asked. I had not read much beyond Marvell. This ignorance was to be remedied, Lowell decided. It was raining curtains outside. Lowell now patted my shoulder in a comforting way, bending down from his Olympian preoccupations to barely notice as I left. I was too afraid of the man to even ask when and where the class took place. I hoped he would not change his mind, would this time remember that he had agreed to my study. He never remembered to fill out the necessary papers for my college, and I never dared remind him.

Although when he saw me before and after class he was kindly and affectionate in an absent-minded sort of way, I was choked up, timid in his presence, and very well aware that at any given moment he could "forget" who I was. Lowell met his class only sporadically during that term, for shortly after this arrangement, he proceeded to have another breakdown. As it was slow in coming, and as I had never seen anyone have a breakdown before,

The author at age twenty, Cape Cod.

the whole series of swings in Lowell's moods seemed very mysterious. What later struck others as "signs" seemed to be normal Lowell behavior. I never was able to shake my slight fear at his unpredictability, the flashes of cruelty that could and did emerge, the wit at others' expense. This, coupled with my awe at the working of his mind, kept our relationship always somewhat formal. I called him "Mister Lowell," and though he asked me to call him "Cal," as did so many of his friends, there was always a slight catch in my throat as I did so. Privately, to myself or to friends, I referred to him as "Lowell": some kind of compromise between the formality of "Mister," and the slangy "Cal."

I admired his wife Elizabeth Hardwick's gently teasing, laughing way of addressing him. The unpredictable, quixotic nature of the man, the manic swings, all were beyond my student perspective. I was, during our association, to come to know Lowell's mood swings well. Though I talked freely with him, much of our relationship was a jokey, laughing one, which made possible an intimacy not directly approached.

Lowell exuded sexuality, and I felt his magnetism. At the same time, a manipulative teasing quality was evident. There was an overbearing, self-centered approach to his courtesy, a playfully destructive core beneath the mild exterior. Curiosity, and streaks of cruelty, might startle. If pulled into the sexual orbit of this extremely attractive person, one would be burnt to cinders. Lowell, with all his genius and madness, would make sure to survive. A girl would not.

At the end of spring term, I returned to Oberlin for my honors exams and graduation. Afterward I returned to Boston. I had already met and was living with my future husband. I had made poetic friendships as well.

Lines from "Robert Lowell: The Church of the Advent"

    — Once he fell asleep reading one of my poems
in his office, just before class, on Gerald
Warner Brace's couch: "Do you mind if I read
it lying down?" he asked, finishing a sandwich,
propping himself on one elbow. His eyes
closed almost instantly. I left him
for class. Lowell bristled in on time,
alert, heady, rumpled. We spent an hour
on a twelve-line poem by Allen Tate, lost
down a well.

    ℗ DONALD JUNKINS

Junkins: Eulogy for Robert Lowell, September 1977. Published in *American Poetry Review* 10,
    no. 4 (July–August 1981).

First Classes at Boston University, 1959–1960

The windows of Boston University looked out on Commonwealth Avenue, traffic, and other buildings. In the late spring, the concrete walls of the classroom would hold the heat, simmering its occupants. We were sitting in Robert Lowell's writing seminar, around a scarred table. Lowell occasionally got up from his place at the head of the table and went over to the window, perching on the ledge.

Lowell always started his writing classes by going around the table, asking the students to introduce themselves and to name their favorite poet. Once, in response to this, a woman sitting to Lowell's right fastened her hand on his thigh. "Robert Lowell is my favorite poet," she said.

Edna St. Vincent Millay was my favorite poet of the moment, I offered, when it came my turn. Lowell cleared his throat, there was a long and awkward silence, and without comment the class proceeded as if nothing had been said. At that time Millay was out of favor. She was considered too romantic, too direct and "out there" — a girl might have a passion for her poetry. But I was in the land of oblique, incomprehensible words, words one had to struggle to understand. I was in Boston, the Land of Harvard, with sophisticates who spoke of poets I had never heard of.

Interesting writers found their way to these classes: Sylvia Plath, Anne Sexton, George Starbuck, Henry Braun, Donald Junkins, and, the next year, Stephen Sandy and Richard Lourie, to name a few. I watched from a vantage of nervous silence and did not learn the names of many of my peers. Either they were also reduced to silence themselves, or they talked compulsively.

Lowell himself was almost unintelligible. He muttered in a strange accent, looking down at a page. Occasionally, he asked rhetorical questions while sitting on the windowsill, his back turned to the class as he stared moodily out toward Commonwealth Avenue below.

Poet George Starbuck seemed the most stable member of the class. He was an ageless leprechaun who had studied with Archibald MacLeish at Harvard. When things got tense — which they did fairly often — George would save the situation with his kindness and wit. He was gentle, courteous, urbane, and relaxed, and he wrote close, technically unflawed poems.

Some of the poems that would become part of *Bone Thoughts* were circulated in that class.

One of the problems with Lowell's classes was the reverence and timidity with which some of his students were afflicted. Although many of his students were already poets, or later went on to become poets, we never got to know each other until years later in other contexts, long after the class had ended. We were much too shy to allow ourselves to seem vulnerable, i.e., friendly.

So many violent points of view, in that early class: to listen to Lowell, Sylvia Plath, Anne Sexton, and George Starbuck (the most voluble members), all talking wildly, all with a high degree of authoritativeness in their voices, stating exactly opposing opinions, was a bewildering but instructive experience. By the time a poem had been thoroughly discussed, it was close to being utterly destroyed. Lowell didn't like the end. He didn't really like the beginning either. Anne wanted more feeling. George thought it didn't scan: the rhythm was off in line five, and in line eight it was clumsy. Someone thought it was imitative. "It reminds me of Empson," Sylvia would say through clenched teeth. "It reminds me of Herbert." "Perhaps the early Marianne Moore?" "Yes, imitative," the class would agree. I bet that few of us had read the poets cited.

Lowell always tried to find something good to say. You could see it was a real effort! His fingers strayed furtively, longingly, to the thin-leaved pages of a leather-bound anthology of nineteenth-century British poetry, which lay next to him at the head of the table. He had planned the class around the classics he loved. But then, dutiful, he returned to the student poem under discussion.

"It lacks music," Lowell would say, frowning. Then, trying to mitigate the statement, "but this is marvelous!" (choosing what the author considered the weakest part of the poem). Eventually the poor mutilated poem would be put aside, and Lowell would turn to the anthology, choosing a "famous" poem that dealt with the same problem as had the student poet, but that solved it successfully. Toward students' work, Lowell's opinions had the randomness of a natural event. Praise or damnation fell equally upon our heads. Lowell's criticisms were erratic. Yet, if a poem inspired him to ramble, it was always an inspired rambling. Never mind that he was just as likely to discourse upon the fate of some British king, or upon his claim to part-Jewish ancestry, as upon the poem itself.

The act of showing a poem to Robert Lowell, as well as to the rapacious class, might be illuminating. However, a kind of nervous-humming fog took over in these classes. This was long before the era of creative writing workshops: this class was more in the category of a random event. And I never knew what I thought of the other students' poems. It was hard enough to understand them. They wrote in daring new ways, about such personal things. And they were so articulate. And so quick to know their own points of view.

Outstanding in that early class were two gifted women poets, Sylvia Plath and Anne Sexton. They differed from each other both in temperament and in poetic style. And in their gifts, they far surpassed the others.

Sylvia was working on poems that were to become part of her early collection, *The Colossus*. They were perfectly constructed and presented. Seemingly flawless, they held beautiful, precise description, but it was almost impossible to enter into the emotions. One sensed that they were there, but held so far back within that the impression of these poems was like gazing upon a perfect hard, cold, marble sarcophagus, trying to imagine the idea of a corpse embalmed inside, its warm life once embodied. Her poems at that time had a general feeling of distant, careful observation; nothing too extreme. She was a dutiful student of the poetic tradition of the time, and she was to break out of it in surprising ways later. But not yet. She was watchful and very careful, holding herself back.

Anne, who had not been to college, was quieter in class when other people's poems came up for review. A quick smile, long sensitive fingers, her listening face drank up Cal's words. Cal, who was working on *Life Studies*, treated Anne as an equal, and drafts of both poets' poems were shared and discussed. Anne was at that time, as far as Lowell was concerned, the bright star of the class, and a colleague in the joint adventure into that thin edge between "confessional" and "poetry." She had a natural and absolutely brilliant image-making ability, and her poems overflowed with passion. Yet they were still contained by form. At that time Anne's poetry combined discipline and feeling. And the result went right to your heart!

Both Sylvia Plath and Anne Sexton were sensitive to the subjects of madness, breakdowns, and suicides. There were times during Robert Lowell's classes when the two women exchanged knowing glances and withdrew into themselves. During one class in which Lowell seemed agitated, we had the distinct fear that he was going to throw himself out of the window. The class sat completely hushed. Anne fixed me firmly with her green eyes, as if to communicate something. Lowell hospitalized himself directly after this class meeting. Anne's poem "Elegy in the Classroom" documents this moment:

In this thin classroom . . .
I find this boily creature in your place.[5]

While still in boarding school, Lowell had been nicknamed "Cal" after the Roman emperor Caligula, by his schoolmates. Cal, "the underside of Lowell," the man I knew and loved, was famous for bad behavior; he had a reputation to be feared. People who ostensibly knew him better than I whispered about it. I did not know how I would handle the breakdowns I had heard about, should they ever occur in my presence, nor the nonstop monologues that Cal was prone to at those times.

Sylvia, Anne, and George Starbuck had a special relationship born out of the class. It was only after the publication of *Ariel* that those of us who had *not* gotten drunk with George and Anne and Sylvia at the Ritz realized the extent of Sylvia Plath's desperation. She had seemed reserved and totally controlled as well as unapproachable to the younger writers. Anne herself felt a barrier to friendship with Sylvia; it was not until Sylvia had left the country that openness grew between the two rivals, and then only by letter.

After Sylvia's suicide, Anne felt a mixture of emotions: anger, betrayal, and abandonment. But most of all she was jealous that Sylvia had actually managed to kill herself, something both women had discussed endlessly. Anne was obsessed with death — one has only to read *Live or Die* to see to what extent. Anne felt Sylvia had achieved immortality by her suicide. Sylvia beat her to it!

W. D. Snodgrass, who wrote about his divorce in *A Heart's Needle*, and Anne and Cal, who wrote about mental breakdown and its effects on family life, were taking risks. Anne's early poem "The Double Image" is based on the Snodgrass sequence in its attempt to deal with real experience, but with a certain formality and structure. Her poem deals with a breakdown and its relation to motherhood: "I made you to find me."[6]

While Anne was working on poems that were to be included in *To Bedlam and Part Way Back*, Robert Lowell was finishing *Life Studies*. In Lowell's class, Anne rewrote and revised diligently. Though Anne's work has been called confessional, the urge to write directly from personal experience was being explored by Snodgrass and Lowell as well. During that time I saw drafts of Anne's "You Doctor Martin," "Music Swims Back to Me," "The Bells," and "Some Foreign Letters." When Lowell passed out copies of Anne's poem "The Double Image" and asked her to read it aloud, Anne read it feelingly, in her hoarse terrific voice. "You are still small, in your fourth year . . ."[7]

It was this kind of writing — passionate, yet formally constructed — that made Robert Lowell consider Anne his most interesting writing student at that time. Nevertheless, Lowell shared his doubts about the personal direction such poetry was taking, reading drafts of some of his poems in *Life Studies* aloud, such as "Waking in the Blue": "This is the house for the 'mentally ill.'" He mused aloud about the validity of writing about these experiences. Lowell was struck by the work of W. D. Snodgrass, who was writing directly from painful experience. To students brought up to admire T. S. Eliot and Pound, this was revolutionary and daring, as it seemed to Lowell himself.

But when Anne continued writing about her breakdowns in her later books, Cal was not pleased. Anne, who had managed to combine and contain the pain of her experiences in brilliant imagery and form, now seemed, in her poetry, to fly apart. At the time of the class, her poems were firmly centered. Later, her extreme fragility fractured the poems entirely. This disappointed Lowell, who, in his writing, was returning to the loose sonnet form. When Lowell talked about Anne in later years, it was as with a sense of painful regret, rather as if the dearest of his talented students had been lost to him, in her work, and in what he considered the indiscretion of her illnesses and her life. There was a sense that she was somehow a prodigal daughter, that her work had strayed too far off center as her illness took hold, and that the lack of self-discipline in her poetry as well as her life was a source of stubborn grief.

In a later interview in *The Review*, Robert Lowell said, when questioned about Sexton and Plath:

Anne Sexton I know well. It would be delicate to say what I thought of her. She is Edna Millay, after Snodgrass. She has her bite. . . . She is a popular poet, very first person, almost first on personality. . . .

Sylvia is not the most enchanting, she's perhaps my least favorite, but she belongs to the group [of major women poets] and has her half dozen supreme, extreme poems. Years ago Sylvia and Anne Sexton audited my poetry class. Anne was more herself, and knew less. I thought they might rub off on each other. Sylvia learned from Anne.[8]

The class met at Boston University on Tuesdays from two to four in a dismal room the shape of a shoe box. It was a bleak spot, as if it had been forgotten for years, like the spinning room in Sleeping Beauty's castle. We were not allowed to smoke, but everyone smoked anyhow, using their shoes as ashtrays. Unused to classes of any kind, it seemed slow and uninspired to me. But I had come in through a back door and was no real judge. . . . At first I felt impatient, packed with ideas and feelings and the desire to interrupt his slow line-by-line reading of student work. He would read the first line — stop — and then discuss that line at length. I wanted to go through the whole poem quickly and then go back. I couldn't see any merit in dragging through it until you almost hated the damn thing — even your own, especially your own.

⟨ ANNE SEXTON

Henry Braun was my great friend in that class and for years afterward. We always walked home afterward, across Commonwealth, across Beacon where we'd split, he to go on to the Gardner Museum where he and his wife Joannie lived — she did restoration work on the paintings there — and me to Warren Street where I lived in the married graduate student apartments. I remember one day when I commiserated with Henry the whole way because he thought Lowell would be angry with him for his criticizing a poem Lowell had written and slipped anonymously into the class discussion. We had just done a Snodgrass poem, everyone praising its delicacies and phrasings, and Lowell passed out "The Drinker." . . .

Henry and I were pretty rough on it, but Henry actually banged his fist on the long table we were all sitting around and said, "This simply won't do!" Then Henry praised the Snodgrass poem more. Lowell was actually quite delighted, but Henry was in great despair as we walked home, saying more than once, "My career is ruined," but laughing as he said it, not really believing it but feeling chagrined with himself for having committed what he thought to be an indiscretion. Actually, Henry was dead right, and I kept telling him that what he said was great and Lowell loved it. Lowell refrained from printing that poem for two books, then greatly revising it.

⟨ DONALD JUNKINS

Sexton: "Classroom at Boston University," *Harvard Advocate*, November 1961.
Junkins: Essay in a letter to Kathleen Spivack, 1990.

Sylvia Plath, 1959–1960

As usual, I arrived much too early for the class at Boston University. The chairs were in disarray around the seminar table, and the windows looked out on busy Commonwealth Avenue below. Robert Lowell was, as usual, a bit late, and most of the class arrived ahead of time, so there was always an awkward wait. There was little talk; a low murmur to the person most immediately proximate, but students did not interact easily. It was rather like going to church, edging into a pew, trying not to call attention to oneself, and waiting for the service to start. People said hello self-consciously, but mostly sat and prepared for what was to come.

The woman next to me was "astonishing in her stillness," as she was to write later.[9] Sylvia Plath appeared perfectly composed, quiet, fixed in her concentration. She was softly pretty, her camel's hair coat slung over the back of her chair, and a pile of books in front of her. Her notebook was open, her pencil poised. Everything seemed neat.

I had read her poem "Doomsday," which had appeared in *Harper's Magazine* while I was in high school. I loved the music of it, the reckless nihilism. I had memorized the poem, but had forgotten the author's name. The author's note in *Harper's* had stated that Sylvia was a student at Smith College. It had been inspiring to me that a young college girl had been able to write — and publish — this poem. The poem had stayed with me through college. I had always wanted to meet the author, a woman who seemed to be living the literary life I craved. I had solaced myself on many a gray day by reciting grandly, as I walked to and from school, her lines: "The idiot bird leaps out and drunken leans . . ."[10] The poem ranked in importance to me with Frost's "Acquainted with the Night," a poem I still treasure, for I too had walked "out and back in rain."

After we had introduced ourselves, I somehow put the poem and the person together. Faltering beneath her intent stare, I said something about how much that poem had meant to me. But Sylvia was not interested in her "juvenilia." Nor in the juvenilia in Lowell's class. Focused around her own goals, she was pleasant but noncommittal.

We talked a bit before class from time to time, as we both got there early. Sometimes she seemed restless, agitated beneath that extraordinary still-

31

ness. She hardly interacted with the other students, her head bent in a book, pretending to ignore the comings and goings, the chair scrapings, nervous throat clearings, and so forth that accompanied the beginning of class. It was not that she wasn't polite: she was, but seemed nervously preoccupied. I thought she might be worried about Lowell's opinion of her poetry, for a greater tension overcame her when he entered the room. She seemed inordinately serious, her head bent over her notebook. Was she taking notes? I wondered. Sitting next to her, I saw that she was scribbling, over and over, the ink marks digging at the page. Maybe she was doodling.

Her *Journals* from that time record how distant she felt from the class, but I think volcanic emotions lay beneath even the feelings of boredom. Outside of class she was already beginning to write *The Colossus*, and other poems. Sylvia was controlled and sophisticated, both in terms of her writing and her education.

What she had to say about poets she read was always interesting. She had a fierce, competitive edge that made one rather afraid of her. The control of her poems, the precision of them, was impressive, but there was no real way in, only external admiration of them. They were "perfect." "The Manor Garden" appeared in the class, and later in *The Colossus*:

The fountains are dry and the roses over.
Incense of death.[11]

Sylvia had a neat, co-ed prettiness. She wore pleated skirts and buttoned-down, pink long-sleeved shirts and a little pin; a kind of frozen woman student's uniform. She often wore "liberty" blouses, buttoned to the glottis. Sometimes she would fold her camel's hair coat about her shoulders. She carefully positioned herself at the long table in Lowell's classes, often at the foot of the table directly opposite Robert Lowell. Her voice had a kind of rasped, held-in drawl, with the syllables clipped at the same time. Although she spoke softly, she seemed definite in her opinions. She had read almost everything, it seemed. Lowell's obscure references were not obscure to Sylvia; she was the best educated of the group.

She had absolutely no sense of humor. Ever! Lowell's offhand, jokey manner did not evoke a smile from Sylvia, as it did often from others. She was serious, focused on the matter at hand, almost pained. Lowell was intense about poetry, totally one track, but after a long exploration of a poem, or of the work of a "famous" poet, he might turn with a deferential smile and make a funny, light little comment. To Sylvia, these were annoying distractions. She could not deflect her attention.

The person in class and the person revealed in Sylvia Plath's letters, journals, and eventual poems were entirely different. Longing, anger, ambition, and despair appear to have been motivating factors for that gifted poet. These Furies expressed themselves outwardly frequently, as they did even more totally inwardly, toward herself and her achievements. As in a Greek tragedy, in which the elements of destruction reside within the character of the protagonist, the elements that led to her suicide had been apparent even in the early stages of her adolescence. Her desperation, so tightly reined in, increased throughout her life.

Sylvia recorded her first impression of Robert Lowell's class on February 25, 1959:

> Lowell's class yesterday a great disappointment: I said a few mealy-mouthed things, a few B.U. students yattered nothings I wouldn't let my Smith freshmen say without challenge. Lowell good in his mildly feminine ineffectual fashion. Felt a regression. The main thing is hearing the other students' poems & his reaction to mine. I need an outsider: feel like the recluse who comes out into the world with a life-saving gospel to find everybody has learned a new language in the meantime and can't understand a word he's saying.[12]

She had told the class, at our first meeting, when we went round and introduced ourselves, that Wallace Stevens was her favorite poet. She sat very straight as she said this, seeming quite sure of herself. Lowell seemed to approve. Sylvia was erudite and classical, unlike the flamboyant Anne Sexton. The achievement of her poetry at that time seemed to lag behind the scholarly achievements of her mind and critical ability.

Sylvia might occasionally venture a comment on a student poem, although Lowell did not invite this very often. When she analyzed a student poem, she was critical, brilliant, and a "good student." She knew about such things as scanning, rhythm, and structure. She was quiet most of the time, and only when she spoke of someone else's poems did that hard edge surface. She was precise, analytical, and could be quietly devastating to another student poet. I would never have guessed that she taught her own classes at Smith College, since she did not have an encouraging warmth that prefaced her critical comments. Her remarks were distanced.

Her own poems were very tightly controlled — formal, impenetrable, but without the feeling that was later to enter them. They were good, like perfect exercises. They did not have the wild passion of some of the poetry from her "Juvenilia": that passion had been replaced by duty and structure.

Lowell did not particularly praise Sylvia, for although her poems were perfect; they had a virginal, unborn feeling to them. As Sylvia herself did at that period. It was hard to imagine her married, passionate, or caring about anything really. Of course she cared intensely about her life, but she hid behind a perfect mask. Lowell tried to push her on her poems a bit, trying to get at the feeling underlying them. He did this gently; he also sensed how brittle she was. Anne Sexton, on the other hand, was writing warm poems. Her poems seared, hot with feeling, and Lowell's critiques attempted to rein them in a bit, to get Anne to make her imagery consistent, and to work more with form.

That year, Lowell was always on the verge of a breakdown. The class was generally awestruck, and trembled with a resonance to the fragility of his mental state. The experience of being there was nerve-racking. Lowell's idiosyncratic brilliance took turns with the more obscure parts of incoherent soliloquies. As each class extended longer than scheduled, and the afternoon got colder and darker, we hunched in a kind of numb terror of frozen concentration over the student poems presented and over the other, more famous poems that Lowell would read aloud and dissect.

Like the rest of us, Sylvia Plath was probably scared to death whenever she had to present a poem in the workshop. She withdrew behind dry defenses. Lowell admired her work, as we all did. He respected her, but assumed a hands-off position on her poetry. Lowell was brief in his comments with Sylvia, unlike the more relaxed, casual, and comfortable manner he might sometimes choose in his approach with others in class.

On a particularly lucid day, Lowell passed out copies of Sylvia's poem "Sow."

I can still recall his somewhat nasal Southern–Virginian–New England voice, oddly pitched, as if starting to ask a question, saying to Sylvia and to the class "This poem is perfect, almost." A slight breath-gasp, nasal and outward, as if clearing his sinuses silently, "There really is not much to say." A kindly but bewildered look. Long, struggling silence. Lowell looks down at the poem, brow furrowed. The class waits. Sylvia, in a cardigan, does not move. She listens. No one else moves either. "It appears finished." Long silence. Lowell looks agonized, but then he always does. Anne fidgets. Realizing that her arms draped with charm bracelets are making noise, she stops. Sylvia leans forward, dutiful, expressionless, intense, intelligent.

"But. I don't know. There's something about it . . ." Lowell's nasal voice trails off, helplessly. "Does anyone else want to say anything about this poem?" No one apparently wants to say anything. We are all too intimidated. We have learned that Lowell will bite our heads off if we say the wrong thing. We're all afraid. If he is entering another breakdown period, he might turn and lash out at anyone who accidentally irritates him. Who knows what is going on in that tortured New England mind? Lowell frowns with effort. Another long, unsatisfying silence. There is the almost inaudible sound of Lowell's nasal breathing. He is thinking. Everyone tries to refrain from saying something stupid. The room gets darker. Sylvia does not move, watching. "I'm sure this will be published," Lowell comments to her offhandedly, with a sly kind nearsighted glance. But perhaps the poem already has been published? No one dares ask.

There is a feeling of unsatisfied poetic process in the room. The poem is formal and beautifully presented, as is Sylvia herself. Everyone senses that Lowell has damned with faint praise and has managed to sidestep real engagement with the poem. One can't get beneath the surface of the poems Sylvia brings to class. And yet one can't define that, or change it, either. There is an air of disappointment, an accepted frustration.

And then Lowell launches for some reason into a reading of Randall Jarrell's poem "The Death of the Ball Turret Bomber," another "perfect" poem. "Now *that's* the genuine article," he says, looking up, and smiling gently, as if surprised anew by the perception. Lowell looks exactly like Little Jack Horner, I think. (*He reached in his thumb and pulled out a plum, . . . "What a good boy am I!"*) He regards us all triumphantly, about to crow. We all know how much he loves the work of Randall Jarrell. We have already gone over "The Woman at the Washington Zoo" in a previous class. The tension is broken, at least for the moment. Lowell, cocking his head, squints toward Sylvia encouragingly. Sylvia slightly relaxes her dutiful straight posture, and I catch her eye. Anne shifts, smiles at Sylvia across the table. The bracelets dangle, the skirt slithers as she re-crosses her legs.

Neither the poetry nor Sylvia herself really got due recognition from Robert Lowell, who was more dazzled by Anne, his other female visitors, and most of all, by his own poetic process. He was deep in *Life Studies,* and W. D. Snodgrass as a current favorite poetic role model interested him more. Sylvia's formal poetry at the time seemed confining, a path Lowell had already traveled in his earlier work. He expressed his astonishment at the bursting forth of raw emotion in later work, after Sylvia's death.

In class Sylvia's comments on other students' work could be scathing, as well as full of obscure references. She managed to suggest that everyone — except herself, of course — had plagiarized poems from dead British or American writers.

Later, at a meeting of Plath biographers at Smith College, I was not surprised to hear that Sylvia, in her earlier days as a guest college editor at *Mademoiselle*, had been photographed nudging and stepping on another guest college editor in order to be in the foreground of the picture. There was much controversy at this gathering: the various biographers had or had not been allowed access to the Plath archives. The biographers were very funny about it; they introduced their presentations by announcing either, "I'm on Aurelia's [Sylvia's mother's] side," or "I am on Olwyn's [Ted Hughes's sister's] side." The mother and the sister-in-law controlled opposing versions of Sylvia and, correspondingly, opposing access to quotes from her work.

What was later to be Sylvia's self-destructive anger showed itself only in the tight control and rather clenched-jaw way of criticizing work. Sylvia seemed to live a very glamorous and grown-up life with poet Ted Hughes, later privately dubbed the "Demon Lover," and there was a controlled poise about her. Both *The Bell Jar* and even the (edited) Plath *Journals* reveal the hate, disgust, and anger Sylvia felt for most of the human race. Although these emotions would eventually be directed toward herself, in that early class Sylvia was perfectly polite as she intellectually tore poems apart. She had a fine mind, for she had read far more than any of us, and was a superior scholar. The class, and even Lowell, was not at ease in her presence. I never dared show her a poem I had written.

Taking pity on me, Sylvia invited me for tea in her apartment on Beacon Hill. There I first met Ted Hughes. He was very tall, and he hunched over in order to enter their small apartment. He folded himself into a sagging armchair and lounged in an exhausted manner. Hughes had a formidable presence; he was darkly handsome and appeared rather inward. Sylvia served tea: she fluttered nervously about with hot water, a kettle, pot, real tea (not tea bags!), cups and saucers. In the English way, she warmed the teapot and poured milk into cups first, then the tea. She wanted me to notice, and I did.

She offered homemade shortbread cookies. Ted said very little, unfolding himself only to reach for more. He had an allure, and seemed preoccupied with poetic thoughts. Who knew? I had not read his poetry at that time. It was winter in Boston and gloomy, and it seemed like a very "grown-up" and formal occasion. "Tell me about yourself," Sylvia said dutifully. But there wasn't too much to tell. Oberlin College and its required chapel attendance seemed far from Beacon Hill. The Plath-Hughes apartment smelled of old books and clogged drains. "What made you come here?" I couldn't really explain why Lowell had taken me under his wing. Had my poetry merited it? This was the unspoken question. It hung in the air. Sylvia was already so accomplished — and so skeptical!

Probably despairing of having a real conversation, Sylvia showed me her library. We discussed books. Ted and Sylvia told me about British poets — young, bright contemporaries of theirs, unknown in this country. They were soon off on a conversation of their own, discussing the merits of the poems. Ted's accent grew thicker, Sylvia's too. They were more articulate for having an inarticulate audience, me. They said very "British" things like "Nonsense!" and "Rubbish!" to each other, clipping their consonants as they disagreed. This impressed me no end! It was an occasion for each of them to shine. I felt perhaps they did not talk this way when they were alone together. But here they seemed companionable, lively, interested in each other's opinions, and also in besting each other in front of me. Ted munched a lot of shortbread. Sylvia kept pouring the tea. I was filled with the sense of all I had not read, and admired this literate, cultivated couple.

After the end of that academic year, Sylvia returned to England, and we, the members of Lowell's class, did not see her again.

Years later, listening to a recording of a broadcast of Sylvia reading her last poems for the BBC, I heard the anger in her voice, the barely suppressed impatience, and a shaking tightness, much more present than in those earlier days. But even then, she presented herself rather like what I imagined an English boarding school "Head Girl" to be.

Alfred Alvarez's work on Sylvia Plath is still, to my mind, the most interesting account of the last of her life. He wrote, in a memorial tribute: "She was a tall, spindly girl with waist-length sandy hair, which she usually wore in a bun, and had that curious, advertisement-trained, transatlantic air of anxious pleasantness. But this was merely a nervous social manner; under it, she was ruthless about her perceptions, wary and very individual."[13]

Lowell and Elizabeth Hardwick visited Sylvia Plath and Ted Hughes in their Boston apartment, according to Sylvia, but it appeared a duty visit, and a warm social friendship did not develop. Elizabeth Hardwick, in private conversation, instead remembered having the couple to dinner and said, "Sylvia was very quiet."

Plath probably felt most comfortable with Anne Sexton and George Starbuck, both poets near her age. She wrote briefly of their famous after-class meetings at the Ritz. Anne Sexton has written more about these times as well. It is interesting to note the sense of competition in Plath's brief entries concerning these two poets: "Retyped pages, a messy job, on the volume of poems I should be turning in to Houghton Mifflin this week. But A.S. is there ahead of me, with her lover G.S. writing New Yorker odes to her and both of them together: felt our triple-martini afternoons at the Ritz breaking up."[14] She also wrote: "All I need now is to hear that G.S. or M.K. [Maxine Kumin] has won the Yale and get a rejection of my children's book. A.S. has her book accepted at Houghton Mifflin and this afternoon will be drinking champagne."[15] Sylvia did not win the Yale Younger Poets prize that year, but George Starbuck's collection, *Bone Thoughts*, did.

While her *Letters Home* to her mother are dutiful and saccharine, a parody of a happy girl of the 1950s, her *Journals* are full of contempt, hatred, and self-aggrandizement. It was interesting to read Sylvia's versions of the same event: the public face; the private one. I had been doing preliminary research for this book at Yaddo, an artist's colony in New York State. I read everything she had written that I could get my hands on. I knew I would write about the Sylvia Plath that I knew in those first years in Robert Lowell's class but wondered what shape this book would take. Plath was already a cult figure: she had emerged transformed in her work from the seemingly docile young woman I had known.

While working there at West House, I came upon a letter in which Sylvia tells her mother about her experience at Yaddo. I realized I was reading the letter in the same room that Sylvia had worked in when she wrote *The Bell Jar*. It made me want to write about the young woman whose work had developed visibly, and whose early poetry I had so admired. I felt I had been privileged to see the early images emerge and begin to take form.

Sylvia Plath's later poems, with their honesty and daring and imagery at their best, are incomparable. "Daddy," "Lady Lazarus," "Tulips," "The Arrival of the Bee Box," "Stings," "Death & Co." — the list is endless. These poems are classics, triumphs of both form and feeling. The promise we had witnessed in her earlier poems was more than fulfilled.

According to Anne Sexton, Sylvia was paid $50 by her publishers as an advance for her first book, *The Colossus*. But following her death, several publishers advanced prospective biographers more than $20,000 each, an unheard-of sum of money in those days. So suicide increased Sylvia's worth, much as she could have used the money in her lifetime.

Sylvia died before she could put her last poems together in a book. Her husband, Ted Hughes, organized the book after her death, and it was published. The force of the poems was amazing. In his original arrangement of the poems in Plath's *Ariel*, Hughes showcased Sylvia's rage, disappointment, and madness.

Much later, long after her death, Sylvia's daughter, poet Frieda Hughes, reissued her own arrangement of Plath's *Ariel*.[16] Frieda Hughes wrote a beautiful and very fair-minded, I thought, preface to her edition of the book. She honors the achievements of both her parents. However, in Frieda Hughes's rearrangement, the *order* of the poems is entirely changed. Her version of *Ariel* ends with relative peace and happiness, as Sylvia gives birth to her daughter, Frieda, and celebrates new life.

Since her death, Sylvia Plath has been acclaimed for giving voice to women's rage. She had the courage to express anger in her poems, not only victimization. But she did not live long enough to express a more complete vision. Death had always seemed an attractive option. She turned to death as a way out of disappointment and exhaustion. But she thought of death — had thought of death before — as a solution, where another woman might have chosen a less terminal way of collapse.

Sylvia had tried so hard to be perfect and desirable. Her letters to her mother reflect a desperate cheerfulness, a striving to present herself as living the life of a '50s-style "normal American girl" and, later, a "good wife and mother." This period of Sylvia Plath's life is formative; she tried to match herself to the dutiful stereotypes of the 1950s. Even her first meetings with Ted Hughes, as she recorded them, have an air of unreality about them, a sense that she was trying to live a story, some fantasy of romance and attraction/destruction. There was a duality in Sylvia, a conflict born of her time in history. We can see, in both her *Letters* and *Journals*, that when she wrote about her poetry and her poetic process, about trying to find a good last line to a poem, she constantly interrupted herself to record an ordinary domestic life: as a girl, dating (very important), or later, as a young mother, shopping, cooking, tending children. She tried desperately to present herself as perfect and desirable according to the standards of her time: the perfect student, daughter, pin-up and bathing beauty, wife, mother, writer. In England, when her marriage failed, it was clear she had not been "perfect." If many of Sylvia's letters to her mother from the last period of her life talk about domestic things — making dinner for Ted, taking care of babies, and so forth — she also documents her writing of poems that were to be collected in *Ariel*. The writing kept her going.

But her life must have been unbearably dark that winter. She had recently moved into a new flat after the disappointment of separating from Hughes. She was in a foreign country that mostly rejected her work. She had few acquaintances outside of those she had made through Hughes. Now he had gone off with someone else. She had suffered an enormous blow to her self-esteem, to the myth she had built about herself. The '50s *Woman's Day* stereotype of the perfect life had broken down. She must have been deeply disappointed in herself as well as in Hughes.

She was far from home, away from her mother, despite whatever ambivalence existed in that relationship of mutual dependency. Who among us, living through a similar situation, exhausted, alone with two young children in the midst of the flu, without heat, in damp cold and freezing darkness, in an early morning, not having slept for nights, would not want to end it all — at least for a couple of hours? Even taking into account Sylvia's history of mental breakdowns, any woman might crack under the same circumstances. One doesn't need a psychiatric background to understand that Plath's circumstances were overwhelming.

My sympathies are with both Hughes and Plath, actually, for as we know from all the written material that has surfaced since both their deaths, Sylvia cannot have been an easy person to live with. Nor, apparently, was the young Ted Hughes prepared to deal with this complexity of emotion. Nevertheless, the loneliness Plath suffered during that terminal period in London would have made far stronger people want to get a bit of sleep, even if one had to put one's head in a gas oven to get it. Perhaps Sylvia felt for that moment that she could not go on; just for that moment, perhaps, she wanted desperately to rest.

What is most touching about the life of Sylvia Plath, however, survives in her poems, and also in the youthful photographs of her. The girl in the bathing suit, the newly married wife, the radiant young mother with her children, the smiling woman with her husband; all look not so very different from the photographs we all have of our young, happy, forward-looking times. Looking at the photographs, one feels we were *all* that hopeful young woman: literary, educated, full of illusions, talent, optimism, and fierce possessive love. That promising young man, Ted Hughes, how could he have become "the enemy" so quickly?

My mind sifts through its own internal photographs of Sylvia Plath: that soft, extremely quiet young woman sitting next to me in class, filled with a passionate ambition. There is a barely perceptible change in atmosphere: the class has ended abruptly, loosening its knot of concentration. Like an exhalation in unison, a scraping of chairs lightens the room, signaling to us all that the moment we have shared is over. Anne and George walk out together.

Sylvia remains in thought for a moment. Lowell hunches over his papers and books, stuffing them into a huge cracked leather briefcase. A few deferential students murmur round him, but the rest leave. Outside the classroom door today Ted Hughes silently waits for Sylvia to get her things together. He helps her with her coat, her books. I can see her shy smile as she looks up at him; I watch them walk down the hall together, know she will be telling him all about what happened that afternoon, what poems were talked about, what Lowell said, what she really thought of it all . . .

It is poignant, looking back, to realize that the secret of Sylvia Plath's last irresistible blaze lies lost somewhere in the checks and courtesies of her early laborious shyness. . . . She showed us poems that later, more or less unchanged, went into her first book, *The Colossus*. They were somber, formidably expert in stanza structure, and had a flair for alliteration and Massachusetts's low-tide dolor. . . . Somehow none of it sank very deep into my awareness. I sensed her abashment and distinction, and never guessed her later appalling and triumphant fulfillment.

ROBERT LOWELL

Lowell: "Sylvia Plath's *Ariel*," in *Robert Lowell: Collected Prose* (New York: Farrar, Straus and Giroux, 1987), 124–25.

Robert Lowell's Appearance

Lowell's appearance was untidy, abstracted, as if he were always gazing off into the poetic ether. He was pale, with a high forehead and thick glasses that magnified flashes of emotion — humor, malicious wit, tenderness, and love. He had an intense inward gaze, and often appeared not to be listening, focusing downward into poetic brooding. Lowell's forehead, and the strained and troubled look to the upper part of his face, suggested eyestrain and weak vision but, at the same time, a focused, third eye that looked into the heart of poetry itself.

The rest of his body expressed a hunched determination around the subject of literature — he slouched, shambled rather than walked, bending over to whisper some slight aside or mockery, some bit of gossip or slander, with a wicked softening of the mouth and glint of the eye, or a mild kindness, the face glazing slightly. He wore tweeds and looked professorial and usually a bit rumpled. He was tall, and gracefully bent to one's level deferentially, as if polite. But of course he wasn't really deferential; he quite knew the worth of his intelligence.

When he spoke, his eyes flashed through his glasses, and his body inclined toward one. He had a mischievous smile, a proud, *enfant terrible* exultance at some particularly brilliant insight of his. He didn't quite crow, but you felt he might. Except that he was too well mannered for that. His voice was hesitant, medium pitched, but broke the air first with a strange high-pitched interrogative beginning to the sentences, in an accent that was a mixture of a quasi-Southern drawl borrowed from his teacher, Allen Tate, and his own Boston Brahmin upper-class way of articulating things. He would utter a sentence clause by clause, with a rising note at the end of each, pausing to muse almost inaudibly between them, with slightly outward nasal breath-pauses, as if snuffling slightly, questioning. Or the voice would angle downward, trailing off, with an invitational lightness. He had learned to sound tentative, but one was aware of the gift being proffered. He had a way of seeming to assume one understood what was being talked about. He invited one to join him in investigating further. He could be clever, with a kind complicit incline of the head.

Through the thick lenses his eyes brimmed at one with a faint smile, as if inviting one to share a joke. Or, at serious moments, frowning inward with

Lowell and his mentor, Allen Tate.

a quiet, bemused, straining look. Always there was a quality of engagement, as if his thoughts were conversation, inviting the listener to participate. Meanwhile, his long hands turned pages searching for just the appropriate quote or lines to be read aloud, as if touching pages were his favorite form of exercise.

Years later I was to work for Erik Erikson, the psychoanalyst and author who taught at Harvard, and notice the same abstracted, inward look, as if nothing was listened to outwardly. Yet Erikson, like Lowell, heard and saw everything, and in a rambling slantwise fashion, would discourse upon a subject with penetrating brilliance, should one wait long enough for his mind to work upon the small scrap of rough speculation offered.

Casual reflections on class poems were buttressed by comparisons with earlier poems, obscure or great, recalled by Lowell, smoking cigarettes at all times, gesturing above the poems he addressed. He singled out individual lines to dissect; to excoriate and often then, surprisingly, to praise — almost in the same breath. The tone of those hours was set, dominated by Lowell's soft, tentative voice with its educated Boston vowels skewed by the Southern drawl and punctuated by periods of thoughtful stillness . . . all awaited the entrance of Lowell as if attending an audience. Cal came in, towering, bent, disheveled, a Rip Van Winkle figure with a bit of exhausted menace in his bearing. He carried a pile of mimeo sheets of student poems, the thickness of numerous phone books. He passed out a poem to be discussed; quite before it had gotten around the room he was asking for responses. A student complained that he had not had the chance to read the text. Lowell removed his glasses, stared at him, then turned to the next student. Silence. Lowell began to speak, the courtly Southern drawl and Brahmin poise reasserted. He talked well about the text, a poem of considerable merit; he quoted Dante and Anthony Hecht. He praised the student — and reached for another text from the tall pile at his elbow.

⚇ STEPHEN SANDY

His private personality, on the other hand, was genuinely casual, even languorous (and yet still more vivid, I think, in the memory of anyone who knew him well). He preferred to speak in impressions rather than judgments: "One feels that . . ." He carried his large body in a headlong, fumbling way he himself called "fogbound"; and preferred slumped, lounging postures when seated. (He was happiest of all lying full length on a sofa.) He liked to live in a certain amount of disorder; he joked in a poem that the President of Columbia's study after the student takeover was "much like mine left in my hands a month," and once scandalized and delighted a friend by saying that his cat lived "on what she picks up around the house."

⚇ ALAN WILLIAMSON

Sandy: "Robert Lowell: Memories of B.U. and Harvard," typescript, 1990.
Williamson: "Robert Lowell: A Reminiscence," *Harvard Advocate*, November 1979.

Lowell's Way of Teaching

Lowell's way of teaching was rhetorical, as if the class were a frame for the expansion of his own opinions. This was punctuated, or rather, elongated, by long, agonized silences, while the class held its collective breath and hoped to come up with adequate answers. Lowell strained, looking at a poem, and sometimes asked questions. He had the class do close textual analyses of poems. Sometimes these were poems written by members of the class, but often they were "famous" poems, anthologized. He also occasionally shared his poems with us, reading a draft of "Ford Maddox Ford" in a groping voice. What on earth was it about? I wondered. I prayed silently for help, tried not to roll my eyes. Oh, please! "The lobbed ball plops, then dribbles to the cup . . ."[17]

A poem examined in class might be only a springboard into Lowell's imagination. After Lowell read a poem aloud, he pressed the class for deeper and deeper meaning. I remember one grueling session with "Homage to the British Museum," by William Empson. A fairly straightforward poem, Lowell was determined to wrest deep significance from it. Part of this, I suspect, may have been Lowell's extreme Anglophilia; nevertheless, the class was bewildered. "What does this poem really *mean*?" Lowell urged, going around the table from one student to another. It was like an examination, in which everyone was bound to fail. Lowell pressed on. We fumbled. At the end, Lowell, his forehead wrinkled, hunched with irritation at the class, talked about the poem. It was a brilliant explanation, but impossible to follow. What did he say? What did he say? Though Sylvia Plath was nodding obediently, Anne Sexton looked skeptical.

As Lowell neared his recurrent breakdowns, these sessions, explaining poems, got more obsessive. One cold, gray December day, Lowell turned to John Donne's "A Nocturnal upon Saint Lucy's Day, Being the Shortest Day," a poem like a dirge on winter and decay. As the class slouched intently over the poem, the room got darker and darker. The class was too reverent to make a single unauthorized gesture. "Tis the year's midnight . . . the sun is spent . . . and I am rebegot of absence, darkness, death," Lowell intoned. The room was chilly, dim, and rapidly getting darker in the late afternoon. "What does this poem *mean*?" Lowell kept insisting. But the class was too depressed to answer him.

When you handed in a poem for class, you never knew whether you would get a reaction to the poem or Lowell's free association to the poem. Embarrassingly, Lowell's comments were often better than the poems themselves. He could be extremely penetrating — devastating, in fact. But he had some standard reactions, too, which became (quiet) class jokes.

Frowning at a long, complicated, and much-worked-over poem, he would hopefully suggest: "Put the end at the beginning and the beginning at the end." This was guaranteed to throw a student-poet into a panic. The next class one handed in the revised poem, dutifully decapitated, and re-shuffled, as per his suggestion. Lowell squinted, looking down at the page as if he had never seen the poem before. After a long pause came the soft distinctive Lowell murmur. "This poem would be better if you would put the end at the beginning and the beginning at the end . . ." Then he would turn to the stack of leather-bound books at his side and pull out the Wordsworth poem he was really interested in talking about that day.

How did Lowell manage to train so many poets? Perhaps it was the fact that if one survived those classes, one felt tough enough to survive the outside world, even as a writer. These classes were more in the nature of an ordeal, a fascinating one, to be sure, than in the nature of entertainment.

Poems were often submitted to Lowell without names on them; most of us preferred to remain anonymous as much as possible. But of course, being poets, we wanted to have our work recognized — and praised — as well. Slyly, Lowell would flush out the unfortunate author. Passing out those smeary carbon copies with a seemingly tentative bend of the head, a kindly smile, he would somehow get the author to confess ownership.

Quietly, outwardly, you might appear to be sitting in a seminar room, listening politely to what was being said about your beautiful poems. But inside, all was blank. For poetry, and being a poet, is a convenient disguise; that is, very few people understand what it is the poet is trying to say. It's a stealthy sort of betrayal in a secret code-language of its own. But at the same time, a poem cries, "Hear me! Hear me!" Who can understand poetry? (Let alone want to?) Nevertheless, the poet needs to be listened to, understood — and most likely, comforted. That's why poets walk such a narrow line between abject humility and — disgraceful vanity! Rejection is always just around the corner. Poets are, I think, people who were never really listened to as children. They are still suffering from that neglect. They might appear ever so "humble," but they never stop wanting to be heard/recognized/praised/published. It's never enough for us poets! So even though we didn't want our poems to be massacred in Lowell's class, it would have been far worse not to have our poems discussed.

We were on tenterhooks either way. If we had handed in poems for discussion and Lowell forgot about our (student) poems and digressed for the whole period, this could be a disaster. The class had run out of time. (Our poems were worthless in his eyes: *brood, brood.* Deep weeklong depression.) But if one's poems did come up, this could be — often was — far worse! Lowell was not the kind of teacher to blather on about how much he loved our little efforts. He usually would make one or two kind and condescending comments and then go straightaway to "real" poems, i.e., poems in a Real Live Book. Or to his own poems, on which he was working endlessly. Either way, the poor author was left with a pounding heart, utter exhaustion after an adrenaline surge, and a weak and shaky sensation.

The pages of onionskin paper we used to make the carbon copies whispered ominously as they were passed around. Truthfully, I have no idea what he said about my poems in class; I was in an inner frenzy of trying not to wince while my poems, my children, were in other people's hands. It was all I could do not to snatch them away and tuck them into my backpack before they could be (psychically) torn apart. Pierced by a migraine, I had no recollection afterward of what had been said about the poems.

Later, when I first began giving poetry readings, it was exactly the same sensation. I remember reading the poem "But You, My Darling, Should Have Married the Prince"[18] (Lowell liked that one a lot for its autobiographical detail) in Lamont Library at Harvard University in the early '60s. Somehow during the reading of that poem I managed to nervously empty the entire deep-black inkwell reservoir of a fountain pen down my long white sleeve. (A weird kind of "shooting-up," I suppose.) I didn't notice I had done it until the evening was over.

It was easier to get an impression of other people's poems in class. With the author sitting there in front of us, a frozen mute, the more daring classmates began to speak at once. No one was able to escape Lowell's classes without being convinced that Elizabeth Bishop was one of the best American poets writing. They were friends, and he respected her fine, exacting poetry, with its perfect mastery of form and attention to detail. Reading her poems taught us all that poetry demands accuracy of observation, even of the smallest things. I remember Lowell reading her poem "The Man-Moth"

49

aloud. The poem is about a strange creature that haunts the underside of the city, fluttering up buildings and through the subway system. Going home on the subway from class that afternoon, I knew *I* was the Man-Moth.

> He does not dare look out the window,
> for the third rail, the unbroken draught of poison,
> runs there beside him. . . .[19]

It is hard to convey the quality of silence and intensity to which Lowell subjected both himself and his companion readers. He read and re-read the poems, word for word. Poems were subjected to scrutiny until their meaning was revealed. He did not have ready interpretations for a poem, but rather brought to each piece of writing a ready, investigative curiosity. Not only did the poem mean something, it was constructed in a particular way to reinforce the meaning. Always Lowell looked at poems from the point of view of a maker-of-poems, rather than as a literary critic. He wanted to know how Blake or Whitman, for instance, shaped the poetry for deepest emphasis. What I remember most in recalling poetic sessions with Robert Lowell was the intensity of concentrated silence, with occasional mutterings in between. Yes, he was brilliant in his comments, as others might attest. But he might also be maniacally elliptical, difficult to follow.

The poets Stephen Sandy and Henry Braun, in later discussions, also had the same impression of the quality of silence brought to bear on interpretations of poetry. Racked with nerves in the face of long silences, Braun and Donald Junkins would start to explicate like mad in order to fill the everdarkening space. On and on they rambled, growing more desperate by the minute. They seemed, to me at least, incredibly well read, brilliant — and obscure! Lowell called them the "graduate students."

Interviews and essays show Robert Lowell articulate, clear, and easy to follow. So he was, in conversation, or print. But in class, when discussing a poem, he sought only to discover what the poet meant, and how this was achieved. Poetry was meant to be understood. He was merciless with a student who presented an "obscure" poem, and had little patience if he could not understand it. No amount of explanation by an eager student writer would appease his irritation. But he was infinitely patient in his attempts to penetrate a poem, and asked that of his students as well. One figured, when presenting a poem, that if Lowell could not finally understand it, no one ever would.

There have been some attempts to document exactly the quality of Lowell's interaction with poetry and with a class. Others who were at one time or another a part of this circle have written some reminiscences, which are included in this memoir. Some took extensive notes; others, afraid to miss a word, did not. Although his influence can be seen from many angles, the sense that he changed the lives of those who worked with him is pervasive. Yet it is hard to pinpoint exactly how that happened.

Elizabeth Hardwick tried to define Lowell's approach to poetry. "You might say I was a student of Cal's during all those years. He was teaching day and night. He was even teaching in bed!" Then, as she slipped deeper into remembering, her recollection slipped into the present tense. "He is original, he changes one's way of looking at things, deepens them."[20]

I took a part of a class at the University of Iowa. He was teaching the *Iliad* in Greek for people who didn't know Greek. We had to pretend to translate, ten lines from Greek we didn't know. It was a wonderful way to teach it. You made a sort of stab. It was fun. And he was marvelous. It is so hard to describe . . .

✧ ELIZABETH HARDWICK

Nothing mattered to Lowell but the poem. His office hours were held in the mornings in his rooms in Eliot House. A pilgrimage arrived, made up not only of his Harvard students but of people from all over Boston. Architects, lawyers, teenagers, retired librarians. We were all the same to him. One by one he would study the poem laid before him, like an examiner of dollar bills trained to expose the counterfeit. He read each line aloud, as if holding it aloft between his fingers. He could be ruthless. Never to the poet, but to the line.

One boy came in with a poem about the recent death of his mother. Lowell stared at it. "This doesn't work at *all*," he said.

For us in the workshop a great sadness descended when we could see Lowell's mind begin to sink into gloom. At that point the ruthlessly honest man would become merely polite. He would smile wanly and say, "That's rather nice" — his highest compliment — about lines that were not rather nice.

✧ ROGER ROSENBLATT

Hardwick: Conversation with Kathleen Spivack, 1990.
Rosenblatt: "The Writing Class, Memoir," from a note to Kathleen Spivack, 1988.

Anne Sexton, 1959–1974

Anne Sexton was at the beginning of her poetic career when she attended Robert Lowell's class at Boston University in the spring of 1959. Anne, ten years older than I, had been writing for several years. Lowell had decided that I needed to be befriended by the women writers of his acquaintance. He had written to them, formal letters of introduction. These letters worked wonders. I was invited by each one of them. For these occasions, I dressed up; "heels and hose," as my college would have said. I wore white gloves too. Teetering on the heels, nervous, it was intimidating to "call on" Plath, Rich, and Sexton. But such was Boston in the late '50s. While many of Lowell's women-writer friends were kind, if slightly patronizing, Anne Sexton, irrepressibly exuberant, was genuinely warm. She had a way of drawing me right in.

Anne was generous and immediately invited me to her house. I was to spend a lot of time there in the coming years. Her study was her sanctuary, invaded only by her two large Dalmatians, who curled at her feet and looked up at her adoringly as she composed her poems. For fifteen years we continued to work together, laugh, talk, swim in her pool, write, read poems, gossip, and commiserate. For a number of years, I had a job in the Counseling Center at Brandeis University, near Anne's house, and saw her several times a week. Anne's house was where I would go to relax. Though I knew of course — who didn't? — of Anne's attraction toward death, the focus of our friendship was on joy, even frivolity, shared experiences, and on that most complex preoccupation, poetry.

After her death, many Sexton-imitators appeared on the scene, eager to suffer, write about it, and kill themselves. ("Get rich, get published, get famous, get *even!*") But few had Anne's imagination and image-making ability. The poet as mad, the poet as suicide, the vulnerable deranged woman: Anne was a believer in, as well as a victim of, that archetype. But her vision encompassed the range of women's lives: work, family, children, love. At the same time she journeyed into a more shadowy private world of self-doubt, pain, hallucination, and terror. All this is recorded in her poetry.

Anne treated me like a little sister; she teased and encouraged me. And I looked up to her — her poetic gifts, her imagination and humor and beauty. She was a magical "older sister": so gifted, glamorous, supportive, and funny. But what I actually lived with Anne Sexton was informal and relaxed. We sprawled in her study, reading poems, or lounged in the sun on plastic lawn chairs in her backyard, glasses of strange-colored fizzy drinks by our sides, typescripts on our laps, as we talked about poetry. There was often the clink of ice cubes around Anne, and she smoked cigarettes just as Lauren Bacall did in the movies. She even looked like Bacall — and also a bit like Hedy Lamarr: wedgie sandals, longish hair, long legs, full skirts, plunging silk blouses, creamy lipstick, eye makeup. A "war bride" out of the '40s. She was smart and talked "tough" and had a ready laugh. In summer we hung out at her swimming pool, experimented with nail polish, commented on each other's figures — for who ever sees "figures" during layered Boston winters! — and talked about men and children and poems and letters of rejection.

Anne came to Lowell's seminar with a desperate ambition and tremulous nerve. She was not yet thirty, but it was considered that she had started writing "late in life"; late, that is, when compared with the undergraduates who dominated the class. Her fine poem "The Double Image" had appeared in the *Hudson Review,* and a few others had been published here and there. *To Bedlam and Part Way Back* was still in manuscript. Lowell advised her on the organization of that first collection.

Anne Sexton was, on the surface, entirely different from her contemporary, Sylvia Plath. Anne was "heart" and shaking hands; Sylvia was "head." Anne had an outstanding natural poetic — that is, image-making — ability, and "The Double Image" was a tour de force of rhyme and form. She had vulnerability and was touchingly raw. Chain-smoking or observing thoughtfully from large, tilted green eyes, she was a soft presence in the class. The poems she brought in were to appear in her first and second books. Cal recognized Anne's talent. Eager to learn, Anne showed him all her early work. "Who is your favorite poet?" asked Robert Lowell. Anne's favorite was William Carlos Williams, a strange choice when considered against the kind of personal poetry she was to share with the class. Anne was often late, because she was too nervous about coming to Lowell's class to get herself there. Her entrances were dramatic: she stood at the door, rattling her bracelets, and dropped books and papers and cigarette butts. The men jumped to their feet, found her a seat. Everyone wanted to protect her. Anne wore silky flowing dresses and flashy jewelry. Her hoarse voice breathed extravagant enthusiasm and life. Her hands shook when she read her poems aloud. She smoked endlessly. Anne's poems were ragged; they flew off the page. She was an instinctual poet rather than, as Sylvia Plath, a trained one.

It was commonly thought that Anne Sexton had rushed into print, experiencing no difficulty in getting published once her first brilliant poems had been created. This was untrue. In fact, Anne had tried to publish consistently for several years before the acceptance of her first manuscript. The first time I went to see her, she pulled out masses of rejection slips from her file drawers and waved them in front of me, laughing. She had two file cabinets full of magazine rejections. Some were printed rejection forms; others, nasty letters. It was somehow comforting to see her fling them about, to know that the struggle to publish was a common one and that everyone got rejected.

Anne actually seemed to enjoy the process of sending out material. She had envelopes addressed to the magazines she favored, and when her poems came back in the mail, she immediately transferred them to new envelopes and sent them right out again. She insisted I do this too. She never condescended to me, or acted as if my poems were not worth being published. We were conspirators together against a harsh anti-poetic world, she seemed to imply. Our poems would prevail. *"Don't let the bastards get you!"*

She liked to read me her rejection mail. She'd have it out on her desk, ready to read, when I walked into her house for lunch. "Oh Kathy," she would exclaim. "Listen to this." She'd roll her eyes heavenward, recite the note dramatically, and then stuff it away in a file drawer, only to find another one to read. "You see," she would say to me throatily, "You just have to keep trying." Then she'd pause. "The bastards . . . ," she added. A dramatic sigh. She'd stub out her cigarette, light another, lean her head back, exhale. "Don't let the bastards *win*, Kathy! Don't ever forget it. Promise me."

Anne smoked cigarettes like a movie star. She was beautiful, magnetic to watch and listen to, and very funny. Her timing for telling a story was excellent, and she loved to be the center of attention. Her friends enjoyed her liveliness, even when she described her depressions. A letter she wrote to me began: "Dear Kathy, All is rush or pain or shit or glory . . ." That was Anne!

Later Visits with Anne Sexton
Reflections on Psychotherapy and Sleep

I drove out to Anne's house on Black Oak Road in Weston two or three times a week after I met her until she died. She always made me feel like a treasured visitor, a special girl, her pet younger sister. She created this complicity between herself and her chosen friends. She seemed delighted to welcome me, the dogs jumping eagerly around. We took our cups of strong coffee into Anne's study, a dark, hushed room with books and papers throughout. Anne inevitably carried a glass of wine with her as well, the glass, set down, making rings on the furniture. In warm weather, the rug bristled plushly against our bare feet, and the air didn't move. Anne had the blinds closed and her study desk faced inward. I couldn't imagine writing without looking out a window. She had a secretary who kept the place organized, typed her poems, and dealt with her correspondence. Anne wore shorts, and she curled up in a chair, tucking long tanned legs and impeccably pedicured feet beneath her. She could have come out of a James Bond movie.

"Read this. I just finished it," she said, handing me a poem. She watched me as I read her work, a speculative, quizzical look on her face. She really wanted to know what I thought. And she went over drafts of my poems. She was a most supportive critic, and tuned in to the subjects that male writers did not, such as the loss of a child. "Oh, Kathy," she would exclaim, tears in her eyes, looking up from a series I was working on.

It was easy to show poems to Anne. She was generous and could enter one's work totally, so I relaxed into a waiting mood when Anne looked at a poem of mine. Not nervous or defensive, just watching that expressive face, those quizzical green eyes, the long fingers, almost as if she was reading braille. I waited, receptive to what she might say or suggest. If Anne, in tune with my writing, didn't get the meaning of a line, then obviously the line needed work. Poems should be clear, chiseled, and beautiful as well. They needed to shimmer.

Anne could get right into the subject of a poem. She was most often supportive. "I love this, I love this!" she would exclaim over a line. Then the dreaded "Kathy, may I steal it?" This was, she felt, her ultimate compliment. "Nooo!!!!" I countered. What a horrible request! She had her own images to harvest, was the best image-maker there was. I think she liked that in my poems as well; that and their music. She was a keen critic though for a false line, an image that didn't work, a weak poem pushed too far. I trusted her ear and eye.

It helped of course that Anne genuinely liked my poems as well as me, and that she understood what the poems were about. She was humble; she considered herself a student still. But up until now, the poets around me had been male. There weren't many women writing about subjects from their own points of view. Women mostly wrote to please. To please: a father/man/lover/husband/teacher/critic/editor. The whole establishment was male! If you wanted to make it, you had to attach yourself to a man or try and become the man in some fashion: change your name, disguise your identity, so an editor of a magazine would read your work rather than throw it away. The field was full of misogyny. Seductive, vulnerable, and frothily feminine in her outward bearing, Anne was often criticized. But she was too good a poet to care; she wrote what she wanted, and the images carried her poems away.

I saw drafts of almost all her later poems. I was struck by her imaginative imagery, the daring swoop of her poems. Sometimes the poem flew off the edges of the page, especially in her later work, which veered off into areas of mystical religion.

In between, Anne told me all about her personal life. I was younger, and didn't know what to say. But I loved listening to her dramatic telling of stories. We would reward ourselves by breaking for lunch, foraging in her refrigerator, which was full of strange stale things, turning bluish-green. Faced with that, I would offer to make my one specialty, an omelet with cream cheese in it, or a salad. Or whatever I could throw together from the uninspiring contents. "Kathy! You're such a good cook," Anne purred, as if it were truly gourmet, which of course spurred me on. Then we would take our lunch back to the study or, if it was warm enough, outside to the swimming pool, bringing our copies of poems with us. There was a sense of infinite leisure about our times together.

I think Anne's husband actually did most of the cooking around there, coming home from his job as a carpet salesman to get the house and children and dinner organized. Or he sent his mother over to do the job. They were a "fifties family": we know from Anne's letters how much she resented the mother-in-law trying to take over. Kayo, the husband, seemed to be a large, roast-beef affable man who appeared totally bewildered by the wife that fate had handed him. He seemed friendly, but stepped carefully, guardedly, around his wife, as if she were a loaded gun. "Kayo" stood for "Knock Out."

Sometimes I stopped by to visit Anne after work when her children were coming home from school, and we would have a glass of wine together. Anne was one of my few friends with children, and I enjoyed seeing her daughters, with pigtails and lunchboxes, run in the kitchen door. They were warm and affectionate with their mother, and she seemed easy with them. Other times, Anne came in to Somerville to see me, and we sat in my kitchen, in which there was a green-clawed ceramic stove, and I cooked the same omelet there. Later, when I moved and had a baby, she came to my house in Watertown. She held my baby, complimented me, cooed and — she made the omelet! She always brought her supplies of cigarettes and wine with her as well as the drafts of poems she wanted me to read. I always felt honored by her visits, as if an exotic butterfly had somehow found its way to my house. But she loved having her friends come to her house: she was so much more at home in her own setting.

As I drove up Black Oak Road to Anne's house in Weston, a rock marked the entrance to the driveway. When I looked at it, I could imagine Anne writing the lines of one of my favorite of her poems, "The Fury of Sunrises": "not to die, not to die."[21]

Anne had a great gift for friendship. Her closest friends were the writers Maxine Kumin and Lois Ames. Lois was later designated by Anne as "my official biographer." Both women were immensely loyal. Lois accompanied Anne on many reading tours, providing support, security, and companionship. She dragged Anne home from the poetry groupies and the bars after her readings, made sure she took her pills, got her to bed. Maxine gave strength and nurturance to Anne during the many difficult periods in her marriage. Both Maxine and Lois are unusually gifted professional women in their own right. They were managing nearly full-time jobs as well as writing and caring for their families. Lois, whom I got to know better, was warm, empathic, and extremely kind. Anne kept up with her friends on a more-than-daily basis, in person and on the telephone.

I remember going out with Anne, Lois, and Maxine to a restaurant on Anne's fortieth birthday. I had just passed my thirtieth. They assured me that the forties were wonderful, without the mortality brooding that accompanied the early thirties. Because I was expecting my first child, and their children were more or less grown, there was some rueful laughter around the subject of child care. They teased me as if I were their little sister: my teeny-bikini body would never return, I would become groggy from lack of sleep, I would be telephoning them to come and babysit. My breasts would not be my own, etc.

They drank quite a bit, and Anne and Lois decided to stage a blowsy poetry competition. Lois had given Anne a necklace, engraved, "Don't let the bastards win." Anne had then given Lois one, which read, "Don't let the bastards get you." Which was a better line of poetry? I chose Lois's on account of the rhythm and heavy accent on "win." Anne's mood changed, and she referred to this with dismay for years. How could I have been so disloyal?

Maxine Kumin and Anne had a close poetic friendship, showing each other poems and discussing their choice of words. They communicated almost daily about their work. Interviews with both women document this closeness, but it was interesting that neither poet wrote at all like the other. Yet they were able to support each other's unique voice. Anne had a great sense of drama and mock-drama. She could be very funny and animated even while recounting the most horrendous stories of her life. There is a sequence of photographs of Anne and myself, taken shortly before she died. A photographer, Ann Phillips, had come to Boston to photograph me. This made me horribly self-conscious, and I tried to think of other things she might photograph that would be more interesting. I took her to visit Anne.

That afternoon, as Ann Phillips, who was then working for *Newsweek*, peered at us through her lens, Anne Sexton started to tell me intimate details of highly personal aspects of her life, things about her husband and her relationships that she had not shared before. She regaled me with a melodramatic rendition of her woes in Weston, Massachusetts. Anne spoke of her failing marriage, of physical fights, of her sense that God lived in her typewriter and spoke to her, and of her despair at losing God. "God is in my typewriter," Anne said. It sounded really crazy to me back then. Now, on days when writing is a real struggle, I know what she meant!

The photographs taken by Ann Phillips document the quality of Anne's conversation that day, her theatrical vivacity, and her enjoyment of the dramatic moment. One sees how animated, glowing, and expressive Anne is in these photographs as she chronicles the extent of her agony. She visibly enlarges, her posture regal. I am getting progressively more depressed.

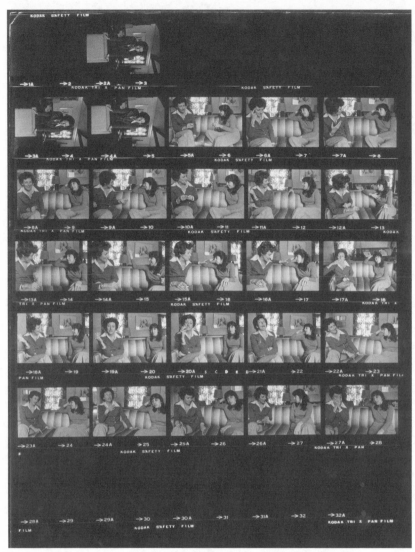

Anne Sexton and the author. Photographs by Ann Phillips.

Anne warms to her subject, as I sit beside her. Dismayed, I am getting a terrible headache. But Anne keeps talking, laughing, gesturing: refreshed and beautiful as Venus emerging from the sea. Ann Phillips, numb and stunned behind her camera, keeps taking the pictures. She is as bewildered as I am; she doesn't know what else to do. Nothing will stop Anne now, she is in her glory. "Don't tell anyone," Anne keeps saying conspiratorially as she brings forth one outrageously juicy bit of personal drama after another. She touches my arm to make sure I am really listening. By the end we were all exhausted.

Ann Phillips and I stumbled out of Anne's driveway at the end of that day with relief. Our young lives seemed charmed, if mundane and prosaic, after Anne's saga. What an intense afternoon it had been. How typical it was of Anne Sexton to choose such a public moment to reveal herself and her marriage. "I won't tell anyone," the *Newsweek* photographer vowed. She had had quite enough! We drove in a daze to Harvard Square and drank a lot of coffee.

Psychotherapy played a large part in Anne's life and work. She had started writing poetry at the suggestion of one of her earlier psychiatrists, after a breakdown. She tape-recorded most of her psychiatric sessions and played them over to herself. Later, these tapes were exploited by the psychiatrist, who, with the permission of Anne's daughter Linda Grey Sexton, sold them to a biographer, Diane Wood Middlebrook. But he kept some back for himself, intending to make more money on them later.

Both Anne and Sylvia were obsessed with psychotherapy within a Freudian framework. That was the fashion then. The constant focus on "self" in both poets' work perhaps accounts for an airless, sometimes self-indulgent quality. They also both devote tremendous attention to their anger, which in their imaginations transforms the poets into demons, witches, madwomen, and man-eaters. There is some relation, I think, in both Anne's and Sylvia's work, between the view of themselves as object or victim and a fear of the largeness of their anger toward key figures in their lives. The poem "Her Kind" was especially important to Anne. She always started her poetry readings with these lines from it, standing onstage, still, looking at the audience directly with her magnetic gaze as she recited: "I have gone out, a possessed witch . . ."[22]

Vibrant and beautiful, Anne was very attractive to men in an appealing and vulnerable way. One of her many psychiatrists used the therapeutic situation to make love to her (documented in *Love Poems*). I knew this psychiatrist; the whole community knew about the affair. But none of his colleagues intervened. Anne talked this over extensively with me as well as with other friends, who naturally advised her to break it off. She described the thrill of making love with the therapist on his office rug, while outside the closed door to his waiting room the next patient waited for her appointment.

Anne felt it was a mark of her being special. Her therapist cared about her; so she took it to mean. The word "exploitative," the concept, was not one available to or in usage by women at the time. Anne had several exploitative psychiatrists, one worse than the next. Although it was driving her crazy — or crazier — Anne was unable to break free of her sexual relationship with her doctor. It resonated to earlier abusive experiences, yet there was no framework then for exploring such topics. When finally the psychiatrist got frightened about his wife perhaps finding out about his sexual relationship with Anne, he ended both the therapy and the affair suddenly, without warning. Anne was devastated. This rejection had far-reaching effects. She made a suicide attempt, at least one. The Good Doctor, of course, continued to practice in Boston.

Anne's psychiatric expenses during the last year of her life were enormous (over $60,000). Is he a psychiatrist or a male prostitute, we asked her. Perhaps he should be paying *her*. We knew she could do better than that! Even she had to laugh. Though she had stage fright before her poetry readings, which made her feel unusually vulnerable and exposed, she took a number of engagements to meet her bills.

Recent biographical material based on the transcription of the tapes that Middlebrook bought reveals painful personal material surrounding Anne's life. Anne spoke often to me, as she did to others, of difficult personal material: her husband's violence against her, traumatic events related to her early life, and so forth. Her relationship with her daughter Linda was problematical. Anne listened to the tapes of her psychiatric sessions. I often came over to her house when she was in the midst of listening to the tapes.

Anne was not reticent about sharing her private life if she felt like it. But she did not share these tapes! Her psychiatric sessions were "confidential." They were for her alone. She wanted to learn from them. She wanted desperately to get well, and she had a piteous hope that her doctors would help her. It is my belief that if she had wanted to share the tapes of her psychiatric sessions with others, she would have, particularly with her closest friends, Maxine and Lois. Or with her daughter Linda. She didn't.

Anne committed suicide partly as a reaction to her psychiatrist's making love to her during her sessions and then suddenly jilting her when he was afraid his wife would find out. The violation of Anne's trust by at least two of her psychiatrists was appalling. Not only were they unable to help her during her life; they seem to have been unable to control their lust for sex, financial profit, and notoriety through her. It is blind profiteering that has led others to justify this exploitation. What is clear is the extreme violation of ethics.

The argument that Anne Sexton would not have minded this rape of her privacy is untrue, and self-serving to her emotional rapists. Anne was a beautiful, vulnerable, sensitive woman who trusted her doctors, and whose trust, as we can see, was badly misplaced. The abrupt rejection, the despair — all contributed to her self-destruction, I am convinced. At the time when we all met in Robert Lowell's writing workshop, there was a great prejudice against "women writers." This particularly referred to women who tried to combine female and poetic roles. Exempt were those few poets of stature: Elizabeth Bishop and Marianne Moore, who had neither married nor had children. "She writes like a man" was still the highest male praise given to a clear-minded woman. Both Muriel Rukeyser and Denise Levertov had disqualified themselves, according to Lowell, by celebrating the vagina, thereby managing to offend both Boston propriety and male prerogative in a few quick scribbles.

Sylvia Plath and, at Radcliffe, Adrienne Rich, had partially managed to become exempt, at least for a time. In Sylvia's case, we know the later hardship she struggled against in order to write and care for her children — a hardship that overcame her finally, so that she wanted only to sleep and sleep. Adrienne, too, struggled to maintain her work. But in a system that rewarded young women chiefly for being worshipful and self-effacing, both these women had managed to win prizes, recognition, and approval from the male establishment.

But Anne was something of a renegade. She broadcast her messy personal life, rather than hiding it beneath a veneer of polite and tightened fury. So Anne, by virtue of her lack of formal education and by her "excessive" emotionality and obvious vulnerability, was a lightning rod for criticisms. She inspired controversy.

Reflecting on the suicides of these two talented women, Sexton and Plath, we can of course find multiple reasons for them. We can never really understand the anguish in another's soul. But as a young poet, I was saddened to be deprived of their maturity, and of the fruition of their talents. I admired the work of both Anne Sexton and Sylvia Plath. I wanted to see where their gifts would lead them. I also wanted to understand why so many poets of their generation — and before — committed suicide. Rage, shame, abandonment, and loneliness and exhaustion were at the heart of Sylvia's and Anne's choices. Perhaps if someone had been there at that desperate moment . . .

It is significant that both women chose, as a way of suicide, something that resembled sleep. There are many ways to kill oneself, but Sylvia chose to lay her head in an oven and turn on the gas, and Anne curled up in her car and turned on the motor. They were later found, perfect, ladylike, frozen Sleeping Beauties for eternity. In our minds they are fixed in "their cold perfection," pale with suppressed rage. But their postures suggest they were seeking rest; they were exhausted, and for that moment they just felt they couldn't go on.

I will talk more about this later, but for the moment, I want to stay with this memory. Anne Sexton was a great artist in her energy, the intensity of her feelings, and she was an exuberant and loyal friend. We spent many happy times together, engrossed: curled up in her study, sharing a meal in the kitchen, or sitting outside in the sun.

Anne had used her fellowship from the Radcliffe Institute of Independent Study (given at least partially to women on the basis of need) to build herself an outdoor swimming pool. This fact did not please the worthy ladies of Radcliffe! Nevertheless, that swimming pool gave Anne a great deal of pleasure, as well as the frequent presence of friends. At the first faintly warmish days of spring, Anne moved her visitors outside under the weak New England sunlight, sheaves of paper around us, books open to thrilling lines of poetry. It was cold, but we dove into the chilly water, pushing aside the dead leaves and new pollen that floated on the surface.

I remember swimming nude in the pool, looking at trees, and drinking Anne's newest drink discovery, Champale, giggling over vague poetic jokes. Or drying off, sitting in the sun, reading each other's poems. Maxine Kumin and her children would arrive. Maxine dove into the pool, cool, competent, and graceful. Anne, on Thorazine, would move a bit into the shade. The phone rang and was dragged outside. Anne's children came home from school. The Dalmatian dragged its puppies outside. Figures were commented on: hips and waists. I had a baby. Lois got her divorce. Maxine's daughter entered Radcliffe. Anne's children grew up. Poems were shared and magazines passed around. We wrote and wrote and read and revised and wrote. We read aloud to each other. Steam rose from the pool; the light grew thin; the leaves fell. And we swam until late October . . .

Teatime with Robert Lowell
and Elizabeth Hardwick

The terms of my fellowship from Oberlin did not involve private study with Lowell. But he insisted I come to his house a couple of times a week. With Lowell, I would spend the afternoon in a private tutorial, much as I had with my professors at college. Often he would show me the work he was doing, and I remember seeing drafts of "For the Union Dead," the title poem of his new collection: "the drained faces of Negro school-children rise like balloons."[23]

Lowell's study was at the top of his house on Marlborough Street, looking out on the famous magnolia tree and the watery spring sky. It was very quiet there. Lowell worked endlessly and carefully on his poems, painstakingly changing a word, a punctuation mark, and reading the poem aloud. He shared the books he was reading and the poets he discovered. He said once, when talking of Auden, that to be able to write just one perfect memorable line of poetry was an incredible achievement. And Auden, he understated to me, by way of gentle encouragement, "had written several."

In those private afternoons, high above the city, in that comfortable study, Lowell was no different in his approach to a poem than he was later to be in his office hours. I don't think that at the time I was fully aware of the privilege of Lowell's having "taken me on" in this private-tutorial way. I took it to mean that he despaired of my ignorance, that he thought I was more stupid than his other students and needed remedial help. "What does it mean?"—that question—completely stymied me. "I don't know...," I would apologize, feeling ashamed of my ignorance. I was terrified of this situation, actually. My stomach growled.

Lowell sat at his desk, his back to the window, facing me, staring down at the book. Or he would slouch on a piece of saggy furniture, an old couch or chair, patiently waiting, it seemed, forever. He mumbled, hunched over a poem. There seemed to be lots of pages about, drafts of his poems. I couldn't make out the minute differences in revision. I sat tensely, with my best posture, and forbade myself to look at the clock. Lowell sprawled, at ease: he had all the time in the world.

I stared out the window at the pigeons on the roof and prayed for liberation. The hours ticked by slowly. Perhaps there was some answer to "What does this mean?" ("you dummy") that eluded me. Lowell would read the line over to me — actually, to himself. Was I being given a second chance? I knew — as does any high school graduate — that a wild guess could get me in trouble. Why, oh why, hadn't Oberlin prepared me for this?

Lowell frowned at the page and rubbed his forehead. He seemed lost in a private reverie. I hardly dared say anything, just a few inarticulate sighs. Time passed slowly. It got dark. Quietly, in a tentative stumbling way, Lowell would elucidate the poem himself. He did this, musing, as if writing the poem at the same time as he deciphered its meaning. A poem, when Lowell had finished delving into it, had no less magic.

My visits to Lowell's study during those early years began right after lunch and lasted to teatime or dinner. Once or twice a week I traveled through the dank Boston streets to the brick house with its magnolia tree in front. I rang the doorbell a long long time, and finally someone would open it. A nurse or maid glared at me suspiciously. Then Elizabeth Hardwick, within, would catch sight of me. "Darling, your student's here," she called pityingly over her shoulder, into the depths of the house. Lowell would shamble downstairs. "Come in," he said absently, not noticing that I was already in. "I was just reading . . . ," he would begin, wandering back up the stairs again. I looked round nervously for a place to leave my coat and boots, and then, fearing to be left downstairs to make conversation, I ended up by carrying my coat and boots and books after his retreating back.

"You know, it's really quite remarkable . . . ," Lowell drawled, already deep in conversation with himself. I was behind and could not quite catch his accent, but no intelligent words were required of me just the same. I was just another hardly noticeable interruption of his thoughts, like a page turning. I followed him up to the attic, with its marvelous view of the river and beyond, and its many books and pieces of scribbled paper, many words crossed out and rewritten. I had never firsthand seen a poet rewrite his poems so much. The surfaces were littered. I stood in the middle of the room holding my things until "Mr. Lowell" cleared a place for them, and for me, and motioned me to the leather armchair. "There," he said, "where was I?" He frowned. "I was just reading the *Iliad* and . . ."

It was quiet on the top floor of the house. So far above Boston, the Charles River gleamed and the late afternoon sun reflected off the State House. It was as if we were on a sailboat together, isolated, beginning an incredible adventure. "There is no frigate like a book," came to mind. I thought of bookplates and libraries and the mystery, the promise of books. Lowell moved from Homer to Shakespeare to Randall Jarrell to his own poems with ease in the heady twilight. In the silences, speculative with reading, a clock ticked deliberately. If I hung on long enough, perhaps the Lowells would feed me. Meals, meals! A social meal with people who might talk to me!

I dreaded going back to my lonely rooming house, and being Rilke! I was reading Rilke obsessively that winter; I was miserable, lonely, just the way he had been! In fact, who knew, I might even eventually die in Boston of pathetic isolation, like most of the people I saw on the streets about me. They shuttled about in the dark wintry streets, their faces contorted with private unreadable histories. I tried to push away these pitiful thoughts, to concentrate on the poetry at hand. But I had already lost the thread of what Mr. Lowell was saying to me. I turned hot with the shame and fear of disappointing my teacher. I hadn't yet realized that there wasn't any thread, had never been one, that reading a poem with Robert Lowell was like giving oneself over to its flashing spokes of light.

After my initial few months of terror, I relaxed. It seemed, once I settled in to the armchair across from Lowell, surrounded by books and words, that I belonged there, had always lived in that world where poetry had such power. I had been waiting all my life for these conversations. Now they were upon me, in that Lowell read and led me to read and inquired into my thoughts on what I read. I found that these hours, for which I had longed so, were the most pleasant I had ever spent. I came alive! I had a real poetry friend! I had a poetry teacher! No matter that I couldn't understand half of what he said about poetry; the man was simply brilliant, that was it, and I was privileged to be there in that brilliance. All I had to do was listen and witness and appreciate and learn. This took incredible intensity, of course. But now it was natural to be reading poetry with Robert Lowell, and, as with an old friend, I did not feel any need to say much. But I began to see into the poems, even to have some opinions. Lowell read aloud to me, with an appreciative gleam in his eyes. He looked up from the page, occasionally asked a question, made a rhetorical, so I supposed, journey into the poem at hand. He smiled with pleasure at the poem he was rediscovering before my eyes. He invited me to share the moment with him. I fell in love and — perhaps — he did too. . . . We were looking at poetry together; we were looking into the mirror of our own hearts. In this now-developing deep whatever-it-was — (*friendship? lifelong love?*) — I was utterly accepted, valued. I felt the strong presence of the man, his dear kindness, his mind, and corporeality. I would feel it always, through personal histories and events that took us in various directions.

My understanding of poetry was beginning to form. Poems that before were difficult to comprehend, coalesced; the meanings revealed themselves. Lowell did me the honor of making me his companion, an adored equal, huddled over those tattered books in that old study high above Boston, sailing among the twilight-darkening cloudscapes into the mystery that is poetry. It sounds like a fairy story achieved merely through the magic of regarding pages next to each other. Though at the time I apprehended this only subliminally, it was the beginning of a lifelong journey together.

At a certain point the session ended, and I followed Lowell downstairs again for tea: lavish English tea with scones and butter and cream and sandwiches in my case, a stiff drink in his. My impression of the Lowell interiors was always gloomy: old wood, lots of old books with their gilt edges and musty smell, delicate china and silver and serving dishes. Elizabeth Hardwick was a light, glamorous, verbal creature. Their little daughter Harriet was brought into the drawing room, where the tea service was laid out in front of a fire, in the arms of her nurse, to be admired in her little snowsuit bunting before going out into the park. The nurse wore a white uniform, as if out of a play. We fussed over the child; Harriet regarded me, the interloper, gravely. Polite conversation would be made, and, as in this writing of it, the talk was usually in the passive tense, with references to "one" instead of "you" or "I," all in true Boston gentlemanly and self-effacing fashion, meant to imply high standards of personal and literary objectivity.

Once downstairs, in Lowell's "real life," I was intimidated and tongue-tied. Away from the realm of books and poetry, I could not enter a more social setting. With Lowell I felt graceful, beautiful, intelligent, and interesting. But in the milieu that was Boston I was overcome by wordless despair. Harriet Lowell was perhaps two years old at the time, and very much the darling of the household. Elizabeth Hardwick was warm and outgoing to me. But it was easier to play with Harriet, to coo over her as she came in from her playtime. Harriet also possessed a much-celebrated and written-about guinea pig.

It grew darker inside, the drapes were drawn, but lights were not lit. A faint melancholy; this was more formal than any afternoon with my college tutor. Elizabeth Hardwick kindly asked if I were hungry. I was too embarrassed to say yes. My hands shook as I spilled tea into the saucer, and I was afraid to tip it back into the cup. Asking for two lumps of sugar, please, would have seemed an extraordinary breach of good taste. Boston was to be the first place I would experience an American version of the "class system," and with a vengeance.

Going out into the smoky, hazy, darkening spring dusk and walking home past the magnolias and red-brick buildings back into Cambridge heightened this sense of alienation. Upstairs, alone with Robert Lowell and the books of poems, I could manage. But downstairs, in the midst of the solicitous Lowell-Hardwick household, I felt awkwardly young, lumpish, and tongue-tied. They were so kind to me! A lot of their conversation then was about New York literary figures — the Lowells were planning to move to New York — and there was no way I could contribute, so in awe was I of the persons mentioned.

Elizabeth Hardwick seemed a faerie creature, all light and grace. It was only when Cal had a breakdown, and Hardwick took over his classes at Boston University, that I saw clearly her more rigorous side. She read the class an article she had just written, criticizing the *New York Times Sunday Book Review*. The article was to be the foundation of the *New York Review of Books*, an alternative forum. On the strength of hearing Hardwick read her article, the class all subscribed to the new newspaper.

Later, the Lowells moved to New York. Except for occasional visits to their apartment, I did not see Elizabeth Hardwick as much. Like their house in Boston, their apartment also seemed dark, high-ceilinged, with windows along one wall, heavy drapes, and rows and rows of bookshelves, with a ladder to reach the higher ones. I wasn't able to read their titles. The furniture was formal, curved, with delicate legs. Perhaps it was because Lowell had grown up in this Brahmin gloom, which he wrote about in *Life Studies* and elsewhere, but darkness, dim light, libraries with books so far up one couldn't read the titles, all seemed to suit him. He would talk on and on of poets and poetry while the room grew thick and dark.

One time, in 1967, I had (after a difficult pregnancy) lost a child; I traveled to New York to visit Cal. For months after this loss I had been unable even to get up, the world seemed so dark. It was an absolutely devastating period in my life, one of the blackest. I decided not to mention a word of this child and something in my bearing made Cal keep away from the subject as well. Determined to have a "normal" visit, I was glad to see him and to talk about books and poetry rather than about what had been preoccupying me. And I had brought some poems to show him. He was tactful enough to praise them. We were deep in conversation, and the old bond of trust was there. Then Elizabeth Hardwick came into the room, flushed with the excitement of New York and everything she was doing there. Kindly and immediately, she expressed her sympathy to me. She seemed so offhand, so formally polite. So unthinkably glamorous, as if nothing bad had ever happened to her! My defensiveness rushed to the surface at her expression of sympathy. I hadn't wanted anyone even to know what had happened, nor how I felt about it. How could she comment on my inner situation in such a casual way? Mortifying tears came to my eyes, I found myself unable to speak, and I fled, feeling a total failure.

Long after Robert Lowell's death, I visited Elizabeth Hardwick in their New York apartment. I was astonished to see the large windows open to the light, and the golden light of morning flooding in to what was actually a large, airy room. The interior seemed graceful, livable. Perhaps it was the presence of Elizabeth Hardwick, in 1990 as beautiful as ever. Or perhaps it was the absence of Lowell himself, the depressive quality that darkened his own interior. Elizabeth Hardwick was warm, light, graceful, and brilliant. The rooms sparkled.

Literary Boston in the Late '50s and '60s
Social Milieu, Class, and the Literary Tradition

When I came to Boston in the winter of 1959, I was struck by the city's class-based society. I was witness to the milieu of the Boston Brahmins, which was really something impenetrable. Their Boston carried the weighty tradition of outstanding New England literary flowering to which Lowell definitely felt connected. Boston was Puritan in so many aspects of that word. But it was possibly against that repression that so many of our great writers who came from this region defined themselves.

Coming as an undergraduate from Oberlin College to be Robert Lowell's tutorial student, I was in the middle of the airless atmosphere of puritanical Boston and the Lowells' house there. I met members of his family, his old school friends, and others. I was often around for cocktail hours or meals — too shy to eat anything, too shy to go home. Elizabeth Hardwick introduced me patronizingly as "Cal's little student." So that was my role, my place, as in a Victorian novel: *"the little student/friend/observing/secretly-in-love/Jane Eyre"* in the corner, and I was defined as such within the Lowell circle.

From the late '50s to the late '70s, I was able to observe the culture and its impact on both Robert Lowell and Elizabeth Bishop. I worked at Boston City and State Hospitals, the Whitty Boiler Manufacturing Company, the State House, at Harvard, and the posh *Atlantic Monthly*, peering through the large windows onto the Public Gardens. On the surface Brahmin Bostonians were classically well educated, extremely formal, and well mannered. This society was elitist, literary to the max. But underneath lay a world seething with contradictions, repression, and rebellion.

In the late '50s, the label "Banned in Boston" was a guarantee of instant success. The old North and West Churches, starchy High Episcopal bastions, flanked the Combat Zone. Prostitutes roamed the back of Beacon Hill. Money flashed in the elevators of the State House in broad daylight. So did the ever-hopeful, hairy-legged "flashers" in their raincoats. But openly gay men were locked away in back wards or clubbed to death in the bushes. Gay women, unthinkable: if possible, they went to hide in Europe. Mental hospitals flourished. Harvard cast its long shadow, and Miss Bishop was treated shabbily. Lowell was barely tolerated by the "Academy."

The typical "Proper Bostonian" was white, straight, quietly wealthy, land-rich, Protestant, and, if male, preferably a banker or lawyer. The ethnicities were ghettoized. In public, poets like Bishop as well as Lowell, so conscious of family, society, and schooling, went out of their way to assume protective coloration. The pressures on them to "conform" were intense. As did many New England writers past and present, Lowell and Bishop forged an uneasy accommodation with Boston and the larger region, which did not entirely accept them. In their life and work they sought to understand, escape, be embraced by, and transcend this complex heritage.

Boston, in the late '50s and early '60s, and its satellite, Cambridge, had a mystique that existed in the world of paintings, literature, and thought. It was the home of the *Atlantic Monthly,* as well as the fearsome literature department of Harvard University. The shadow of Harvard was cast everywhere, like a tall tombstone. Revolutionary history marked the streets. Intellectuals sat in the all-night cafeterias discussing great thoughts. Most of the shops sold books, books, books: used ones and new ones and foreign ones. Small whiskered men darted in and out of these shops. There were stores with art prints in their windows. There were stationery shops, a typewriter store, and very little else that was not devoted to the life of the mind.

Men wore corduroys or tweeds and heavy crew-neck sweaters. Women wore their hair up in buns, black lisle stockings, oxfords or heels, skirts and blouses. The clothing stores sold liberty blouses, primly buttoned on mannequins, plaid and pleated skirts, and cardigan-pullover sets. Girls wore camel's hair coats or, occasionally, pea jackets. The presence of a "boyfriend," however, allowed one to wear his sweaters or shirts.

The scene was conformist in its way, relentlessly bluestocking interspersed with young Harvard men's athleticism. The old Hayes-Bickford Cafeteria was open until the small hours of the morning. It served watery coffee, bread or rice pudding, toasted English muffins, beef stew, and boiled meats — the standards. So did the Waldorf Cafeteria. Bums as well as students could be seen in them at night, as well as the Harvard Square hangers-on, dropouts who had somehow found their way there and were posing as students. A fast-food delicatessen, Elsie's, was available for more solid fare. Its roast-beef-special sandwiches were famous, and the lines at Elsie's stood five deep. The air reeked of grease: Bartley's Burgers never changed its frying oil, and the charred hamburger smell permeated everything. The grease saturated the food, and the limply curled french fries sagged under its weight. In the winter air, the oily smoke fumed out of the place, rising. It was warm when you walked by, almost like the subway grates. Inside there was sawdust on the floor reminiscent of elementary school, of kids being sick and janitors. Waiters hollered out their orders, and banged the crockery down. Mr. Bartley presided over all this, palely reddish-haired, at the register.

I had arrived in winter. I visited the Museum of Fine Arts, the Gardner Museum, and the Boston Public Library. I walked the Freedom Trail, looked at the Burial Ground and Old North Church and fainted in stale Filene's Basement. There was an atmosphere of deep gloom upon the city; cold and dark had walled in its inhabitants. On old overheated trolleys that screeched madly, old people sat with their bags and bundles. I stayed away from my rooming house as long as I could, waiting for Robert Lowell to reemerge from a breakdown and teach me. But eventually I would have to give up, go back, and settle in for a long and lonely evening.

I was terrified of my landlady, Mrs. Ryan, with her stout, corseted body and her face perpetually apoplectic. And equally terrified of her small, spindly husband. I subsisted on the simplest of fare: bouillon cubes, oranges, raw carrots, and raisin bread. There were other people in the house whom I got to know much later. Laura Nader, Ralph Nader's sister, lived there, finishing her thesis on anthropology. The British scientist Molly Gleiser was working at MIT. And poet Mary Carleton Swope, in her last year at Radcliffe, had an apartment below me. She was finishing her studies with Archibald MacLeish, who favored the men in his class.

I tiptoed through the musty hall, past the ever-prying eyes of Mrs. Ryan up to the looming dark of my room. Once I tried to wash my sheets in the bathtub, and the Ryans came upstairs and yelled at me. Didn't I know they sent them out to the laundry? I didn't know, had no idea that linen might be sent out somewhere to be washed.

I read my favorite writer, Rilke, obsessively. I was deep in *The Notebooks of Malte Laurids Brigge*. This journal based on Rilke's stay in Paris was my guidepost. It offered some reason, some previous counterpart, to the poverty, alcoholism, and madness I saw on the streets and streetcars of Boston. And it offered a counterpart to my agonizingly self-conscious loneliness in a city where I knew no one. "So, then, people do come here in order to live; I would sooner have thought one died here."[24] And further on I read, as if written from my own interior landscape: "I am learning to see. I don't know why it is, but everything penetrates more deeply into me and does not stop at the place where until now it always used to finish." In Rilke I found my double in self-consciousness, my own thoughts expressed in the most poignant way. I read and reread his work. He had written, as if for my eyes alone: "And you should not let yourself be confused in your solitude by the fact there is something in you that wants to break out of it." But I was waiting. I waited perpetually for Lowell to come out of the hospital and teach me something; I waited to enter the poems I could not yet write; I waited for something or someone to appear and illumate the solitude.

Cambridge was a red-brick and cobbled town in the environs of Harvard Square. In the fall the town showed itself best, with crisp days, the click of hurrying heels, and the colors of trees against blue skies. Just a few short blocks away was Central Square, with its dirt and grime, the whine of the subway, the blowing paper and despair on the streets. Woolworth's seemed the centerpiece of Central Square, with its red crowded entrance. Stale Halloween candy-corn still rotted by the cash registers in February, and limp, red, crepe-paper streamers, once festooned hopefully, now sagged from the low fluorescent glare of the ceilings. No party here. Bag ladies with hennaed hair shuffled through the aisles seeking a bit of warmth, or hung out at the counters just wanting to talk to someone/anyone. Outside, old men in worn slippers pulled crushed newspapers out of the overflowing trash cans, wiping their noses on their sleeves.

I watched the formidably Smart Young Things in smart clothes moving quickly about pretty, red-brick Harvard Square. One subway stop away, the homeless characters — right out of Rilke! — haunted Central Square. Harvard University paid no taxes to the city of Cambridge, enjoying its privilege, so Central Square with its sooty maw of a subway, its grit whirling about in the winter wind, its neon fast-food ugliness was a result. "Life: A cautionary tale."

Harvard Square had its share of grime and despair, of course, but nevertheless it provided a successful intellectual island. I attended, in those early years, meetings of the Poets' Theatre, a theater for verse drama, and some of the early meetings of *Audience*, a literary magazine. Poets Ruth Whitman and Stephen Sandy were friendly, but the arcane intellectualism of both settings was hard to penetrate. Pretentiousness was the order of the day. The *Harvard Advocate*, the undergraduate literary magazine, was a prime example. Women were scorned, except as bedmates. The young male editors postured and drawled. Cambridge seemed an imitation of England, an England out of books: P. G. Wodehouse primarily, with stuffy young prigs in abundance.

When the need to be among people, no matter whom, became great, I would go to the reading room of Widener Library, where people would eye each other between the turnings of newspaper and magazine pages. Friends of mine, students at Simmons College, would go to Widener to pose as Harvard students and meet Harvard "men."

The coldness of the Boston literary scene was not to be believed, and first attempts to broach that were impossible. I wandered into the Grolier Bookshop, a small store that specialized in poetry. Gordon Cairnie, the owner, was courteous. Deciding that it would be nice for me to know some young writers, he telephoned a poet, Arthur Freeman. Arthur's voice crackled distinctly over the phone. "I am not interested in meeting a lady poet from Ohio," he said clearly. I was mortified. Before talking to Gordon, and even buying books at the Grolier Bookshop, one had to run the gauntlet of the "male club" that pre-empted the place. I wanted to be as unobtrusive as possible; I waited outside, peering in the window to see whether the coast was clear before I would enter. Large, knowledgeable, roast-beef men sat on a sofa, talking familiarly about local poets. Later I was to become close to Gordon, and also to his young helper, Louisa Solano, who took over the store after Gordon's death. It was difficult to enter in those days; the men sat on the couch, comfortably, and the others, women or unknowns, scuttled in and out as quickly as possible. The new owner, Louisa Solano, transformed this poetry bookshop; she created an entirely different place. Louisa and I had met in the summer of 1958 when we double-dated two roommates from MIT. The young men faded from our lives, but we remain friends to this day.

Louisa worked during the week at a bookstore in Boston and helped Gordon Cairnie at the Grolier on Saturday afternoons. She was already set on a career as a bookseller. During the course of her ownership of the Grolier, Louisa became one of the great booksellers, especially of poetry and all things concerning that art. Her archives of the period are at Harvard; they show an extraordinary record of American poetry during the later part of the twentieth century. When she retired, Louisa sold the Grolier to a mutual friend, the poet and philosophy professor Ifeanyi Menkiti. After her retirement, the city of Cambridge dedicated a street to her name. Ifeanyi

Menkiti and his wife, Carol, continued to respect the tradition established by Louisa, while adding their own multicultural flavor to the shelves.

The list of writers and artists in Cambridge at that time was impressive. But, dear reader, if you have come this far, skip the next pages! For they are interesting only to those who lived this time. Like any in-group, we witnessed each other's development. But there were writers/artists growing up all over the United States, in California, New York, Iowa, and everywhere! And writing with nostalgia about their good old days. It's boring if you haven't lived this, fascinating if you have. So skip this, skip this — Reader, we were no Jack K(erouac) — and if you're looking for the Merry Pranksters in what follows, turn the page.

For how can I convey the excitement, the sheer conversation of these times? Even then we were aware of mythologizing ourselves though we didn't have a Sartre or Simone de Beauvoir to do it for us. We found each other in the little coffee shops of Harvard Square. We met almost daily. We discussed everything: philosophy, poetry, personal lives, and of course, during those years, we all participated in political activism. We still are politically active. We still read, write, work, think, share creative work, and personal issues — those of us who are still alive. We thought we would talk to each other forever, for the rest of our lives. And so we have.

Back then, Cambridge was our Paris! The center of the universe! And Harvard Square our Montparnasse. The Café Pamplona was our Deux Magots; the Hayes-Bickford Cafeteria our Brasserie Lipp. Out of the steamy windows of the cafeterias we saw famous people — wasn't that Robert Frost? — hurrying, coat collars up, huddled against the cold. The snow piled grimy in the streets. The lowering skies threatened sleet and grim weather. But inside the cheap cafeterias, the warming counters offered, swimming in the wells, languidly tepid, overcooked string beans and graying corned-beef hash. Flecks of cream curdled in the coffee, sloshing. We drank lots of it. Dunked crushable English muffins or "Hermits." Eggs over easy, tapioca pudding, white toast, pea soup, rice pudding, gluey Boston beans. In the mouth, food fell to nothing: gummy, off-white, slippery, and oysterish. Old-people food, down-easy.

Who noticed? We were talking, talking. The air vibrated with intellectual excitement. We were living in an era of greatest American poetry, and these poets were living in our midst. Chomsky, Erik Erikson, and many other great professors: Galbraith, Fairchild, Warren Ambrose, Howard Zinn, and others influenced us also. It was the late '50s. It was the '60s. Anything could happen.

The writer Sara Sagov lived next door with her fiancé, Pronob Mitter, a physicist, in a building in which James Alan MacPherson, the fiction writer, was the caretaker. Louisa Solano, our poetry specialist, lived there also. Avant-garde psychologists like Philip Helfaer, who founded the Institute for Bioenergetic Analysis, was at that time writing his thesis. Myron Sharif, a therapist and the biographer of Wilhelm Reich, lived in the same building as Susan and David Jhirad. Louis Kampf was part of this group, along with Heather Shain, Ellen Cantarow, and others. John Marshall and Tim and Patsy Asch were making films of Bushmen and Yanomamo Indians. Writers Robert Melson, Gail and Mike Mazur, Jacques Kornberg, Gordon Fellman, Celia Gilbert, Gail Freidman, Florence Ladd, Marty Peretz, and others huddled in dark places in intense conversations. The seeds of their interests were already evident. Everyone was becoming a writer or an artist or filmmaker or scientist. We were "becoming" what we would later "be." There were endless discussions, parties, romances, breakups, new romances, political passions.

Massachusetts Avenue was a small stretch of stores, on one side Harvard, with its great libraries, on the other, the small vertical streets going down toward the Charles River. The cobblestones of Plympton Street throbbed with literary life. It spilled over in dank, dark cafés — the Pamplona, always good for whipped cream and discussion, or the old University Restaurant. "Bartley's Burgers" mouth-watered the air. The waiters and waitresses everywhere were all writing books or undergoing psychoanalysis or trying to write their Harvard doctoral theses. (Often these activities took place simultaneously.) The pungency of sweet-and-sour from the Hong Kong restaurant merged with the acidic smells of the copying machines underneath.

The Grolier was often in financial trouble, as it supported its overhead by the sale of poetry books alone. To raise money for the store, poets, led by Bill Ferguson, Barney Holland, and others, set "famous poems" in type on a press in the basement of Lamont Library, and printed a fine edition. Another time we put on a theatrical extravaganza organized by poet Bill Corbett, where poets read and spoke. I dressed up as Gordon Cairnie and did a funny piece about the store, the poets who came in, and Gordon himself. The highlight was a bump-and-grind parody of some of the goings-on in the store, called "No Bones," which I had written in John Berryman's style. As I performed it, I stripped off Gordon's tweed overcoat and cap, flung them into the audience, and finished in a bathing suit and fishnet stockings.

No Bones

Those literary gennelmun
one could do better than to run
wif dem . . .

Significant Other, 1959–1977

I had been given two names to look up in Boston, besides Lowell's. It was months before I summoned the courage to contact them. One was an old childhood friend. Now married to an artist, with two small children, Aggie Smit provided me with a substitute family. The other was Mayer Spivack, whose two cousins had gone to Oberlin with me. "If you have some time, call him," they had said, writing down his name and number. Finally I did, and a warm, friendly voice breathing out of the abysmal loneliness of Cambridge answered.

Mayer lived in a house shared with Henry Geldzhaler and artist Johnny Shahn (Ben Shahn's son). The Japanese artist Yoshi Shimizu and others also lived there part of the time. The toilet, doorless, was in the hall; a shower occupied most of the kitchen; and Henry sat reading in his room with sunglasses on, no matter what hour of day or night. Poet Alan Dugan and his wife, artist Judith Shahn, were often visitors. Mayer seemed very much in the center of Cambridge life. He hung out at the old Café Mozart, staring intensely into the woodwork, and also helped run the old Club 47, a center for folk music.

Mayer was dark and intense and brooding. He was in art school and spent his time in the cafés, sketching. Later, when a friend, Heather Shain, found out that I was involved with Mayer, she exclaimed, "Well, I certainly hope you can bring him out!" She had dated him once, found him taciturn and sullen. They had driven to Worcester and fought about how to get there. We were whispering about this in the reading room of Widener Library; her sudden expostulation shattered the sacred library quiet.

The first evening we met, Mayer gave me his black turtleneck sweater and a crystal ball. He announced that we were going to be married. He then telephoned his mother and told her. I was alarmed at his rash declaration. His mother said, quite reasonably, "But shouldn't you get to know her first?" "I'll know her as well as I'll ever know her," Mayer proclaimed in grand and arrogant fashion. Since we had spent exactly four hours together at this point, I was surprised. But thrilled and fascinated as well. What a romantic statement! Mayer was an artist as well as "crazy inventor," with thick, curly black hair standing straight out as if he were permanently wired. He thought associatively, in a unique way. Life with him was exciting and fun.

What a romantic character! "Reader, I married him . . ." But that was almost a year later, at Christmas. Neither family came to our wedding.

My parents disapproved of the relationship with Mayer. Though they had never met him, they opposed any idea of a forthcoming marriage and threatened to cut me off if I went through with it. There was more pressure. Robert Lowell offered to take me in to stay with his family for a while, his home becoming my "official address" when I moved in with my future husband. My parents wanted me to have a steady job and marry a stable man and couldn't understand my desire to write.

In 1959 all I wanted to do was re-create the lives of Simone de Beauvoir and Sartre, and just *live* with Mayer Spivack. Mayer's parents pressured him to "stop living in sin." Mayer's parents were getting nowhere, so they changed tactics: they wanted us to be married, quick! so that he could, as his father put it, "make a decent woman out of me." I didn't especially want to be a "decent woman": I had read too many novels.

Robert Lowell was resigned to the fact that I could not completely focus on poetry, given the emotional turmoil of the moment. By this time the tutorials had expanded to long conversations about our lives, cups of coffee after class, tea, dinner, and so forth. "Let me meet your young man," he offered. We arranged to meet Mayer on a street corner near the B.U. Bridge. It was a dark, rainy afternoon, and the wind and rain whipped through our thin coats. The class had, as usual, run later than expected. I shivered. Lowell put his arm about me. Mayer was late. Lowell talked vaguely about Randall and Allen (Randall Jarrell, poet and friend, and Allen Tate, the literary critic and Lowell's mentor-teacher) as we waited. Finally Mayer arrived. Lowell was soaked, though gallant, and the three of us had tea and made conversation in The Pit, a dive on Commonwealth Avenue. Both Mayer and Cal were frowning with the intensity of the moment, though I could see that both were pleased. They continued to have a cordial association throughout the years.

"I'll go to New Jersey and talk to your parents." Lowell did, told them I was a promising poet and that Mayer was a fine young man — and my parents were totally bewildered. And even more worried. How would I make a living? What was this fairly unintelligible Bostonian trying to tell them? A poet! And a mad one at that — that was hardly an endorsement for their first-born daughter. They did not take kindly to what they saw as Lowell's interference. Lowell came back and reported to me about the meeting and was so foggily kind to me for weeks that I adored that man forever.

"It's good for a poet to be married," Lowell said, patting my shoulder and offering a large white handkerchief. (It was the era of ironed handkerchiefs.) The strain of so many pressures and decisions had overcome me, and I wept in his office at Boston University as well as at Marlborough Street. These words seemed to reassure me; I did not consider the source. "There, there." I was literally crying on his shoulder, no doubt having a little nervous breakdown of my own. Lowell was at that time the only "grown-up" to whom I could confide, since my parents, so long my confidants, were opposed to my marriage. Lowell was understanding, kind, and he listened. Pressure on me from all sides — my family, Mayer, his family — was overwhelming. For one, both sets of parents thought we were too young. Then, we had different backgrounds. These were only the start of their objections.

When Mayer and I later took the train to New Jersey so that he could meet my family, my parents were so agitated that they had a huge fight. "I'm leaving!" my mother cried, calling a taxi. "I'm leaving too!" shouted my father, and he called the same cab company. There were only two cabs in town, and my parents rode around Montclair Plaza in their separate cabs, shrieking out of the windows at each other. "It's your fault!" My brother and sisters wailed, bereft, and Mayer and I looked at each other. I was mortified. Mayer told me that his parents had never, in all his life, had a fight or even a cross word.

The next day my parents decided that we would play "charades," which they pronounced in the British way: "shah-rhawdes." They had invented their own version of the game, which was based on one word only. My father chose Mayer as his teammate, and the rest of us comprised the other team. Mayer was bewildered, but he did as he was told. For almost an hour he crouched on our cold porch floor, while my father, in a silk dressing gown that he also wore when he did his imitations of Martha Graham's modern-dance compositions with his faculty cronies, hovered above him brandishing a large fly swatter.

"Zhh Zhh Zhh!" my father thrilled, fluttering his kimono sleeves and making motions to us to try and guess what he and Mayer were enacting. He was swatting at Mayer enthusiastically now, just barely missing him. Of course we couldn't guess. Mayer was cowering. Finally our team all gave up.

"Mosquito!" my father crowed triumphantly, waving the fly swatter one last time. "Mosquito!"

I had the idea that to be a writer, a "real" writer, one had to know "real" life. Although I had been partially supported on fellowship moneys that Lowell found for me, I decided to experience something even more real. The "ashcan school of realism" dominated literary perception in the late fifties. Paddy Chayefsky, Arthur Miller, these writers had influenced our ways of looking at things. I knew nothing about "realism." I took a job in a boiler factory in Allston. I rode my bicycle across the river from Cambridge each day to grease and rivet various metallic protrusions. Perhaps a non-writing job would leave my mind free for poetry. But the noise of the Whitty Boiler Factory was so deafening that my mind was good for nothing both during and after the workday. "What's a nice girl like you doing in a place like this?" my fellow workers asked me. "I want to be a writer, a *real* writer!" I cried. "I want to know everything and write about it!" But after my days at the factory, I was too tired to even think about writing. Back home, my father was tearing his hair. This was the beginning of various job experiments, writing jobs versus non-writing jobs. I wanted to be relevant, like William Carlos Williams, or Chekhov. They at least were doctors; they were doing something people would have considered "useful."

Mayer got a job at MIT, and that gave us the financial wherewithal to marry. I reasoned that if I went and simply got the marriage over with, everyone would come round in the end and I would be able to stop crying. Mayer's boss, Edwin Land, a few friends, and some non-parental relatives came. The minister of a Unitarian Church married us amid his collection of strange fertility statues and fetishes. We were relieved that a decision had been made, finally, and hoped this would take family pressure off us both. Actually, we went on to have a lovely young marriage and two wonderful children. We were to recall our lives together with great affection, humor, and love.

Oberlin had been a great folk music center, especially during the beginning of the civil rights struggle. Mayer and I shared a lot: humor, an ironic sense of life, and a desire to be artists. We were both amateur musicians. Together, we played backup with various musicians who came to town. Mayer played the ocarina and banjo, and I, who had studied cello, played guitar, autoharp, harpsichord, and other keyboard instruments. They all sounded appropriately twangy. I also knew every sad love song in the book: "*Once I had a lover and now I have none . . . warble warble.*" That sort of song.

At Club 47 we heard Joan Baez, Mimi and Dick Farina, Maria Muldaur, Mitch Greenhill, and other young singers perform, and we jammed with them after hours. We played backup with the Jug Band and other musicians and groups of the time. It was the era of folk singing and music-making in peoples' homes. Theodore Bikel, Cynthia Gooding, are still in our old record collections. Pete Seeger, the Weavers, Odetta all gave us songs. At the Newport Folk Festival, we camped at a friend's place, played, and, historically, watched Bob Dylan transform his music, much to the dismay of Pete Seeger.

We also sang madrigals at home with friends. I played cello in amateur string quartets, and music-making united the times. Folk music was a very small club scene at the time; even B. B. King played in a tiny smoky bar in the Combat Zone. Most music took place in peoples' kitchens. The *do-it-yourself* sixties movement was launching itself. Mayer was very supportive of my writing and came to every poetry reading I gave. He did the beautiful covers of my first two books. In the seventies, performing, I remember looking down from the stage of the American Repertory Theatre to see Mayer and our two young children lip-synching along with me, every word, smiling encouragingly: they had heard me rehearse so much.

The first year in Boston had been poignant, sharp in the relief into which the city was thrown. I never experienced such terrible loneliness again. But the impression remained. Later I wrote a poem about the experience through Rilke's eyes.

Sojourning alone in Paris,
he thought, now finally
he was a poet . . .[25]

Adrienne Rich, 1960s

Robert Lowell, when he was at a loss as to what to do with a young woman who had come to Boston just to work with him, called on the women he knew to help. He introduced me to women poets in the area. These were "formal" letters of introduction, handwritten on cream vellum, not to be ignored. The women invited me to their homes. "Formal" meant one dressed for the occasion. Homes in the Boston area were large and looming, too dark and serious. I wore stockings and heels, my best dress, the coat my mother had bought me for "good" occasions. In this way, wobbling past yew trees, nervous, up front steps, to wait while a doorbell sounded somewhere far inside a dark interior, I was let in.

Adrienne Rich was the young woman poet in the early 1960s whom Robert Lowell admired the most. He held out her writing as an example to me of something to work toward. Adrienne Rich had won the Yale Younger Poets prize with her first book of poems. She was at that time a formally classical poet with restrained feeling. She had a clear, noble, crystalline quality to her work, and a strong, opinionated way of looking at poetry.

She had invited me to her house in the late afternoon. The house was dark, spread out and generous nonetheless, on a gracious well-treed Cambridge street. Opening the door and leading me in, Adrienne Rich inclined her chiseled head toward me with intensity. Her sleek feathered hair and focused glint created an impression of a proud young eagle. Her career had already launched itself, splendidly. She had a suppressed impatience about her being, a hardly tamed striving that showed itself only in fine strain marks about the eyes. They warned one.

I sat in her kitchen, drinking tea and listening to her beautifully intelligent sentences while her children puttered about upstairs. She seemed to me outstanding not only in her promise, but in her achievements at that time. She struggled with painful arthritis, with motherhood and writing, but all with an apparent grace. It was not for many years that I was to realize at what a cost such grace and control were obtained. I remember offering, feebly, to babysit. She was far into her life as a faculty wife at Harvard, and that entailed stylistic reserve, a show of strength that I could not possibly understand. In the face of her rapid articulation, I felt my own inarticulate intuitions about poetry groping and painful. I had to take time to figure out what I thought about a work. I never felt comfortable enough to show her my poems.

The kitchen in which we sat was drafty and old-fashioned. She lived in an ark of a faculty house off Brattle Street, dark and too cold and depressing, with kitchen windows giving off to sad shrubbery in winter. I kept my sweater on and a coat around me. Adrienne was small, but muffled and bunched in sweaters that hid the presence of a waist. Her face was pale and strained toward an intelligent inquiry beyond the domestic setting that was the immediately visible. She had a clear, biting voice, with a sharp, opinionated enunciation even to the niceties. Though the atmosphere seemed dark and muffled, her presence and conversation sizzled.

Upstairs, during that first visit, I could hear her children moving about. Adrienne was ironing. Even then she limped; it was clear she was in pain. Her small, dark, intelligent strength was impressive. She was serving me tea, ironing, leaving the gloomy kitchen from time to time to go upstairs and supervise her children's activities — once in a while there would be a loud bump on the floor, raised voices — and then she returned to the ironing, and to her literary conversation. Later I was to meet her husband as well, Al, or Alf, Conrad, who seemed, to my young eyes, a perfect blond foil for his dark wife. The Conrads' children were in school, in a class taught by a friend of mine, Kate Summey (Frank), and Kate would often get us together socially.

Adrienne's poems, particularly about Boston and Cambridge life, impressed me. She had written a beautiful one in which rowers on the Charles River become mythologized, and the Charles, which I had come to love, and by which I walked often, becomes the Styx. And she had also written a poem about lovers living together in that same collection, called "Living in Sin," with which I identified. Against the wishes of both sets of parents, my future husband and I were then living together in a somewhat furtive and impoverished fashion.

Although Adrienne Rich had already won the prestigious Yale Younger Poets prize for her first collection of poems as an undergraduate at Radcliffe, Harvard University would not allow her to attend its upper-level English classes. Professor Harry Levin and others maintained that the courses with the "real" professors at Harvard were reserved for the men; the Radcliffe girls could make do with the teaching assistants. But now Adrienne seemed to be living an ideal, courageous life, near Harvard, in a big shadowed house, with husband and children and poetry and marriage and sophistication and success. I did not at that time sense the foment underneath what looked ideal.

Later, the Conrads moved to New York, and I did not see Adrienne much. I knew she had gotten involved in antiwar activism and that she was teaching with the same passion she had applied to poetry. Almost ten years later, after I had a long-awaited baby, she telephoned me from New York. "Aren't you angry?" I remember her asking me. I was stunned by the question. I had lost an earlier baby, and had wanted a child desperately during the intervening years before the birth of this one. Anger was furthest from my mind. Gratitude and relief were the overwhelming emotions. "No," I answered, puzzled. Adrienne told me how angry she had felt at some of the confinements of motherhood, a feeling I was later to read about in her books of prose. In *Of Woman Born*, she brilliantly explores the ambivalence of motherhood. I felt the searing force of her personality during that phone conversation beyond the conventional niceties I had seen before.

She visited Cambridge then, and, after her husband's suicide, we had lunch together on one of her visits. She spoke clearly, crisply, with a bite to her voice that frightened me. She regarded me intently, with the fiery gaze of a hawk. As she told me the details of her husband's death, I sensed her fragility, fierce pride, and sensitivity, unspoken, unacknowledged, beneath a rage and distancing. She spoke defiantly, closing the subject with each statement. Not daring to offer a word, I listened, feeling both troubled and helpless in the conversation. Adrienne sat across from me at lunch, her small body gathering some strength as she put all this behind her. She changed the subject: "What do you think about Anne's latest work?" she asked. "Such a shame, such a waste of her gifts." Adrienne launched into an intelligent dissection of Anne Sexton's career and poetry, and we settled back in our chairs as if we had managed to skirt treacherous rocks.

Adrienne's work, while it alluded to her husband's death, did not address it directly at that time. She became an open lesbian, and she spoke courageously for women's issues, against suffering, against political injustice wherever it appeared. She was also uncompromising. Adrienne refused to read or teach if men were present in the audience. I remember going to Sanders Theatre at Harvard to hear her give a poetry reading. There were a couple of men present and she insisted they leave, or she wouldn't read. The deliberation over this lasted longer than her reading would have. Finally, after several of hours of discussion, the men agreed to leave. These endless political debates were exasperating. It was the era of meetings, debates, and polarization. You had to like sitting a lot to get through a poetry reading by Adrienne! Rich's political positions were non-negotiable. Years later, I heard her read again at Radcliffe. This time the audience was mixed, and she read more general political poems. But, in subsequent readings, she never forgot her unjust treatment at the hands of Harvard.

Adrienne Rich's search for the "common language" is a theme uniting all her work. She feels the painful lack of it, as one sees in her earlier poems about marriage and relationships between men and women. It is only later, and then only with women, that the "dream" becomes more tangible. In all of Rich's work there is a sadness and sense of alienation, a search for the merging-with-the-other that is finally impossible and unobtainable.

Language, so highly prized, with all its rigorous attention to conventions, must be fractured as humanity is fractured by injustice. Images of ice, snow, frozen lakes, and distance persist. In her later work, Rich unbuilds her carefully constructed poems, writing almost as if in shorthand, so that what exists is the space between words and phrases — as important as the phrases themselves.

The kind of anger Adrienne expressed caused a rift between herself and the non-lesbian women of the time. The "women's movement," which found itself trying to deal with the problems of all women, polarized into lesbian and non-lesbian, as well as along race and class lines. It was difficult for me to square the earlier picture of Adrienne — a loving wife and mother of three sons — with the woman who would insist that all men banish themselves from her poetic and actual presence.

She has spoken of that paradox herself, and in *Of Woman Born* tries to address her anger at her children, her closeness to them, and her feelings toward men and a male-dominated society. *Diving into the Wreck,* her *Love Poems,* and the *Ghazals,* all deal with the attempt to understand survival, to make relation out of fractured chaos. Her use of form gives the poems an underlying subtle structure. And even when she appears to abandon form, the structure is still there, lacily and lightly drawn, as in a Japanese brush painting. She has an ease, mastery, a crystalline passion to her work, and a sort of impatient perfectionism to her political perceptions.

Adrienne felt — even in those early days — that right was on her side. I was in awe, and, despite Lowell's formal letter of introduction to her, would never have wanted even to admit that I, too, wrote poetry. Young, tongue-tied, I was afraid to speak up, to possibly disagree. Her voice thundered like an Old Testament prophetess. At best, she was the voice of an avenging angel. At her worst, she came close to a passion of righteousness.

Robert Lowell respected strong women and chose them as friends. Cal loved talking poetry with Adrienne. He felt she was one of the most intelligent and gifted writers of the time, and he repeatedly spoke of her poems and poetic conversations and critiques with admiration. For her formal yet passionate poems were, to him, far better than those of either Sexton or Plath. He frequently referred to Adrienne as an example of a really fine, well-disciplined, and daring young poet. He felt she was developed and mature, and appreciated her as an equal.

It was a blow to him when later, during his divorce from Elizabeth Hardwick and his marriage to Caroline Blackwood, Adrienne publicly rebuked him in the *American Poetry Review* for using "Lizzie's letters" in his books *The Dolphin* and *Lizzie and Harriet*. That review broke the friendship. After that issue of the *American Poetry Review* came out, Cal could not stop obsessing about it during his classes and "office hours." He talked painfully on and on about Adrienne as a poet. "Major or minor?" he asked the group. "Minor, definitely minor," he answered his own question. "Wouldn't you say so?" He sought reassurance from Frank Bidart, who tried to hedge. Lowell's spiraling monologues about Adrienne Rich were the precursor to what later turned out to be another mental breakdown.

While a visiting professor at the University of Paris, I had the opportunity of teaching all of Adrienne Rich's poetry to the highest level of university students in France, who were then preparing for the "aggregation," a most demanding qualifying exam. I was obliged, both because of the requirements of preparation, and also because Rich's poems in English were doubly difficult for French-speaking graduate students, to go slowly through all of her poems, word by word. The students were expected to memorize them, every line! Her poems stood up to this enforced scrutiny: they gleamed with lyricism and conviction.

The Two Sets of Classes

Boston University and Harvard, 1959–1977

There were two sets of classes with Robert Lowell in Boston: the early ones at Boston University and the later ones at Harvard.

The Boston University classes were "star turns," featuring the older, more glamorous poets. In addition to Anne Sexton, Sylvia Plath, and George Starbuck, people who were in those early classes at Boston University, or who visited, included Henry Braun, Helen Chasin, Don Junkins, Richard Lourie, Jean Valentine, Sayre Sheldon, Hugh Seidman, and others. We had heard of the Iowa Writing Workshop. But there was no such workshop in the Northeast where poets could gather and devote themselves to the discipline of poetry. Poetry, it was felt, could not be "taught." Lowell's classes were known for the attempt, so poets came from all over to study with him. Members of the class were rarely introduced to visiting poets: it was assumed that we possibly knew them. Afterward Lowell would hastily disappear with them into a distinguished huddle.

Along with the women enrolled in his classes, Cal attracted a certain number of older, adoring women who came to audit and watched him raptly. One could speculate on these relationships — and we did. Sometimes these women would be completely silent for an entire term, sometimes they barely dared speak. They all seemed beautiful and mysterious; romantic attachments were imagined. One woman sat at the foot of the class table for months. She glistened with silk and jewels, never gave her name, and spent the semester gazing at Lowell, unblinkingly.

There were always women like the thigh-grabber in the original Boston University class, ones who had actually enrolled in the courses. One could always rely on students to provide strange, unthought-of poetry and poetic subjects. One of the more entertaining moments I can remember came from a woman who had written an epic poem about — ? Hard to tell. Lowell ran through his "what does this mean?" number — and he was not being deliberately obtuse, as one often suspected, when he did this with a poem and the meaning seemed obvious. Lowell would not let this go. The class struggled with the poem for two hours until the author triumphantly revealed her identity and her subject matter. The poem, it turned out, was about her climbing a huge mountain while in an advanced state of pregnancy, standing on the mountaintop with an enormous belly, and then clambering down the other side of the mountain, accompanied by her husband. On the other side of the mountain, conveniently, there was a huge ocean, which our author entered. The poem ended with her giving birth to her child in the pounding surf.

"Aha!" we all said. "No wonder we couldn't get it!" Such "Aha!" experiences happened fairly often, and I must confess to waiting for them; they provided such a relief from the heaviness of the Lowell aura. The author smiled, and Cal was for once speechless. Thirty years later I re-met the poet, Nancy Rice, and although I had trouble remembering her name, her poem sprang, fully etched, from my memory.

After moving from Marlborough Street in Boston to New York, Lowell was appointed to teach at Harvard. He commuted to Cambridge to do so, and this signaled the beginning of the second wave of classes and a wave of younger poets who came to study with him. In addition to his Harvard classes, Lowell decided to hold "office hours," open sessions that poets could attend — working poets — who were not Harvard undergraduates. These office hours were dedicated and intense.

Writers such as Frank Bidart, Robert Pinsky, James Atlas, Sidney Goldfarb, Robert Grenier, Lloyd Schwartz, Alan Williamson, and others were part of the later generation of writers who continued to attend, year after year. Some writers from the earlier Boston University classes also showed up. The level of talent and ability of the people who passed through the office hours was amazing: a thoughtful undergraduate, Jonathan Galassi; Andrew Wylie; Sandy Kaye; Roger Parham Brown; Richard Tillinghast; Steven Sandy; Geoffrey Movius; Bill Corbett; Sidney Goldfarb; Bill Byrom; a young Texan poet, Barney Holland; Anne Hussey; Arthur Oberg (who died tragically); and others. Among the women were Anne Mazlish, Ruth Hanham, Peggy Rizza, Jane Shore (with her alert gaze that seemed to take in everything), Judith Baumel, Estelle Leonteif, Gail Mazur, Celia Gilbert, and Alice Ryerson (who was later to create the Ragdale Foundation). These talented men and women all appeared in classes and office hours, although some of them were so intimidated they did not talk much nor dare present their poems. We met each other randomly, outside the Lowell context, and friendships developed.

Occasionally I would run into writer James Atlas, so funny and literate, browsing morosely through the magazines at Reading International, the bookstore, taking a break from his biography of Delmore Schwartz.

The awe, reverence, and timidity in Lowell's classes were so overwhelming that it was not until years later, when I met Roger Rosenblatt, then director of the National Endowment for the Humanities, that I realized we had sat opposite each other for an entire year, without identifying ourselves. But eight years later, we could still remember each other's poems and Lowell's devastating comments about them.

Ambitious as the first group at Boston University was, this second wave of poets was equally so. I can remember getting together with Richard Tillinghast, Steve Sandy, Bill Corbett, Gary Miranda, or others as we encouraged each other in the publication struggle. Billy Byrom and Grey Gowrie attended, each on a fellowship from England. It has been fascinating to follow the careers of the poets who gathered around Robert Lowell and to see their impact on American writing today.

Lowell fostered both talent and competition. It was exciting to see what would happen during his office hours: who would be there, and what anonymous poem passed in by a student would spark his interest. I remember one hour in which Lloyd Schwartz turned in a dramatic monologue. Lowell leaned forward; he asked Lloyd questions about the monologue. Quiet, polite, Lloyd demurred. We all felt the daring and originality in his poem. Lloyd had first come to office hours with his friend Frank Bidart, and though quiet at first, his grace of personality was apparent. Both Lloyd and Frank were intelligent, supportive of other students' poems, and thoughtful in their comments.

Robert Pinsky visited Lowell's office hours fairly often. An athletic, pleasant man, he was well liked. He was modest, soft-spoken, and extremely knowledgeable. When Lowell asked Pinsky for his opinion on a poem, Robert would answer in a most delicate and tentative way. He was extremely polite and respectful, for he didn't want to intrude upon Robert Lowell's opinions. His discourse was tactful and gentle, and he was completely committed to poetry.

Frank Bidart illuminated the office hours with drafts of poems that would later appear in his first book, *Golden State*. Frank was from California, tall and modest. His lines were long, open, in the way I pictured the California landscape to be, revealing. He was quiet, hardly owning the astonishing

The Block poetry course. Ned Block is in the center foreground, and the author is on the far right. John Harris is at the top with the panda; Bill Byrom and Susan Carey are below him.

poems he was handing in. His later poems were to be heart-stopping. Frank Bidart, Lloyd Schwartz, and Robert Pinsky stayed on in Boston to write and teach. They continue to be exceptional in their talents, as well as in their graciousness, as I observed. The other writers too — we met each other, read together — we shared a special bond.

I also met the poet Peter Davison, who I was to get to know better when

I worked on the *Atlantic Monthly*. In his memoir, he wrote about the literary climate in Boston.[26]

Bill Byrom was a British writer who had come to study with Robert Lowell. He organized a poetry reading course for his friends, titled the "Ned Block Poetry Course." Ned, who was a graduate student in philosophy, supposedly needed educating. Each week Billy mailed us all a famous poem, along with his annotations. Once a month or so we got together to talk about the poems, but most of all to eat and dance. Paul Levy, Emma Rothschild, Grey Gowrie, Ned Block, John Harris, Susan Carey, and others were part of the Block poetry course. Billy photographed us once under a picture of the famous Oxford University circle, wearing the appropriate costumes and poses.

Lowell's classes waited, breathed upon his good opinion. Whole terrible, downcast weeks followed when he was in an oblivious or pre-breakdown mood. Even now, survivors of his classes, both at Boston University and later, at Harvard, remember with acute embarrassment some throwaway, yet negatively tinged, comment Lowell made about poems of theirs. For the most part, though, his general attitude was encouraging and kind. He was above caring what his students did, except what it could teach him, and was much more interested in his own work and that of the great poets.

When Lowell asked, about a line written by Auden or Yeats or Hardy, "What does this mean?," he asked the question in the deepest, most careful sense. We groaned inwardly when the question was posed. Yet he was always generous in the face of what he considered real poetry. I remember one class at Harvard, years later, in which a young student, Andrew Wylie, handed in a translation of "Le Bateau Ivre," by Rimbaud. Lowell praised the poem. Then he took this approach to the same poem from his new book, *Imitations*. Going over both translations, word for word, he proceeded to show the class, and Andy, where the translations differed, and where he thought Andy's in places surpassed his own. It was a most generous moment of teaching.

One's own poems aside, there was always a lot of silence in Lowell's discussion of poems; endless pauses with occasional flashes of quicksilver insight. Lowell's "what does this mean" was an intuitive brooding upon the poetic inspiration itself, an attempt, it seemed, to breathe in the spirit of the poet writing. His approach to poetry was an invitation to meditate, in the deepest, most spiritual sense, on a poem. Each poem — to use Eastern meditation as an example — became a mandala, a star of light whose lines illuminated, or made sense of, a universe. When, in class, Lowell found a student poem that suggested, either by its abysmally bad quality, or by its good, a poem of one of the "greats," he would immediately turn to the master poem and invite — that is, force — the class to meditate upon that poem.

It is a tribute to Lowell's teaching of poems that the poetry was even more miraculous *after* he had led us through his obsessive textual analysis, than before.

Lowell taught us not just how to improve poems but, by astonishing and unforgettable example, how to think and talk about poetry, care about it, let it be part of our waking lives. Whether by going over the poems people brought (and anyone could attend — undergraduates or graduate students, distinguished visitors or people who literally walked in off the street; you needed only to know these sessions existed) or by looking at whatever great poet he felt like talking about that particular week, he demonstrated that you could be serious about poems without being solemn. I've never had a teacher who joked so much, and teased, and speculated.

⟨⟩ LLOYD SCHWARTZ

Without exception student writers wanted to take Robert Lowell's poetry workshop. The fact that not many advanced workshops were offered at Harvard and that Lowell had a reputation for choosing his classes quixotically added to the anxiety everyone felt on the first day of class. The seminar room was packed. Lowell didn't seem to know what to do with the large group although he must have had equally large first classes before. When he started talking about literature some student was anxious to discuss the most obscure texts to impress Lowell and he seemed to know this and enjoy it. In the end he selected an astrophysicist at the Observatory who'd never written a word, a social studies concentrator who was beginning to be interested in poetry and only then a few of the writing students.

⟨⟩ JUDITH BAUMEL

Schwartz: "Attending Robert Lowell's 'Office Hours' at Harvard," *Boston Phoenix*, December 19–25, 2003.
Baumel: "Robert Lowell: The Teacher," *Harvard Advocate*, November 1979.

Elizabeth Bishop and Ping-Pong,
1974–1979

Elizabeth Bishop came to Harvard to teach, and Lowell took me to meet her. She had arthritis and asthma and was also going through a depression. Perhaps she needed to meet poets in the area, he thought. He introduced me to many of his poet friends. This friendship took.

Elizabeth Bishop had a soft, endearing quality: wistful eyes, a sweet expression, and an irrepressible laugh. "Loveable" was a word that came to mind when one thought of her. This was in direct contradiction to her reputation, which focused on the more distant aesthetic qualities. This reticence, a reserve to the point of shyness, showed itself in the public sphere. It gilded her poetry.

I visited Bishop in Cambridge at least twice a week. I adored her! It was light and fun and interesting, and our slant-wise, wacky personalities suited each other. She was idiosyncratic, unconventional. We played Ping-Pong, read poems, drank and ate extraordinary meals, laughed and talked of so many things. I was usually invited at 11:30 in the morning and did not leave until the late afternoon, just before dinner. Her conversation was fascinating.

She loved hearing about other peoples' lives: their domestic doings, their interests. But sometimes we just sat in the same room together, reading under the warm lamps of her Brattle Street apartment. She took me under her wing, read my poetry and commented on it, and showed me delicate spidery drafts of her later poems. She was very reserved, and although she alluded to a great many personal things about her life, and spoke more openly about some of her personal difficulties, I have tried to respect her friendship.

Elizabeth Bishop represented, for Robert Lowell, someone between a High Priestess and a Mother Confessor. She was one of his closest friends. He respected her poems, introduced them to his students, and also went to her for guidance in his own writing and revision process. She seemed, in initial presentation, a forbidding and distant figure, her poems technically perfect, polished, and deeply expressive. Cal introduced her poem "The Man-Moth" in his workshop, and also "The Prodigal." "The Prodigal" was exact in its close attention to detail, its technically exact description, the formal construction — all leading to the simply stated end: "Carrying a bucket along a slimy board . . ." I had been moved by "The Man-Moth" when I first heard it, and the poem stood for the pathos of loneliness with which I identified: "one tear, his only possession, like the bee's sting, slips."

This poem, an early one, turned out to be prophetic. Written after Bishop's first trip to New York, and included in her first collection, "The Man-Moth" might be read as an early poem foreshadowing her life: Bishop herself would always "nervously" climb toward "light"; always "ride backwards," as it were, and she would only — then only to trusted friends — or only to the page and then in a sidewise, reluctant fashion occasionally, if you waited long enough, reveal the sadness within. It would not do to shine a flashlight, never — one must (praise ye New England) wait.

Elizabeth Bishop wrote delicately and elliptically. Much was unsaid, left out, alluded to. What is most important is what is *not* said, line breaks, form, slant rhyme, all to convey a breathless quality to the small, precise observation; the reader is left to draw his/her own conclusions. She did not, like Walt Whitman, like Ginsberg, or even like Lowell, thump the incessant drum of "myself." The "I," when it comes in her poems, is a little surprise, and usually comes in as a comment on humanity and the human condition, either distanced from (the "I" the observer, precisely detailing) or merging with, and therefore taking its place within, a larger cosmic worldview ("— until everything / was rainbow rainbow rainbow / and I let the fish go"): a larger fusion-with-world (as in the poem "In the Waiting Room") in which the self is allowed — briefly — to partake. This reticence, which might be said to be Anglo-Saxon, this northern reserve, as well as this transcendental vision of the self-in-world is something Bishop shared with Dickinson. Poetry as code.

Elizabeth Bishop was, at the time I met her, about sixty, and I had been hearing about her for years before. Cal respected the precision of her work, and Bishop had a fastidiousness of verse and person that seemed to be a model. Dignified, restrained, and gracious, she had a quality of reticence and passion about her. Beneath the restraint in her poetry was a tenderness that wrung your heart, and beneath the reserve of the woman, a warmth and hospitality. She had spent many years in Brazil and was a great cook of both Brazilian and other cuisines.

Bishop had a wide range of interests, an open friendly manner, and an enthusiasm for people. At first she seemed not particularly interested in talking about poetry. She was interested instead in art, architecture, travel, and many other subjects. She was a somewhat round, un-intimidating little person with the sweet, open face of a child. Her wavy white hair seemed to contradict and surprise the young, dashing appearance she presented. She wore tight leather pants, smoked constantly, and was badly asthmatic. She wheezed, but this did not stop her from enjoyment of life. She loved fun, throwing back her head and laughing with full zest. At that first meeting, she immediately invited my husband and me to a Brazilian dinner. Many people express interest in inviting one at the spur of the moment, but she followed through, telephoning us a couple of times to make sure we could come, and that we could coordinate the evening with another young couple whom she wanted us to meet. The young woman of the other couple was the daughter of a friend of hers, she explained, and the young man an architect. She was sure he and my husband would enjoy talking with each other.

Elizabeth Bishop had cooked an exotic meal of Brazilian black beans, sausage, and chicken, complete with wines and bread and fruit. It had probably taken the whole day to prepare. We reclined on the floor of her small apartment after the meal. She showed us books on Brazilian architecture and also talked of Mexican ruins she had visited. She was extremely interested in the work of both the architect and of my husband, and the men basked in the attention. She had a sparkle and curiosity, and an ability to make people feel at home. She played us some Brazilian records, too: sambas and indigenous folk music. Time passed too quickly, and it was almost midnight when we all left, promising to see her soon again. I hadn't expected to have such a relaxed encounter with a poet who had been an idol of mine, the poet of whom Berryman had written: "Miss Bishop's too noble-O."

Elizabeth Bishop's Brattle Street apartment came with a Ping-Pong table in the foyer. Her hands were by then arthritic. Soon after our dinner she invited me to play Ping-Pong with her once a week, which supposedly would help her arthritis. Afterward, I was to stay to lunch, a meal she had prepared as elaborately as the Brazilian dinner. She asked me to call her Elizabeth, which I found hard to do. She was so much a "Miss Bishop," so much a person who seemed to know exactly who she was.

These noon hours evolved very quickly into a weekly ritual, as we both enjoyed the challenge of Ping-Pong. Elizabeth dashed about on her side of the table, her charming face pursed with concentration, and bursting into delighted laughter at her tricky shots. Asthma was a problem for Elizabeth, but it did not stop her from the game, clad in those same leather pants and a silk shirt or sweater. Lunch would be simmering: an exotic soup. Or there might be a beautifully prepared salad, always with wine and wonderful Brazilian coffee. After Ping-Pong she would set out lunch elegantly, and then we ate in the living room, and talked.

During these lunches, which lasted well into the afternoon, the conversation ranged over a variety of subjects. She had the quality of surprised youthfulness in her eyes, and gradually, in a quiet manner, allowed one to get to know her. In person, she was quite unlike the austere public persona of "Miss Bishop," but she could be extremely stern and opinionated. One did not want to offend her, nor to invade her closely guarded privacy. She had strong interests, however, and enjoyed hearing about other people's lives and interests. She made friends among several other "younger people" at Harvard, and often invited my husband and me to dinner with some of her other friends.

I met the poet Octavio Paz and his wife at her house, and later we attended a poetry reading and talk at Harvard by the British poet Stephen Spender. Paz's wife, it turned out, was an avid tennis player looking for a partner, and so subsequently she and I played every once in a while at the Harvard tennis courts near the Smithsonian Observatory. Sitting between Elizabeth Bishop and Octavio Paz at that Harvard lecture, and arranging a tennis game with Paz's wife, slim, blonde, elegant, and fast-talking, seemed such a funny juxtaposition of worlds. It was a toss-up as to which of the passions was to dominate the evening: love of poetry, or love of racquet sports! I was overcome with shyness in the presence of these two great poets, and in the presence of Paz, with his fine, intelligent, leonine head, felt humbly relieved that at least I had my tennis partnership to offer. The lecture dragged on, the hall was hot, and the questions by graduate students who just wanted to hear themselves talk — "Mr. Spender, wouldn't you agree that . . . etc., etc." — for twenty minutes seemed interminable. Coats on our knees, knees jammed against the seat backs in front of us, we all, with the exception of well-bred Elizabeth, fidgeted. Paz looked as if he was asleep, but I was sure he was thinking great international literary thoughts. Paz and Bishop had a fine friendship, based on a long history, an interest in Latin America, and a shared poetic stature. They got on very well, and Paz's wife, too, seemed quite cheerful and upbeat and at home with Elizabeth.

Robert Lowell had represented Elizabeth Bishop as a taskmaster, and she did have that aura about her. But she also had a supportive ease. Once, during a reading by Frank Bidart at the *Harvard Advocate* — the most gloomy of places to read poetry — she came to listen, and was given the only overstuffed chair. She had only consented to attend out of her friendship for Bidart — "I can't stand hearing people read their poetry," she said. But Elizabeth Bishop loved Frank, as did Lowell. She also developed a great friendship with Lloyd Schwartz, who was doing his thesis on her work. Lloyd, so kind, gifted, and thoughtful, was wonderful to Elizabeth Bishop, and they became close. At the *Advocate*, Miss Bishop was treated as the guest of honor and made to sit in the front. The rest of us crowded into the back, sat on the floor, or stood. My husband was sitting uncomfortably on the floor during Frank's reading, and at one point Bishop patted his frowzy, curly head, offered him her legs for a backrest, and murmured, "Just put your head in my lap."

A great traveler, she carried her mementos with her and displayed them. She showed me photographs and postcards. They were of people, views, and architecture in Brazil, mostly. There was a sense of a tragic void around that country and her reminiscing. For some unspeakable reason she could never go back. I listened, as to a delicate, shy bird. I came to understand that Elizabeth had spent many happy years in Brazil with a woman friend Lota (de Macedo Soares) who was passionately interested in architecture and urban planning. Somehow, after many years, there had been a falling out. Elizabeth had had to leave, and returned to New York. Her friend killed herself. Elizabeth Bishop never uttered the words "lesbian" and "lover." She was extremely reticent, and I was also very reserved. She had had other friends, she told me, a nice woman referred to as "Suzanne" in Seattle, where she had gone for a stint of teaching, and someone here in Cambridge, "Alice" (Methfessel), who was always presented tactfully as "the secretary of Kirkland House."

But nothing could ever replace her feeling for "Lota." That death was a blow from which she would never recover. Her hands trembled as she talked. She did seem a bit lost to me, perhaps drank too heavily, smoked too much. I did not at that time grasp the full implication of the shock the death had caused. She seemed to suggest her friend had died in her arms. She had a violent dislike of extreme emotions, and only showed them when she had too much to drink. But even then she was a "lady": she was undoubtedly an alcoholic, but it never disturbed the delicacy she showed in my presence.

Later I was to hear Carmen de Oliveira present her work on the relation of Bishop, Lota, and Brazil at a conference on Elizabeth Bishop in Worcester, Massachusetts. I was amazed! My "Miss Bishop" had presented herself to me as the stable one. "Lota," she claimed, was difficult, alcoholic, and majorly manic-depressive, although creative and brilliant of course. Surprise, it emerged that some Brazilians had a totally different picture! Their beloved "Lota" may have had her problems, but unfortunately she met up with the falling-down-drunk, unreasonable, demanding, depressed, and scene-creating "Elizabeth." If Elizabeth had not come down from the North to Brazil and plonked herself on Lota's doorstep, if she had not made all that trouble, no doubt their glamorous, brilliant, talented Lota would have been just fine!

Bishop's poems show the depth of her feeling beneath the contained exterior. But to me, the person, as well as the poems, revealed themselves slowly, with a sense of unutterable pathos, heartbreaking in the mixture of held-back longing and loss. While her poem "Invitation to Miss Marianne Moore" ("please come flying") is full of high spirits, "The Shampoo" has a delicate, quiet tenderness, a gentleness of touch that makes the heart hurt.

Elizabeth Bishop spoke of her attempts to reintegrate after Lota's death, and of her analysis with her doctor, "Annie," in New York. She had a close relationship with her doctor, a European woman in whom she could confide. But her sense of excruciating loneliness pre-dated the events of her adult life. Once, when showing me photographs, she took from her bookshelf a photograph of herself as a baby. Together we gazed into that child's eyes. Her troubled early life is well recounted in her poems and small prose pieces, but when she showed me her baby picture, I saw her strength and careful observation of the world, even then. That little girl possessed the forthright gaze so evident in the woman. One knew this was a baby who really looked at things. The direct steadiness of that young look, the open vulnerability of the baby, touched me as I saw it mirrored in the face of the sixty-some-year-old woman. One felt, also, the weight of pain the baby was to undergo, the suffering and loss that would bring this secure, definite, little person to the edge of despair, the abyss that underlay Elizabeth

Bishop's seemingly polished, accomplished life. I sensed the fragility of the little person she had been, and saw it expressed in her adult eyes.

After several months of spending time together, one late afternoon Miss Bishop told me she wanted to read something aloud to me, a story. It was cold and snowy; she didn't want me to leave. It was as always a winter evening, and the heat hissed; she didn't have enough lamps for my taste. It was gloomy and cozy at the same time; she poured us a drink, and we settled in. She made me sit in her big armchair while she sort of perched on a footstool. What she wanted, deliberately chose, to read to me was her story "In the Village."[27] I didn't know it, had not read it, and I was only familiar with her first book of poems. I didn't even know she wrote short stories. But this was not a short story that afternoon; it sounded as if practically a diary entry. It was raw, although of course exquisitely polished. But the raw emotion of this story is unmistakable, less disguised than in the poems.

The story begins: "A scream, the echo of a scream, hangs over that Nova Scotian village."

This is the scream, the naked, overt cry that will haunt Elizabeth Bishop all her life. It is the scream of her mother, who is mad, and who has come home from the mental hospital, "the asylum." To which she will return when the child Elizabeth is five years old. Bishop read quietly, deliberately, wanting me to understand. The reading was direct and shockingly intimate; a personal side of herself that Bishop never showed in her "public" readings of her work. Miss Bishop had decided to tell me more about herself by her reading of the story; she was not presenting the story to me as "art" or "artifact," but as something meant to allow me to understand her better. She wanted to convey to me her autobiography — things that she could not say directly, that she had not been able to say in her poems. Following her mother's breakdown, Elizabeth Bishop had been exiled, sent to live with relatives here and there, condemned to wander, longing for maternal union forever.

She read in her matter-of-fact voice, wheezing between phrases, sitting, pouring a second drink, then a third, as the winter sun set outside. The calm, subdued manner of her presentation of the material, coupled against the passion of the situation itself, was a deeply moving experience. As I spent time with "Miss Bishop," she slowly allowed me to get to know her better. Between thoughtful silences, broken by the struggles she had in breathing, she talked. Her eyes were faraway, the silences poignant. She gave me the *Diary of "Helena Morley"* to read, and talked about her kinship with the author. She talked about the deep isolation Helena Morley had experienced in her early years, and her identification with that. She talked to me of Brazil, which was in her mind a lost paradise by the time she came to Harvard.

Later she telephoned me at night. I picked up the phone next to the bed. It was after 11 p.m. Had I read *Helena Morley* yet? I hadn't, I admitted. A job and two small kids had kept me from doing so. More than a little vexed, she read parts of it aloud to me over the phone. I was exhausted, but didn't dare hang up. The reading ended long after midnight.

She also read me "In The Waiting Room." In this poem "the cry," both separates and unifies. The child is in the waiting room of a dentist's office, looking at old copies of the magazine *National Geographic* while her aunt has her appointment. As usual in New England,

> It was winter. It got dark
> early. . . .[28]

In that little breath-catch, the line break before the word "early," there is the sense that always there is a little catch of breath, a little hurt, already associated with the idea of "early" darkness. In that poem her relation to everything in the universe comes into question (how can it be?), for she has felt distant and outside of what is happening up until now. She tries to understand how this fusion might come about, what it means: she fuses/ merges with the women portrayed in the magazine, with her aunt, with the feminine — about which she is ambivalent.

Once hearing Elizabeth Bishop read aloud, one understood the writing was, in every way, written "in her voice." Seemingly quiet, composed, matter-of-fact, her poems held a passion underneath. Elizabeth Bishop hated "public" readings. She read, as my friend Fanny Howe put it, "Like a buyer from Macy's." When she read aloud in public, Bishop was a small touching figure, hunched over the poems, murmuring, it seemed, more to herself than to the audience, and dressed in quiet, subdued, ladylike clothes: black dress or gray suit, string of pearls, that sort of thing. But in her apartment, in the easy chair, the slacks, the baggy sweater, her whole body curled up around the reading expressed the deep concentration in each word she wrote.

Bishop wrote slowly, maddeningly slowly, she felt. She experienced what she termed "a writing block" during some of her time in Cambridge and Boston. She showed me some drafts: small exact handwriting, neat straight tiny lines, and many words crossed out, lines too. I had trouble reading her writing, so small and fine, but noticed of course the large numbers of cross-outs and revisions. Later she worked on a typewriter, and the same was true of those typed drafts. She worked for months on a poem to find the exact word or positioning of lines she sought. Her output, she thought, was small, although she valued the work and care it took to produce the poems. But when we look at her life's work, it is full, and each poem is a gem. There was not much waste or slack to her writing process. The poems are carefully deliberated and polished.

I showed her my first manuscript, *Flying Inland*, and she read it through carefully, commenting in small, neat handwriting on words or lines she thought needed changing. Her suggestions were precise and to the point, and I went over the manuscript with new energy after she had talked with me about it. It had taken her, she told me, many years to get her first book, *North & South*, published, although many of the individual poems in it had been published. Finally it won a contest at Houghton Mifflin, although the firm had rejected it on its own before. Later she combined the book with her second, *A Cold Spring*, and the combined volume won a Pulitzer Prize. She encouraged me to keep trying to publish my first book, although it was easy to want to give up when the rejections came in.

At one point I had to go to New York to see an editor who was possibly interested in my manuscript. "Where will you stay?" Elizabeth asked me. I didn't know, so she arranged for me to stay as her guest at the Cosmopolitan Club, an exclusive Manhattan residence club for upper-class women, where she was a member. The Cosmopolitan Club was elegant, with quiet elegant women, beautifully dressed. My room had flowered wallpaper, with flowered sheets and lampshades to match. The closet was bigger than my bedroom at home; it was made to house the wardrobes of debutantes "coming out" in New York. It was one of the first times I had been away from my two young children, and I felt very glamorous as I sat in bed with my breakfast tray, a rose upon it, propped up by flowery pillows, and reading the *New York Times*. I sank into the huge claw-footed bathtub, immersed in delicious warm water, and later, thick towels. I couldn't believe such luxury, such solitude. I promptly telephoned everyone I could think of, in a kind of manic ecstasy, including Elizabeth Bishop in Cambridge. "My" editor came to see me at the Cosmopolitan Club — the potential of that proprietary word "my" with "editor" — those two words repeated themselves in my head like historic fiction. Men were not allowed above the ground floor at the Cosmopolitan Club: we had a drink, of course, in one of the quiet rooms downstairs.

I tried to appear as if such occasions happened to me all the time, as if I had been to the Cosmopolitan Club born. "Suave and debonair" ("Swove and dee-boner," as my college roommate joked). It was like living a sophisticated literary dream. I could scarcely stand up after "the drink," but managed to glide elegantly back to my room upstairs. It was difficult to come down to earth after this visit, back to my children, whom I had missed, of course — their angelic fantasy presence, not the reality of diapers and hard work. And it was to be a few more years before an editor took my book.

Although her first books had taken their time coming out, Elizabeth Bishop was by now a formidable literary presence. She was formal and reserved, and one would not have dreamed of troubling that exterior.

She was horrified by the women's movement. She couldn't understand it, she said, although she had a keen interest in discussing it with me. What did I think? She thought it was strident, unruly, undisciplined. Elizabeth Bishop could be opinionated. The "Movement" was not something she wanted to be associated with. She seemed to prefer to surround herself with friends who were married, friends with children. She had an interest in children and child-rearing. And she had instant rapport with children; saw the world from their eyes empathetically. She would have loved to have children, she told me wistfully. She often "adopted" younger women and mothered them, as, in a more distantly associated way, she took an interest in my development. She always wanted to hear about my children, enjoyed knowing my husband as well as myself, and had many close friends nearer her own age and stature. She liked domestic life: creating and participating in it. The women's movement did not suit her fastidious romantic nature.

In those dark afternoons I spoke up a bit feebly and then subsided. Lowell and his gang had already dubbed me "the feminist," though in fact I was probably on the more conservative side of my contemporaries. Bishop was on a definite toot about the subject, and I did not dare cross that stern, scolding, outraged presence. It is one of the few subjects I saw her get really worked up about — something she only occasionally did on the subject of "bad" poetry.

No More Masks, one of the first anthologies to be devoted completely to the work of women, was in its preparation stages. The editors, Florence Howe and Ellen Bass, had written to Elizabeth Bishop for inclusion of her work in this anthology. Elizabeth was furious, and refused to be included. First of all, poets were to be listed by their birth date, and the issue of age was demeaning, she felt. But most of all, it was an anthology devoted to the work of "Women" and she said this word with outraged scorn. As if there weren't good men poets in the world! She didn't think of herself as a "Woman" Poet, and she was insulted to be included in this category.

She wrote an outraged letter to the editors about her feelings on this subject. The next week she read it aloud to me, put it in an envelope, sealed it, and sent me out to the post office to mail it. I, however, who had very few publication opportunities, was delighted to be invited to be included in *No More Masks,* and had no scruples about my birth date or sex. A month earlier, with no hesitation whatsoever, I had mailed off my own poetry submissions to the anthology. Elizabeth was irked at me for that, and felt I had let down poetic standards. Although I saw Elizabeth Bishop's point of view, I had also experienced quite a bit of discrimination at being a woman and poet, and thought it wonderful that some opportunities were opening up at last. She was adamant in her stand to be recognized as a "writer," a category transcending that of gender.

Interestingly enough, or perhaps predictably, Bishop, when questioned about women's writing, said scornfully, "Women's experiences are much more limited, but that does not really matter — there is Emily Dickinson, as one always says. You just have to make do with what you have, after all. . . . Some women can write like Emily Dickinson, the kind of poetry with no common experience to speak of at all, where there may be some women dying to get out and climb Mt. Everest. . . . A lot of nonsense."[29] In one way, one might say that Elizabeth had had good luck in being recognized as a "poet," rather than as a "woman poet," since she was of the time that slightly demeaned the category: "Woman (read: Three-Name) Poet."

A few years later I heard Muriel Rukeyser read at Harvard. Rukeyser was old and had suffered a couple of strokes. She had flown up to Boston but had to use a walker to reach the stage. Invited by the *Harvard Advocate,* she tottered onstage and, in a barely audible, trembling voice, read her magnificent strong poems. It was an incredible reading, a chance to see and hear one of the most outstanding American poets of our time. The students who ran the *Harvard Advocate*, the literary magazine, had on impulse invited Muriel Rukeyser, and she had agreed to come. But now they were overwhelmed with her care. Not one member of the Harvard English Department attended that reading. The students were left alone with the full responsibility for Miss Rukeyser, who was extremely ill. So did Harvard treat its women poets. When male poets of Rukeyser's stature came to Harvard, the university took better care of them.

Despite these kinds of attitudes on the part of her employer, Harvard, any conversation about the beginnings of what was to become the women's movement, any suggestion of women's poetry readings or women's anthologies, received a firmly negative response from Elizabeth Bishop. She entirely disapproved. For one thing, I think she equated such activities with women's separatism. As a (very quiet) lesbian, as a woman who moved freely in many circles, lesbian separatism, or even women's separatism, was something she abhorred. The women's movement was just starting, and the issue of separatism would not come up until much later. Lesbians were still "in the closet," and the movement would not polarize for years. Although her love life held central importance to her personally, it was not to occupy that position in her social or professional life. Adrienne Rich has written about Bishop's reserve from the lesbian point of view. There were many complex issues underlying her refusal of the *No More Masks* inclusion.

Robert Lowell exalted Elizabeth Bishop, and his third wife, Caroline Blackwood, was terrified of her. She was afraid to meet her, for if Elizabeth did not approve of Caroline, then Caroline knew she would have a hard time of it. They were to meet, but it was never comfortable for either of them, especially as Elizabeth Bishop had taken Lowell to task for his use of Hardwick's letters in his poetry. Elizabeth did have a "St. Peter at the Gate" quality about her, a stern, bleak, sardonic way of looking at things. And she would tolerate no disagreement once a final opinion was uttered. But she also shared with Lowell an extreme psychological vulnerability, had had breakdowns, drank a great deal, and was fragile both physically and emotionally. One felt protective of her at the same time as one felt in awe.

Elizabeth Bishop and Anne Sexton were eager to meet each other, and since I was a friend of both, they asked me to arrange it. "Invite her for lunch at my flat," suggested Elizabeth. "Have her come out to Weston," said Anne. Both women were reluctant to meet on the other's turf. I found myself in the middle of delicate negotiations. The summit meeting took weeks to arrange. "I'm shy," each protested. Well, that was only partially true, as I watched the prima donna aspects of each poet surface. Finally, a restaurant was agreed upon, a time and a date. There were, of course, several cancellations and postponements. Also, each poet insisted I pick her up and accompany her. Anne was afraid to meet Elizabeth Bishop because Lowell had touted her as the best woman poet in America, and because Anne admired Bishop's work so much. But Elizabeth was afraid to meet Anne because she feared that Anne would be "confessional," and she was repelled and appalled by what she considered Anne's raw and sexual outpourings, and because of Anne's openness in writing about her breakdowns, a topic Elizabeth feared and about which she could never bring herself to write directly.

However, Lois Ames agreed to serve as Anne's second, to pick her up and bring her into Cambridge to the Iruna, a Spanish restaurant where we would all meet. After I had met Elizabeth Bishop in her apartment and we had played a rousing set of Ping-Pong games, the four of us actually managed to sit down at a restaurant table. I waited for great words of literature to fly about my ears. Here were my favorite women poets meeting. What a wonderful conversation would ensue, I thought.

"Tell me, Anne," Elizabeth leaned over, "How much money do you get for a reading nowadays?" "At least a thousand," was Anne's immediate answer. And the two poets were off, talking about contracts and money and publishers who had or hadn't done them wrong. Lois and I sat there amazed. If we had thought one word about poetic process was to be exchanged, we were mistaken. The two women talked about business with relish all through lunch until the dessert course, when Anne dramatically turned to Lois and exclaimed, "Lois, did I ever tell you how much it hurt, having my babies?" Now it was Anne and Lois's turn to talk, while Elizabeth Bishop and I sat silent, as Anne and Lois outdid themselves on each gory, painful detail of their various childbirths. As I walked Elizabeth back home, she was thoughtfully silent. "Well, really," she said at the door, dismissing the whole encounter. As far as I know, the two women never saw each other again.

Elizabeth Bishop, like Lowell, rewrote constantly, often complaining to me that she was "blocked" when unable to solve a problematic line. I would often see drafts of poems, and sometimes she would crackle open a page and show me. Her handwriting was tiny, and pages of poems, in teeny handwriting, lay crumpled on the windowsills. Often, she would gather them up and hand them to me when I walked in; some were on the window by her bed, or in the ashtray, others, crumpled near the wastebasket. Bishop agonized over the form of her poems. She was a master at the use of line breaks as well as punctuation to indicate a little suspense, a held breath, a little pause/rest before the next idea. Her use of line breaks, and poetic spacing and punctuation, is impeccable; and her rewrites, like those of Lowell's, focused a great deal on different constructions of the line breaks.

Elizabeth Bishop was asthmatic, had been so since childhood. She wheezed and chain-smoked — and had trouble breathing always. Asthma is thought to have a strong psychological component, and one point of view is that it can be considered to be the body's way of expressing suppressed crying; grief comes out in that fashion. It is triggered by allergies and irritants, but it is one of those illnesses that is also considered to have a strong psychosomatic aspect: that is, there are strong affective components to what is expressed as a physical dis-ease. It is often thought that it is triggered by abandonment, as when a small baby is abandoned in infancy by its mother. The cry is suppressed, the despair is too great to bear, the baby gives up a part of its will to live.

We see the asthmatic rhythm and hesitations perhaps most clearly in Bishop's poem "One Art." At the time I was visiting her, Bishop was working on this poem, which is so lovely that it is almost sacrilege to talk about it. There are at least seventeen collected drafts of this poem in a library collection at Vassar College,[30] and probably at least forty drafts, many more, that were torn up and thrown away, that never made it from Elizabeth Bishop's apartment into a library. They made it into the wastebasket. Some of these drafts had only one or two words on them. In her apartment, I would find them crumpled everywhere: on the Ping-Pong table, on the windowsill, in the bathroom.

"One Art" is all about loss, loss lived and loss expected. The attitude it seems to take toward loss is casual: loss is nothing, you learn it, it's not difficult to learn "The art of losing." "Lose something every day," says the poet philosophically. That's how you learn this "art." (Learning by doing.) Gradually the losses pile up. The losses are described by their "thing-ness," depersonalized: "my mother's watch . . . loved houses . . . two rivers, a continent." The poet repeats, "The art of losing isn't hard to master."

Mother is "lost"; houses, meaning love that existed within those houses; the rivers; the continent — all this predicts/foreshadows the possible, unbearable loss of her lover. "It was nothing," the poet seems to say, in her bravado. But suddenly, in the last stanza, she falters. She can no longer continue to conceal the real situation: faced with yet another loss, the immediate imagined upcoming loss, her ironic distance shatters. But it shatters so purely, so quietly, that you hardly notice. The impeccable control, as exemplified by the conventional grammar and punctuation, breaks down.

"One Art" has a strict form, and Bishop seems at first glance to follow it. But then you realize that unlike other villanelles, "One Art" is not based on iambic pentameter. The important lines end with the trochee. This villanelle turns out not to be driven by the energy of the iamb, but instead by the continuing echo of the trochee at the end: "master" "faster." The light brushing of the line with the unaccented syllable, a trochee, is said to be a "feminine ending," as opposed to the "masculine ending," the iamb.

The more one looks closely at the poem, it seems that the rhythm driving it, the rhythm that alters, breaks off, reappears, has, behind it, a catching of breath — a strange breath pattern, asthmatic, like Elizabeth Bishop herself — and, behind that catch of breath (these trochees, that little dash at the beginning of stanza four), the rhythm of suppressed sobs. The trochee, as in "Uh oh" or "Watch out" or the French "Ooh la," is an utterance of warning: something's wrong, be careful. The mounting sobbing lies just beneath the poem while on the surface the poet pretends not to care. It is that tension between *suppressing* and *expressing* that make this poem so heartbreaking at the end. The ending is preceded by a dash, as if adding a little afterthought to the list of losses. That dash, which suggests time, reflection, a choked-back sadness, and then, obsessively, the making of a list . . .

> — Even losing you (the joking voice, a gesture
> I love) . . . [31]

"One Art" is the only poem published in her lifetime in which she uses the words "I love," even obliquely. But in an astonishing late poem, "Breakfast Song," found by her friend Lloyd Schwartz when she was sick, she permits herself that direct statement.[32] Earlier, even in her poem "The Shampoo," the lover is addressed — only once — as "dear friend"; never is there an indication, to the outsider, that this is a love poem. It's all about water and stars and a bowl . . . Or so it seems at first look.

In "One Art," written near the end of Bishop's life, despite the assumed distance and coolness that form the conceit of the poem, personal grief threatens to breaks through. But displays of naked emotion are unthinkable; the cry of grief is "mastered," subdued, suppressed, denied; nevertheless, it finds its expression in the breath-catches of the last two lines. The assumed irony is revealed for what it is; a mask.

> . . . It's evident
> The art of losing's not too hard to master
> though it may look like (*Write* it!) like disaster.

The art of losing is perhaps hard, but still, protests the poet, not *too* hard. It's not until the final line that the reserve breaks down completely. The punctuation lets go its terrible control. "Say it," the poet urges herself, "(*Write* it!)." Writing as betrayal, writing as revealing, writing as truth: these tensions are brilliantly suggested in this poem. The deliberately assumed jaunty tone is meant to whistle away the fear. A delicately tensile structure underlies the surface of the villanelle, "One Art," that carefully polished surface that the poet is going to demonstrate, by the end of the poem, to be just that — *only* the surface. And that surface is going to crack.

I remember Miss Bishop's in-held breath, the struggle with herself, gasping, "Where is the asthma inhaler?" Putting out the cigarette, crumpling yet another page, trying it again, the act of writing, the act of putting the words down, getting it right this time, no, it's no good, the rumpled hair, the small black cramped letters, another cigarette, the inhaler, where did I put it? The awful white page, the tyranny of that page, another go, wheezing, trying to breathe, the word "like" written twice, a double simile, ungrammatical, juddering catch of breath in the last line, a poet never does that, reckless, nothing left to lose . . . "though it may look like (*Write* it!) like disaster." I hear in my mind again Elizabeth Bishop's faltering voice, the unbearable thought — "I shan't have lied" . . . my "losing you" ("though it may look like") — cannot bear to actually face it — asthma. "(*Write* it!)" IS "disaster."

Robert Lowell, ever obsessed by his contemporaries' rank in life, poetically speaking, asked his classes to evaluate Elizabeth Bishop's work. "Major or minor?" he asked. He had already rated Marianne Moore. The class went blank; by now they knew a rhetorical question when they heard it. "Minor," he pronounced Elizabeth Bishop. But it was with a sigh. "Almost major," he amended. Well, at least she was on the list, we thought.

Ping-Pong Sestina: For Elizabeth Bishop

On Monday mornings in your apartment we faced
each other across the net, two poets
having a go at Ping-Pong. Your arthritic hands
gripped the paddle. Determined, you played
against my energy and youth, a tricky game
in which I held myself back, wanting you to win,

not to succumb to your age, or defeat: always to win.
You grinned with delight at the speed of the game,
pressing in for the slow shots, gingerly played
as the ball dripped casually over the edge of the net, handling
your aching body and keeping the poetic
plonk of the white ball going. Wheezing, your face

was childlike. "Please call me Elizabeth." But I couldn't quite face
that. You were "Miss Bishop." Elizabeth Bishop, Poet,
as in "Miss Bishop's too noble-O." Even with one hand
behind your back, whatever smallest edge you had you played
to advantage as if seeing angles were a game
and as if there were only one way of recording, one way to win

that cancelled all other alternatives. You so easily won
friends, admirers, yet always at play
was your encircled suffering, lack of love hinted, gamely
ignored; the poems and stories in which pain was handled
so far back behind the eyes that the poetry
stood for itself, was really *poetry*, not pain. You faced

it only obliquely. Once, showing me a photo, the face
of yourself as a baby, small, stubborn, not at all "poetic,"
protesting abandonment in crumpled white lace, your hands
tightly folded as if your dear life, even then, was not a game,
as if you sensed you had something dark to play
out, a despairing intelligence behind that winning

little person. But it was late now. You were winded,
fighting arthritis, the ball. I found myself mentally playing
both sides of the table, cheering your game
so much more than my own. Did I hold back? Did I hand
you the final point? The match? No, you won on your poems
alone. Your austere inward face

was wickedly triumphant, handing me the paddle. "Shall we play
again?" Lunch was waiting, talk of books and poetry. But facing
winter noons in Cambridge, we started another game.

   ⓥ KATHLEEN SPIVACK

. . . when I was young I had so much reverence for writing. Elizabeth Bishop was
my teacher in college — she was my favorite teacher, and I revered her work,
and I came to love her as a person very, very much — and I remember that later
when she would invite us over for dinner I would get almost physically ill. It
was this combination of conflicting feelings: excitement, discomfort, a sense of
unworthiness. Being with her mattered so deeply that it made me almost sick.
Caring so much, the intensity of my devotion was nearly overwhelming.

   ⓥ JONATHAN GALASSI

Spivack: Delivered at the Elizabeth Bishop memorial service, Poetry Society of America, New
    York City, 1979.
Galassi: "Agents & Editors: A Q&A with Jonathan Galassi," interview by Jofie Ferrari-
    Adler, *Poets and Writers* (July–August 2009) (adapted).

Boston and Its Influence
Bishop and Lowell

IMMIGRATION, CLASS, AND RELIGION
Boston influenced Lowell and Bishop in different ways, Lowell much more than Bishop, in his life and work. Bishop's stay in Boston was actually rather brief. Their origins and family immigration patterns might help one understand the two poets' differing points of view. First, Robert Lowell. His family came over on the *Mayflower* and dated back to the first "Puritans," one might say. They came here specifically to escape religious persecution. They were an immigrant sect, as were the parents of so many others that were to evolve in America — the Shakers, the Mormons, and the like. Escaping the Church of England, they came here, as we were told in the history books, "to worship in their own way." Their "own way," meant an extreme austerity, compared with the church they had left, the High Anglican Church, so close actually to Catholicism, except that after the creation of the King James Bible, services were conducted in English. Their "own way" led in turn to religious and other persecutions, the Salem witch trials being the prime example. Out of this austerity and repression, Hawthorne and other writers flourished. But Puritanism was at the heart of the Lowell tradition. As he wrote, " 'Rome was,' we told the Irish, 'Boston *is.*'"[33]

Lowell was attracted to Latin at St. Mark's School, an Episcopal institution. He loved the classics. He was even nicknamed "Cal" after a Roman emperor, albeit a mean one. In a repressive environment, he found ways to rebel. The family was a largely commercial one; he was a dreamy boy. He lived the classics, and they were to hold his imagination for his entire life. He managed to leave Harvard, a significant accomplishment: for a bright boy, that might have taken a bit of work. Especially when you consider that a Lowell had been president of Harvard: it was a kind of "family business." Next was his later adoption of Catholicism. By Lowell's time, the strict Puritanism of the early immigrants had been watered down. Yet his imagination was caught by sin and redemption, as we see in his early poems. Latin had been cast aside in Anglican services in favor of the King James Version of the Bible. But Lowell was attracted to more formal classical structure — as we see in his work but also in his life. His conversion was, in Lowell's and "puritan" terms, a huge rebellion. The "papists" went beyond Jonathan Edwards; they believed in purgatory. But they believed in confession and forgiveness too. Most of all, the services were conducted in Latin! I think that is one of the things that attracted him. But for his family, the austere, but eccentric Lowells, this must have been hard to take. "What has our problem kid done next? How will we tell the Cabots etc.? Egad, the boy's run off with the 'smells and bells' people!"

Of course there were precedents for this: notably T. S. Eliot's conversion from the more liberal Unitarianism of his family to High Church Anglican. Eliot had spent time at Harvard at the Anglican monastery on Memorial Drive, one of only twelve such monasteries existing in the world today. The Society of St. John the Evangelist still welcomes people for retreats; it is a lovely little oasis that you might want to visit if you find yourself in Boston.

Interestingly, Lowell's burial service took place at the Church of the Advent, the Highest (read "coldest!") Anglican church around, and the closest to Catholicism. The priest spoke not one word about Lowell's individuality as a person or poet, but followed the standard, routine service for the Burial of the Dead.

But during the time I knew Lowell, and I spent many Sundays with him and his family, Catholicism seemed to be in the past. Mostly he lay around while reading poetry aloud to us — Elizabeth Hardwick, and later Caroline and myself. A wonderful article deals with Lowell's religious thinking, and I refer you to it ("Robert Lowell, Death of an Elfking").[34]

For Elizabeth Bishop's family, the immigration to Boston was not allied with the *Mayflower* but came at a much later date. Part of her family had come to New England from Nova Scotia as part of a later labor migration. Boston itself never caught Bishop's imagination; poetry of place was very important in her work, but Boston was not one of those "places." Her moving poems take solace in the north, with the wonder of memories: "The Fish," "The Moose," etc. Or in the south: Key West, Brazil. However, the austerity in her poems might be in some part linked to the strict austerity of the Nova Scotians, who were largely Scots, with all the reserve of those peoples, rather than the ebullience of the Irish population, which overflowed into the back of Beacon Hill. Her sense of religion seemed to be more closely related to a kind of pantheistic mysticism, although "The Prodigal" is based, of course, on the Bible.[35]

THE ROLE OF HISTORY

One of the aspects that characterized Lowell's mind and his writing, as I've mentioned above, was his ability, similar to that of Peter Drucker, my father, to see relationships between historical events and the present. To listen to him talk, to read his work, one was struck by the breadth of intelligence, historical knowledge, and recall. Even *Life Studies*, which was a departure from his earlier work, in that it dealt directly with his personal history, was played out against the tension of his earlier and later preoccupations with Boston history. History, and the history of New England, was central; it was in his bones — not only in his earlier works, but of course in *Life Studies,* and most of all in the poem "For the Union Dead," which he was working on after I first came to Boston. He introduced me to the history behind the poem, and I spent many afternoons or mornings in his study while he worked on it, and tried out various lines. Here he referenced the famous Saint-Gaudens sculpture of Colonel Shaw's regiment. It is prominently placed in Boston. At the time that Lowell wrote this poem, there was a project to establish a parking garage under the Boston Common, and the juxtaposition of this famous group statue, and the advent of "king car" was very much in the news. (Saint-Gaudens's sculptures, which are devoted to American historical events and figures, including Abraham Lincoln, can be seen in Boston, Chicago, and elsewhere, and his work has been the subject of a PBS special.)

Bishop did not write about History with a capital H. Or think about it much. She was more interested in describing exotic places. She wrote about landscape, people — mostly poor ones — and the sociological constraints around them, as well as stray animals. Her imagery comes from the extreme north, or from the south. She was not interested, unlike Lowell, in writing about British and New England history. Bishop peered closely at her environment and had a keen eye for human interest, children, and animals — when we look at her work, it has a close-up charm and humor and observation of detail. Through her friend Lota de Macedo Soares she was very interested in architecture and city planning, and she loved to talk about that and had lots of books on architecture. My husband, Mayer, was also working in the field of city planning and on designing public playgrounds, and we heard all about Lota's work in that field and the political problems that finally led to the defeat of the project.

MISOGYNY

As women began to take an active part in the civil rights movement, working alongside their men, and also against the Vietnam War, supporting their male children, they began to ask for an equal leadership voice in these organizations and in society as a whole. Inequalities that had always existed, been taken for granted, were now impossible to sustain.

The writer Rosellen Brown lived in New Hampshire and commuted to Cambridge during the term of her fellowship. She and I sometimes exchanged residences, so my family got to spend time in the country, and hers in the city. When our books were finally published, we walked around Cambridge together, taking turns going into the bookstores to ask if the books were in, and to order them if they weren't. Later, my friends Fanny Howe, Alice Walker, and I struggled with the breakup of marriages as well as the demands of babies. We had all made a sort of pact to earn at least $3,000 a year on our writing. But a few years later, only Alice had realized that goal.

As women writers, many of us were raising young children and holding jobs as well, as opposed to the carefree male graduate students around us. My closest woman friend within the second wave, though she rarely visited during office hours, was writer Fanny Howe, whom I'd also met through Lowell and William Alfred. We each had become pregnant around the same time and had babies within a few days of each other. I wrote this poem, immortalizing our struggles to write and raise young children at the same time:

> I am writing my heart out here.
> In a kitchen two towns away,
> my friend Fanny is doing likewise.[36]

In the early '70s, writers Fanny Howe, Alice Walker, Rosellen Brown, Florence Ladd, Ruth Whitman, and I, along with artists Pozzi Escot and Flora Natapoff, all held Bunting Fellowships around the same time. Many of us had young children. The concept of child care had not yet been discovered by Radcliffe College. The Radcliffe Institute was meant to model the Junior Fellow Society at Harvard. In fact, we were called "fellows"!

We were lucky to get these fellowships, and it was our fault if the messy facts of personal lives — men, children, money (the lack of it) — got in the way of our taking full advantage of the "life of the mind" so miraculously offered us by Radcliffe. The Institute offered us a place to work, an office away from home, a very small stipend (many of us had to work to make ends meet), but most of all, the company of other writers, artists, and scholars. It was a wonderful concept, a wonderful opportunity for women, developed by Mary Bunting and first director, Constance Smith.

Reality presented obstacles. I remember staring out of my window in desperation on the dewy morning that marked the beginning of my prized Radcliffe fellowship, holding a crying baby, and unable to get in to the first meeting. I had hired a babysitter, but the babysitter was sick and couldn't come. Liberty flew out that window. I saw my whole precious year draining away. The baby cried and cried and I did too! But I was not the only woman with a child. I soon discovered that other "fellows" faced the same situation. Soon we had organized ourselves. One of us watched all the children one morning a week, while the others wrote. Then we took turns, and we often got together in the afternoons with our children. We shared child care, our writing, many happy mealtimes together, as well as literary nurturance.

I was assaulted on Brattle Street in Cambridge one late afternoon not long after the birth of my youngest child, Marin. (The scholar Ethel Higonnet was later killed in the same location.) My book *The Jane Poems* comes out of this experience. It coincided with the war in Vietnam, in which civilians, including women and children, were specifically targeted. Also there were almost no supportive services for women at that time, and it made me want to work with others to change this.

The climate in Boston was more prejudiced than in any other part of the country, perhaps, when it came to actually taking women seriously, or hiring them. A few years earlier, my mother, pregnant with her fourth child, had been expelled from a university physics graduate program in New Jersey. A pregnant woman, it was reasoned, might give the graduate students "ideas." Until the late '80s, the Equal Opportunity Act did not apply to the teaching professions. Women who applied for teaching jobs could not admit they were married; they might get pregnant, which meant that they might have had Sex — and then have babies, which meant they would leave. So women lied for these jobs. Harvard was particularly horrible to women (Boston University, too) — they boasted they could get rid of women Ph.D. candidates by "making them cry."

Ruth Whitman, a poet who had studied classics at Radcliffe and who later married her classics professor, was seen as having the handicaps of big breasts and a big smile. She had titled her first book, unfortunately, *Blood and Milk Poems*, which sent the Harvard community up the wall. Just the thought of women's bodily fluids — *all that dripping* — made their toes curl. I recognize these attitudes in writing about this. Bishop of course did also. Women were supposed to be "attractive" and exist for men. Lowell selected his women students for his classes at Harvard mostly on their looks. He often asked me to sit in while he chose his students, and afterward he was amused that I dared to disagree with that criterion. But in the workshops or during office hours he would often turn on a woman he had selected for her looks, especially as he approached his breakdowns. Have it, don't flaunt it — that was "old money" New England in regard to their cars, their mansions (the so-called cottages at Mattapoisett), and such things.

But women were sometimes invisible to him. Quiet elegance. Discreet blondes, pearls. The protective coloration. In public, Miss Bishop presented herself in that way. When she read her work she wore a suit, yes, with a skirt! Clunky heels, a white blouse, little pearls. "Sign in at the front desk on the first floor." In private, at home in Cambridge, Elizabeth Bishop wore the tightest leather pants, had her own flamboyance, and of course drank and smoked and hacked and coughed. And although she told me in dramatic detail — enormous detail, it turns out — about her love affairs, it was all so vague and allusive and "suited for my ears" that I didn't think twice about the implications.

I think Bishop internalized the misogyny of the time. How could she not? Being a woman, with implicit pre-conscious sexuality — as in "In The Waiting Room" — was problematic. Many women with intelligence grew up with this dichotomy at this time. Bishop had a very ambivalent relation to being a woman plus poet — plus lesbian — in the Boston/Cambridge/Harvard nexus. She had been very hurt by Mary McCarthy's not-so-veiled portrayal of her in *The Group*, as we know. Extremely vulnerable, sensitive, she hid much of her private life. She wanted nothing to do with anything that seemed to involve the women's movement. She internalized many of the male attitudes of the day toward women, who were supposed to be attractive, appealing to men, and not ask for equal pay or a job with benefits. Her meeting with Anne Sexton, in which Anne talked in great dramatic detail about childbirth and her own suffering throughout, was disastrous. Anne played the I-am-suffering-mega-feminine-sex-goddess-pain-of-childbirth card to the hilt.

Bishop had come to Boston/Cambridge demoralized and in poor health, both physical and psychological. Lowell pressed Harvard to hire her, which it did — but only part time and conditionally. This was so they would not have to pay her benefits: she was a woman after all, not considered a great poet — no woman was — and Harvard could get away with this. The subject of lesbianism was unthinkable, except in code-language like Ancient Greek, which the academic fuddy-duddies seemed to find titillating. (According to them, only one lesbian seems to have existed *ever* in all of classical history: *Sappho!* long dead and no real threat to their professorial marriages.) So officially she hid it.

Bishop's published poems go overboard to conceal the very real source of her emotive/affective life. Her letters and unpublished fragments show a huge capacity for affection and love, but her published poems bend over backward to hide that part of her nature. Lloyd Schwartz, Thomas Travisano, and Alice Quinn have shown us that secret part of Bishop's life. And we know that Bishop adored Frank Bidart. I think Bishop would have loved to have children — we see her feeling for children in her poems. And her feelings for Frank Bidart were maternal and concerned, as for an adopted son. I think both Lowell and Bishop shared an almost parental love for Frank Bidart.

Although I saw Bishop several times a week for some years and she told me much about "Suzanne" and "Lota," never was a full name given, and never was the more personal relationship overtly stated. Not once. Bishop had a "secret garden." But the liveliness, wit, spirit of fun, vivacious intelligence, observation, and compassion that come through in her letters is the voice of the person I knew, her many-sided human struggle.

Making a living for a poet, as always, was problematic at the time — but more so because it was before the era of the MFA industry. Lowell, as everyone knew, had a trust fund, so he was able to cope with part-time teaching. Bishop, like many others, was more constrained — sometimes just enough money to get by, but health insurance as she got older became an issue. She didn't love teaching and often dreaded meeting her classes.

Lowell tried to help Bishop at Harvard. Lowell himself, at least in his early years there, was marginal to the university. On his own, he might not have gotten a job there, despite his poetic success at that point. Harvard did not like to hire its own, but it couldn't very well turn down the Lowell name because the Lowells contributed significantly to Harvard's endowment. But he had little say in what the university did. He was at first commuting for one semester to Boston from New York, where the Lowells had moved. He arranged for Bishop to replace him later, and we know there was some tension about that when he wanted to come back. I am not sure Lowell actually had a lot of power or say at Harvard — a Lowell expert might know more — but I gathered he was too erratic, and the community was not set up to cope with his breakdowns, late grades, and frequent absences from teaching. There were complaints. But William Alfred, who kept his private life carefully hidden, was part of Harvard, and a very important figure there. He was professor of Anglo-Saxon, and his classes were overflowing. He was a wonderful man, though often robbed or defrauded by "sons" he had "adopted" to live with him (the "rough trade"), but nothing was ever said. Anyhow, he had the power to force Harvard to give Elizabeth Bishop, finally, a bit of standing and health benefits. One would not be surprised to learn that Alfred might have offered to pay it out of his own pocket.

But although Elizabeth Bishop could be open about her lesbianism when alone with Lowell (while flirting with him whenever they were together in my presence), she was intensely guarded about her private life. It might have cost her the job to behave otherwise. She behaved like a lady of her time, with impeccable manners and laughter, and Lowell was always courtly, jokey, and attentive. However, they maintained a formal distance between them, from what I observed, and I think that distance made their relationship possible.

Lowell carried within him contradictory views. He admired women writers, as we know. Yet he was influenced by the misogyny of his time. He wrote something to Bishop to the effect that "you are one of the greatest American poets. For a woman . . ." Yet in his dealings with women he was unusually supportive. He was a mentor in the true sense. He loved the work of Adrienne Rich, and he encouraged Anne Sexton and Sylvia Plath, as he did me with my work, taking it to publishers and magazines. He was totally supportive of Elizabeth Bishop's work, and never missed an opportunity to praise it. He had an enormous generosity, certainly in my experience of him. And so did Miss Bishop. In classes, pre-breakdowns, Lowell engaged in his "mirror mirror on the wall, who is the greatest poet of them all?" monologues. He always rated the women, including Elizabeth Bishop, as "minor," this with a little pained sigh of regret.

HOMOPHOBIA

An unsophisticated Puritan town, Boston was supposedly ruled by proper heterosexual families, patriarchal men, who participated in manly sports and activities. Actually, when you think about it, women played a huge role, and perhaps they ran the show — Mrs. Peabody, for instance, so active in civil rights — but the flutter was all about pretending that the man was always right. So Bishop, as we see in one of her letters, wanted nothing to do with going public in Boston about her personal life. Lowell, in public, was actively homophobic — perhaps more so because he was a poet. Brahmin "real men" were heterosexual, worked in banks and law firms downtown, wore pink sailing pants, played elegant tennis, drank a lot but held their liquor, and were "real men" in a New England, cultured, refined sort of way — as opposed to the hunting, shooting, fishing, James Dickey–like violent, abusive, alcoholic "real men" who fathered sons like well-known poet-sons-of-alcoholics of the Midwest. Here women ruled: it was really a matriarchal society with all the ambivalence that went with that.

Perhaps as protective coloration, Lowell and Bishop treated the subjects of homosexuality differently. Lowell was openly homophobic; he would complain to me about members of his workshop when he relaxed in his rooms after classes or lunches. He sometimes would taunt members of his later workshops about homosexuality, just to see how far he could go. Lowell made sure we understood that he was differentiated. Yet the people who were most present to him during the breakdowns were men who were available, didn't have children, and had enough money to be able to leave everything and give time to Robert Lowell.

ANTI-SEMITISM

One could always tell if Lowell was approaching a breakdown because he would vaguely claim to be Hitler and come out with other provocative remarks. He would be sure to make some anti-Semitic comments to me, regarding my father's origins, and also to the economist Emma Rothschild, who attended the workshops as a young woman. Then he would always say, "Well, I am part Jewish myself," with an inviting smile to Emma. Of course — if he couldn't be King George or some other such nobility, he could at least be a Rothschild! Emma and I saw it as a certain sign of danger approaching; we retreated from going to Lowell's classes and left the field to the braver men until this quite aggressive phase of the Lowell cycle was over. I think this kind of anti-Semitism was also a barrier in his association with Stanley Kunitz. Although Kunitz was extremely helpful to Lowell, with drafts of manuscripts and so forth, there was a definite reserve on both sides.

SOCIAL ISSUES

The civil rights movement was already gathering momentum, and the country was splitting again along familiar lines drawn during the American Civil War. But there also were strong elements in Boston itself that opposed the civil rights movement. Institutions like the Boston school system were severely split, and hiring practices at businesses and universities such as Harvard did not even start to change until long after. For Lowell, both the civil rights movement, which was already building in the late fifties, early sixties, and the later Vietnam War, engaged him. He saw these events as part of America's history, and they entered his poetry as well as his political life. For all of us in Boston at the time, these were significant historic times, and some of us can remember riding buses to Alabama for voter registration drives, walking in Washington with Martin Luther King Jr., and participating in the many marches against the Vietnam War in Boston, New York, and Washington. So when our great literary figures, Robert Lowell and Norman Mailer, and others, marched together in Washington during the Vietnam era to protest this war, they marched for all of us, inspiring pride and sense of solidarity as writers. Bishop was not in Boston at this time.

On the other hand, when the social climate freed up, this did not extend to the social behavior as far as I could see, of Lowell and Bishop. The hippie culture of drugs and "free love" was entering the general consciousness. Drugs and free love had never been a problem for these poets, but they understood it differently. Neither Lowell nor Bishop, for instance, participated in "the summer of love"; they did not occupy university offices; they were never tempted to become hippies. Marijuana and LSD were not part of their culture. In general, they held to their classical literary values, delighting in new discoveries in that realm only, and even then did not stray too far from their formal educations. The times changed but their values did not. They remained true to their classical educations and well-wrought literature.

Once I had a poem with an exhibitionist in it. He thought an exhibitionist was somebody who did tricks and stunts. He was an embarrassing person to explain to . . .

⊚ ALICE RYERSON HAYES

When I think about him, I think about him smiling to the side a little shyly, in a particularly Bostonian way, and it makes me sad.

⊚ FANNY HOWE

Hayes: Note written for Kathleen Spivack, 1989.
Howe: Note written for Kathleen Spivack, 1990.

Lowell's Poet Friends

Frank Bidart, Lord Gowrie, Bill Alfred

Lowell had very strong friends who saw him and Elizabeth Hardwick through the rough times — and who later, too, came to Caroline's aid. Be it in England, New York, or picking up the pieces in Boston or Cambridge, without their support, things would have been a lot worse. Above all, William Alfred and Frank Bidart, two of the kindest people in the world, were able to go wherever needed in order to help out both Lowell and Bishop.

Of the later students in Cal's life who became his friends, I was most familiar with Frank Bidart and the young Lord Gowrie. Frank first appeared in Lowell's classes as a graduate student. He hunched over the table during the "office hours," slumping onto his hands. He had a high forehead and exhausted eye sockets. He was tall and round-shouldered, and stooped as if staying upright was too tiring. His eyebrows were somewhat raised, and his earnest face and voice were endearing. Frank kept all-night hours and must have had trouble staying awake during the morning meetings of the group. When he walked with me, he would practically curve into a question mark to bend his tall body down to my level. He had long, expressive hands and an agreeable avuncular manner behind which lay strong emotionality.

His poetry was strong and daring. He wrote directly about his subjects, starting a poem titled "California Plush" with the line: "The only thing I miss about Los Angeles . . ."[37] Frank's work projected a deceptive ease over strong technical control. Most striking was his empathy with his subjects. As he wrote poems exploring personae, this ability to almost merge with his poetry became even more apparent. I was later part of a theater troupe that performed the poetry of Frank Bidart and other Boston poets, and Frank's poem exploring the life story of an anorexic girl was heart-wringing in its intensity. Lowell loved Frank and came to rely on him more and more.

Frank possessed an old-fashioned goodness. At first the dependency was one-way — Frank seeing Cal as a father figure. Frank adored Lowell. But later, in the '70s, Cal came to rely on Frank's generosity as well. Ian Hamilton writes of Frank's role in helping Lowell with his manuscripts. Sensitive, without large reserves of energy, Frank gave up a great deal to Robert Lowell. Cal's demands took a lot out of his friends. More caught up in the cycle of Cal's illness than the others, more directly resonating, Frank often appeared exhausted and ill after his visits with Cal. Kind, intelligent, and sensitive, his vulnerabilities were very much on the surface. Not only did Frank Bidart's poetry reach its maturity, its depth of feeling, in his later years, but Frank honored his friendship with Lowell when he edited the thoughtfully annotated edition *Robert Lowell: Collected Poems*.[38]

The Gowries — Grey and his wife Xandra "Bingo" Bingley — arrived at Harvard in the mid-'60s, and Grey sat in on Lowell's classes there. (This was shortly after Frank Bidart came onto the scene.) Mayer described Grey as "this year's Englishman" because of Harvard's exchange program with British universities. But Grey was a star already. Of all the people that I knew, Grey was the most capable of communicating with Cal during his periods of mania. Grey had a gift for conversation and for grandeur. He knew history, particularly English and Irish, and loved talking about it with Lowell.

The arrival of the Gowries livened things up considerably. Grey and Bingo appeared one day on drab Kirkland Street like characters out of a novel or movie. It was like the Jazz Age, or like the movie *Midnight in Paris*, where glamorous people of another milieu suddenly walk into your lives and make you a part of theirs. I was standing in the checkout line at our neighborhood grocery store, Savenor's, when the Gowries first came into view. This supermarket, later the grocery store of choice for television chef Julia Child, was not so fancy then. It was a neighborhood, down-home grocery store on the Cambridge-Somerville line featuring Jewish foods: gefilte fish, chopped liver, pickles, and pastrami.

The formidable Mrs. Savenor held court at the checkout counter, bossing her sons, who worked for her fearfully, as well as her customers. Her sons scurried about the store doing her bidding. The matriarch wore a floury faded apron over her sizable billowing front, her bare arms were huge, and her swollen legs bulged over split black leather shoes. She had a strong accent and an "*oy vey*" sense of humor. Outside, I saw an entourage gather itself, poised to enter the store. Assisted by a number of helpful young women, Grey, a tall, slim, elegant, and dashingly attractive man, emerged from a large black car, double parked, with his small son, a curly-haired precocious three-year-old who, comically, looked exactly like a miniature of his father. The child had a very solemn manner.

Mrs. Savenor and I watched Grey as he pointed the young women toward the shelves. At his direction, they heaped up a grocery cart. Then very quickly, he signed the name "Earl" on a check with a large flourish, and swept out of the store. The little boy and the entourage of young women followed behind, carrying the bags. They all got back into the large black car to the astonished eyes of Mrs. Savenor and a few other customers. As they pulled out from the curb, Mrs. Savenor turned the check over and over, as if a mystery might thereby be solved. "Earl . . . who?" How strange to just write his first name on a check, I thought. Earl. A good name for a country-western singer.

The Gowries had come from Oxford, which already seemed exotic enough for me. Anglophile Harvard had fallen at their feet. Harvard immediately produced elegant housing for them, something it never did for the Lowells or anyone else. Later, the Gowrie house burned down, and with it one of the priceless Francis Bacon paintings from their collection. They had brought their paintings along with them for Grey's graduate study.

Grey was the epitome of lightning intelligence and energy. He had wild, frizzy black hair, tremendous courtesy, and the ability to appear to be interested in everything and everyone. When he talked to or listened to someone, he made that person feel that he or she was the most remarkable person he'd ever come across. Talking with Grey, one would instantly become reinvented. Everyone expanded in the presence of Grey and Bingo, much as one did in the presence of Robert Lowell. Grey's intelligence was an almost-visible aura, crackling. It was accompanied by kindness as well as generosity. He was a great friend to me.

Grey and Bingo swept about the slushy streets of Harvard Square in identical ankle-length lynx fur coats. Like legends from the Jazz Age, they created get-togethers where wine and conversation sparkled. They carried off their reputations in great style. One evening, at Grey's birthday party, I looked down the immense rows of chairs on either side of the table and noticed that various women were seated down one side, in the exact order of their importance and involvement with Grey's life, I imagined. And down the other side were ranged the young men, Bingo's admirers, so I told myself. Bingo was a direct, warm, intelligent woman who kept the Gowrie ménage, at least for a time, more or less on its feet. She was lovely, harder to get to know than Grey, and more "there" once you did get to know her. Grey and Bingo smiled at each other from the head and foot of the long table. It was easy to invent glamorous lives for this illustrious couple.

Aside from dash and flair, the Gowries were hospitable. They were concerned about their friends, and about Cal. Grey Gowrie had one of the few minds that could keep up with Cal. He was already destined for great things. He had an extraordinary career, including art history and modern art. Grey's full name was Alexander Patrick Greysteil Ruthven, the second Earl of Gowrie, which was already distinctive enough. The early promise and brilliance flashed like an aura about him, but within that aura was a man of intelligence, courtesy, and immense loyalty and kindness. After his time at Harvard, he served in the British House of Lords, was a government minister under Margaret Thatcher, and became chairman of Sotheby's and later the Arts Council. He wrote several collections of poetry as well as literary and political essays.

During periods when Lowell was going off the deep end, he would go on and on about British kings. Grey did not mind at all, he loved to talk about British history too. Of the two of them, Anne Sexton quipped: "Oh, a poet who wants to be an earl, and an earl who wants to be a poet!" This was a fairly apt description, but Grey was already a poet and Cal — well, he fancied himself at least an earl, if not an erratic Roman emperor. Later in an interview with Ian Hamilton, Lowell reduced his family's status to that of "the Duke of Something's sixth cousins."[39]

Grey could deal with Cal with a light touch on such difficult issues as Cal's wanting to drink while he was on lithium and/or Antabuse, as well as his hospitalizations. Grey seemed to know what to do. For a time during Cal's many hospitalizations at McLean Hospital, he was allowed to leave the premises if he went to an "approved" house. Cal went either to the Gowries' on those evenings or sometimes to visit me and my husband in our small apartment in Somerville. I was grateful for the presence of Grey in Cal's life.

The Gowries were the same generation as myself, and I shared my perplexity at some of the situations in which I found myself with Cal. On the evenings when Cal was to come to my house, I worried over what to do about liquor. Cal was not supposed to drink; he was heavily medicated. He "compromised" by drinking large quantities of alcohol diluted with milk. Should I have alcohol in the apartment, or not? It never did actually seem to matter, the Gowries would advise. Just try and control the quantity, they said. On their advice, I would buy a few bottles of wine, and Cal would sit on the couch and drink all the wine as well as quarts and quarts of milk, and talk — brilliantly, aimlessly — and I would know that I could never be as brilliant in response. Then he would go into the kitchen and open the cabinets, searching for more liquor. When it got to be a certain time, Mayer would drive him back to the hospital. I never actually saw Cal break down; he was kind and tractable in our presence.

Bingo also had difficulties with Cal's nervous troubles. Uprooted, with a child and a job in Boston, she was sensitive to Cal's upsets, and on more than one occasion, she told me, spent evenings when Cal was "paroled" to their house locked in her bedroom. Bingo looked like a young woman in a George Romney painting: she was the picture of English beauty and shared Grey's grace, laughter and gallantry. But Grey too had his underside.

The Gowries were heroic in their friendship to Cal, as well as in their own lives — all the more so when I saw them, after Cal's death, in their relations with Caroline Blackwood and her children. Divorced by the time Lowell died, Grey and Bingo returned from England together for Lowell's funeral in Boston, and to join with his friends and relatives there.

Lowell had the ability to attract friends, friends who would persist throughout his life. From my Boston vantage point, I observed some of them and knew tangentially of the artist Frank Parker, Peter and Esther Brooks, and others. I also got to know the British poet and playwright Jonathan Griffin, whom I later visited in England.

William Alfred, a man with high comic spirit, had mischievous eyes and a heart of utter kindness. Known as the "only saint at Harvard," or at least, in the Harvard English Department, Alfred's goodness was legendary. (I should point out that there was very little competition, at Harvard, for the position of saint.) Students endured his Anglo-Saxon courses in order to have Alfred as their teacher. He had written a version of *Agamemnon*, and the play *Hogan's Goat*, as well as others. Modest, gentle, steadfast, Alfred's hospitality to Cal, his family, and friends, had an enduring quality that gave comfort, even during Lowell's most difficult pre-breakdown periods.

William Alfred could be seen hunched over, one shoulder higher than another, with a baggy overcoat, a stoved-in hat, and shoes that seemed too large for him, as he shuffled through the streets of Cambridge. He had a merry elfin face, cute squirrel-like cheeks, and his eyes scrunched up when he smiled, which was often. He loved jokes, could tell wonderful stories, and loved to imitate accents, particularly of Irish theater folk.

Over the years I spent many happy afternoons or mornings at Bill's house on Athens Street, which had high ceilings, comfortable armchairs, and a cozy kitchen. Bill was a good cook and often invited me to breakfast or lunch after he had finished his student conferences. When he invited me out to dinner, it was always at the Athens Olympia, a dark, old-fashioned restaurant with high booth dividers, downtown. It was his favorite. He took my arm as he shuffled along, called a taxi, imitated New York theater folk with a strong Irish accent, laughing.

Often we'd settle into his comfortable armchairs (complete with doilies on their arms) and talk about poetry, plays, and his productions, or his problems with his latest "adopted son." He was very proud of his friendship with the actress Faye Dunaway. His coffee table was loaded with books sent him by grateful students, articles they had published, copies of their recently produced plays and other achievements. Afterward, we went into his kitchen where the white metal table would be set — more doilies — and he made me sit down and watch him cook for me. He put on a large apron, joking with me as he flourished a large wooden spoon.

Bill Alfred was always on a diet for his weight or his heart, so he would take great pains to make homey meals for me and then fix only a cup of tea for himself. I felt guilty tucking in to all that food in front of him, but I felt even worse if I refrained from eating these mother-type meals: scrambled eggs and toast, or tuna salad and pudding and tea. "Oh, I wish I could eat that," he would sigh, as he fiddled with weak tea and a cracker across the table from my plateful of bounty. I was "eating for two."

The doorbell rang constantly at Bill's Cambridge house, for students, former students, and friends — the categories merged one into the other — were always dropping by to see him, bringing their term papers, usually late, as well as their spouses and children. He seemed to adopt all of them, sometimes with drastic results. An occasional adoptee turned out to be a thief. Bill would bail the person out. Once that situation was more or less resolved, Bill would turn around and welcome more young people into his life. Somehow in the midst of this, as well as throughout his teaching duties, he managed to write his prize-winning plays and television presentations. Bill had many theater friends, and one was sure to hear about Faye Dunaway, who appeared in many of his plays.

Bill lent me his little pied-à-terre, a tiny apartment he kept in New York, which was jammed with antiques and pictures of the Virgin Mary and photos of celebrities. It had a bathtub in the kitchen, with a board over it so one could use it as a table when not bathing in it. The apartment was full of pictures of Bill and his family, his students and former students, and friends. Most of all, it was full of pictures of Faye Dunaway.

I had been going to New York to see the Lowells. On the shuttle flight to La Guardia I had sat next to the captain of the *Rotterdam*, the famous flagship of the Holland America cruise line, or so he claimed, grandly. (Oh sure, sure, and I'm the Queen of England, I thought.) I told him I was a writer. As we parted at the gate, the captain invited me to come to his office that afternoon and interview with the company. He would like me to meet the president. Maybe I could get a job on his ship, he said. It would be good for the Holland America Line to have a poet on board. He was ogling me, but I didn't care. It was winter, the late 1970s. Perhaps he was putting me on, maybe not. Why not give it a try? I could teach writing to the passengers on the cruise ships. The company would pay me and would pay for my flights to foreign ports to meet the ships. It would be fun. Meet me at headquarters and I'll introduce you to the president. OK!

It was winter, and snowing heavily. I ran to Macy's to buy a floaty, day-glow turquoise nylon dress and little strappy sandals, my idea of what one had to look like to get a job on a cruise line. Never mind the qualifications for the job; as always, the pressing question of "what to wear" was foremost! Dress in hand, I made my way through the slushy streets to Bill's apartment. No sooner had I arrived in the apartment than the door slammed shut behind me. I quickly got into my new "job interview" clothes. (Keep it light, keep it light!) I had thirty minutes to get back across town to the Holland America interview.

As I turned to leave the apartment, I found the door would not budge. It had jammed shut. I couldn't open it and couldn't get out. I banged and banged. The other people in the building came and stood helplessly outside while I, all dressed up for the interview, beat on the inside of the door and called "Help!" My interview time had come and gone. I changed back into my blue jeans and resigned myself to never getting out of Bill's apartment.

Already, only one hour into my visit to New York, I had become a cliché. I would die, friendless and alone, behind locked doors far away from home. I would be the weird lady crying, "Help, Help!" although no one heard. And when, three months later, they broke into William Alfred's apartment — what is that strange smell — there I would be, my desiccated body still in my floaty dress, the little sandals still on my skeletal feet. How sad . . .

The other occupants of the building called the super, a young Puerto

Rican. He decided, his voice muffled almost to nothing on his side of the door, that the only way to solve the problem was to take the door off the hinges and take it to a locksmith. For a week I stayed in Bill's apartment without a door, not wanting to return to Boston and leave his Virgin Marys, his bathtub, his photographs of Faye Dunaway, unguarded until the door, with a new lock, was replaced.

Incidentally, I got the job on the *Rotterdam* anyway, and spent some winter months floating happily around the Caribbean and through the Panama Canal as a guest lecturer, dressed alternately in wispy, lime green dresses, and long, lacy nightgowns, my version of "formal" clothes. I taught writing — memoirs, letters, journalism, and literary writing — to the passengers when they were not otherwise occupied with tango lessons and gambling. I also published a ship's literary magazine. Additionally, for I had time on my hands, I offered to teach spoken English to the Filipino and Indonesian crews who hated each other so much that they could not be in the same class together without knives flashing. "O Captain, My Captain" turned out to be a heavy drinker — surprise! — and ran the *Rotterdam* aground on a sandbar outside of Cartagena.

But back to Bill Alfred, who was always generous. Overcome with admiration for the man, I called him up and jokingly proposed to him. No matter that I was already married . . . I could hear Bill on the other end of the telephone, probably nervously tipping his hat as he answered. "God bless, God bless," he kept saying. I promised he could stay in his own house, could wear his hat and suspenders at all times, and his only requirement would be to tell funny stories and cook scrambled eggs and toast. Clearly this was not enough of an inducement. I am sorry to report that Bill remained immune to the charms of the arrangement.

Bill's role in Robert Lowell's life was extremely important. I sensed that he was Lowell's closest friend in the entire world. Much of Bill's generosity to Cal through the good and bad times still remains unspoken. Bill had an honesty, an ability to cut through verbosity. There was something absolutely loyal in Bill's friendships and interest in people, and he was a source of comfort to Cal always.

At Frank Bidart's suggestion, I had begun attending Lowell's morning "office hours" as it was called in the basement of (I think) Quincy House. A group of fifteen or more, gathered around the large table, ranging from well-known writers to Harvard undergraduates. Unpredictable, intense, rigorous sessions unlike the tinkering of "workshop" or the solemnity of "seminar." His spirit, which I admired greatly, made us all cheerful, eager, alive to our art. What impressed me was that he was so entirely devoted to poetry — he was a *man of poetry*, more than a "great man" or "famous writer." . . . He liked absurdity, and lore, and learning. Above all, the ardent chain of learning about poetry through the generations — criticism, gossip, technique, history, all the broad or minuscule study of the art.

⌖ ROBERT PINSKY

[T]here was a . . . revelation in store for me, and that was the discovery that Harvard offered *writing* courses. Why, this was news! Here was William Alfred, the popular Harvard English professor I had read about in the *New Yorker*'s "Talk of the Town." And here was . . . "Mom!" I rose out of my lawn chair with a glad cry. My mother hurried to the door and looked out through the screen. "This is unbelievable! Guess who teaches poetry at Harvard? *Robert Lowell*." I read aloud: "English 8a. Writing (Advanced Course) . . . The emphasis will be primarily on poetry. Not more than ten students will be enrolled."

"Only ten?" my mother said doubtfully. "That's not so many."

"Oh, for God's sake, Mother. How many poets can there be at Harvard?"

⌖ JAMES ATLAS

Pinsky: Note to Kathleen Spivack, 1990.
Atlas: "Robert Lowell in Cambridge: Lord Weary," *Atlantic Monthly* 250 (July 1982), 56.

Stanley Kunitz, 1971–2006

Lowell introduced me to Stanley Kunitz when I visited him in New York. It turned out that Kunitz and my father had taught at Bennington College during the mid-1940s. His daughter had been our babysitter. Kunitz had many stories to tell of his time at Bennington, and of his friendship there with poet Theodore Roethke.

Kunitz had undergone some hard times himself as a poet and person, and had transcended them. He had been a friend to Roethke and to other poets of Cal's generation, and had survived the same struggles and self-doubts. His poetry has a compassionate quality that is extremely moving. It was as if Stanley had melded himself out of suffering. His poetry and translations reflect this integrity. Despite, or perhaps because of, his own struggles, Stanley had the gift of stepping outside of them, of observing and reflecting. His essays are strong and thoughtful, and his criticism, even of student work, often had a moral component to it. Kunitz had vast experience in looking at manuscripts of his friends, all of whom sought his advice.

Stanley Kunitz later pointed out, in a private conversation, that neither Lowell nor John Berryman could ever have written as much, as deeply, and as well, if they were merely the disturbed characters that emerge from such portrayals as Ian Hamilton's biography, *Robert Lowell*, or Eileen Simpson's *Poets in Their Youth*. Elizabeth Hardwick, Caroline Blackwood, and others echo this. "How could Cal ever have gotten any work done if he was as disturbed as Hamilton made him out to be?" Kunitz commented.

Kunitz spoke of the greatness of Cal's poetry. He also spoke of the greatness of their friendship. Cal had an extraordinary ability to make and keep lifelong friends. How could he have achieved this if he was the embarrassing maniac portrayed? The Hamilton biography distressed Kunitz for many reasons, he said. It focused too much on Cal's mental illness and on the negative things people had to say about that.

In the early '70s, when I was putting together my second manuscript, *The Jane Poems*, Robert Lowell sent me to stay with Stanley Kunitz in Provincetown. He wanted me to stay several days with Stanley until the manuscript was organized to Stanley's liking. I had arranged and rearranged the book, driving myself completely crazy. Kunitz was a genius in manuscript creation: he had worked on Lowell's manuscripts, Theodore Roethke's manuscripts, and others.

I was nervous especially about the order of the poems in *The Jane Poems*. Stanley advised me to put them in the order I had first intended, ending with a lyrical, more upbeat note. Editor of the Yale Younger Poets Series, Kunitz had chosen *Flying Inland* earlier that same year. But then Ken McCormack, my Doubleday editor, who had repeatedly turned down various versions of *Flying Inland*, surprisingly accepted *The Jane Poems* after seeing only the first three beginning poems. Suddenly there was a timing problem. Stanley, after consultation, went to Doubleday and negotiated a two-book contract for me. There were other good poets in line for the Yale series that year but I was totally insecure about my second book, which, I sensed, Lowell and the rest of the male hierarchy thought was entirely unpublishable. Stanley managed to get Doubleday to bring out both books, something that I am sure would never have happened without his intervention.

He invited me to Provincetown to work on my poems. But when the day came, I was very nervous for a number of reasons. The main one being that I looked like hell. The night before I had broken my nose demonstrating my inventor husband's "Body Sail" — something he had invented to challenge the new "Wind Surfer" already on the market. The Body Sail was basically a surfboard on the water with an enormous and loose sail on a heavy boom. To tack, you had to lift the sail overhead while maintaining balance on the plank, twirl it over your head, and somehow land it on the other side. As Mayer Spivack's champion, loyal wife, and model for the Body Sail, I was required to demonstrate the utility of this innovation on water, while Mayer zoomed alongside me in a little rubber dinghy, running a 16-mm camera and shouting, "Smile!" I wore a teeny sassy ruffled polka-dot bikini, gritted my teeth in a grimace, and worried most of all about looking fat.

The Body Sail was also supposed to be good on land. Every year in April, Mayer would also enter the Boston Marathon on roller skates, with his version of the Body Sail, trying to prove that with it he could glide faster up Heartbreak Hill than any marathon runner. He hoped to attract media attention. It was among the most stressful events of the year. Mayer had bought a used, white Volvo ambulance. It was so big that I could not see over the steering wheel. As Mayer roller-skated in the marathon with his Body Sail, I was supposed to drive slowly alongside. A nervous driver, I tried to maneuver the boxy Volvo next to the runners' track on Commonwealth Avenue, otherwise cordoned off. Mayer scowled and gestured furiously at me to drive in closer. The police gestured just as balefully, motioning for me to move off. My stomach ached with tension. Meanwhile, our two babies sat in the back seat and, well trained, waved (clean) diapers out the windows. I honked the horn as instructed and we all shouted, "Go Mayer! Yay!"

Mayer was suited up for the Boston Marathon in tight rubber shorts, and additionally sported huge knee and elbow pads, big leather gauntlet gloves, and an enormous buglike helmet. As he hoisted the heavy, home-made Body Sail onto his shoulders, his long knobby legs wobbled on their roller skates. Each year, inevitably, the Body Sail took the oncoming wind, blowing Mayer and his skates backward down the hill, the sail flapping and whacking the earnest huddle of marathon runners trying to go up. Inevitably the police would move into the middle of the race and escort Mayer and his Body Sail to the nearest station, where they would keep him for the rest of the event.

The Body Sail, Mayer hoped, would have its greatest success on water. Just before going to meet Stanley — it was summer by now, and Mayer was determined to get recognition for his sail — I had spent countless days camping in Wareham, Massachusetts, with our children, demonstrating Mayer's invention, which he hoped *Sports Illustrated* might feature. That evening while struggling with the Body Sail out on Buzzard's Bay, I lost my concentration for a moment ("Was my stomach sticking out?"), the full force of the boom as well as the sail whacked me in the face, and I blacked out and went under — for the third time. As I tried to regain consciousness, I could see the children beckoning from shore as I was swept further and further out. Somehow, I managed to get back on the board and paddle the wet sail and myself back to the beach.

But the next day, as planned, I was in Provincetown at Stanley's door, having taken the bus from Wareham. I could barely see, had a broken nose, a terrible headache, and black raccoon circles under black-and-blue eyes. My hands shook as I held my manuscript. The first thing Stanley did was to show me his garden. He took me round to see each plant. He showed me the spruce tree, which he wrote about later, the decorative spaces, every plant, and grasses I had never seen before. The garden in Province-town was more than just a polite and obligatory garden. It transcended its "garden-ness" — it was heart, soul, and center for Stanley. The light in Provincetown was/is of a special quality; it is said that it is the similar light to that in Arles, which inspired so many painters, including Van Gogh. Provincetown was a haven for artists, and everything grew there bathed and transfixed by the light. When we went inside, I waited as he looked at the manuscript. There was a persistent clicking sound. Finally I realized it came from my own shaking hands, sifting and resifting nervously the deep bowl of beach stones that lay on the table before us.

I was also to stay, during the winter season, fairly often at the Kunitz–Elise Asher household in their brownstone in the Village in New York. There, especially, paintings Stanley collected carried a similar emblematic meaning on the nature/culture continuum. He had close personal relationships with painters such as Mark Rothko and others, and their paintings, it seemed to me, carried the same quality of light as did the nature, wild and tamed, that is found in Provincetown, Massachusetts, a special natural and cultural microclimate of its own. Provincetown, at that time (the early '70s), was home to Portuguese fishermen, mainly, and only a few artists were there in the late fall and winter season, Stanley being one of them. The Provincetown garden, a tamed wilderness, was a deep source for his poetry, and I think he also considered it his greatest poem.

Kunitz's colleagues, Frost, James Wright, and others, were more interested in a larger country concept, the "farm." Even further back, American poets had occupied themselves with the "wilderness." Other contemporaries, Frank O'Hara, later Ginsberg, were urban poets. But a lot of Stanley's poems revolve around nature. They depict the progression from the child who roamed the woods to find solace to the man who tamed nature and finds himself. For instance, as in the earlier *The Testing Tree*.

Both Kunitz and Theodore Roethke taught at Bennington College around the same time as did my father, the mid-'40s. And both poets apparently left Bennington in a huff — though at different times. Alienated and marginalized already, Kunitz and Roethke felt entirely out of the mainstream at Bennington. Vermont was far from the centers of poetry. Both poets had already experienced much rejection and despair. Their careers did not take off; they could not get published; they were bitter, disillusioned, jealous: in other words, they were poets like any others. They suffered depression, which enhanced feelings of being neglected, along with self-doubt and fear of failure. They were outside the mainstream, while Robert Frost seemed to be finally striking a chord. (Where exactly was this "mainstream"? — we call it the "Canon" now.)

In Stanley's poetry, even in his early works, all seems to remind us of the sacred world behind the apparent one, the beauty and great plan behind the work of dirt. Roethke had a different take; he had worked in his family's greenhouses as a child and had a definite love/hate (mostly hate) relationship with it. To Roethke, who was forced to work in dirt as a child, muck leads to madness and the fear of madness and death.

Under the concrete benches,
Hacking at black hairy roots, —
Those lewd monkey-tails hanging from drainholes . . .[40]

In Stanley's writing about this Provincetown garden we see the joy, not the work. Though, like a poem, of course the garden was "worked": planned, revised, moved about, with the transitions carefully thought out. The great thing about a garden was — unlike a poem — that one could plant things and actually, a season or so later, see them published!

At that time, the Fine Arts Work Center, Stanley's brainchild, was a very small community in Provincetown. Roger Skillings and Barbara Baker ran the dilapidated, very small building for a few winter fellows (Cleopatra Mathis was there in the early days, and others). "Fellows" had to vacate Provincetown when the weather got nice, and the Rhode Island School of Design or Pratt Institute moved into the buildings in the summer. But in winter, these "fellows" froze in the unheated rickety noisy building, lived on food stamps, and drank. All the shops and restaurants were closed, except for the "Mayflower," which served the daily fish and chips, Portuguese kale soup, and soggy mashed potatoes. Stanley, Allen Dugan, and Marge Piercy occasionally held meetings — part workshop, part potluck — for the few winter "fellows" in their homes. The cold wind was bitter. Visiting writer/teachers, like myself later, came for a winter month at a time (my position for instance, arranged by Stanley). We were given a place to live near the Red Inn (unheated, but on the water) and worked with whichever writing "fellows" were not too depressed to turn up.

The typical Provincetown poem written during those winters, it seemed to me, went sort of like this:

Here I am.
It's so lonely and cold.
I am stuck out here in winter
At this eastern-most point of the United States.
Beyond me is nothing nothing nothing . . .
And I contemplate my own death.[41]

It was so cold and windy during those Provincetown winters that the fellows' poems moaned and lamented as did the weather.

Stanley nurtured the poets who came to him, his friends, his students. Not only did he create and support the Fine Arts Work Center in Provincetown, which grew enormously under his stewardship, but in New York he did the same for Poets House. When it came to gardens and poets, Stanley was an optimist.

For many summers, long after my first stay with Stanley in Provincetown, and after my separation from Mayer, my friend Joe Murray ran the sailing school in Provincetown. I worked there and also taught writing. We lived on Joe's boat, *Boss Lady*. Every few days I swam into shore to visit Stanley and help him with his papers. We never did too much, and Elise Asher made us lunch. On Stanley's orders I shifted things from one pile to another. He handed me articles to read from the *New York Review of Books* and watched as I read them. Stanley spoke to me of life, who he was reading, who were his favorite students, his regrets and pleasures. There were many other people who loved Stanley, students and helpers, I am sure, doing the same thing, shifting piles of paper under Stanley's direction from one stack to the other.

My friend Joe, who had his own gardener's relation to Stanley, came in from the boat in the afternoons, and he began to help Stanley with the garden. He too bonded with Stanley. I have photographs of us all, and especially of Stanley pointing with a kind of bird-dog, quivering intensity as he showed Joe where he wanted a plant to go.

A young couple, Greg and Carol Stockmal, had bought the house in Worcester, Massachusetts, that had been Stanley's childhood home. In the back garden was a pear tree Stanley's mother had planted, and it still bore fruit. Stanley had written about that tree.[42] Every year the Stockmals sent a box of these pears from the Worcester tree to Stanley in Provincetown. I was there one time when the package arrived. Stanley opened the box of pears with great care. He picked one up reverentially and cut it into thin, delicate slices. The sweet slices of Perfect Pear melted on our tongue like communion wafers.

Stanley asked Joe and me to visit him the day after his hundredth birthday, as the celebration itself had passed in a wild whirl. Stanley had dressed for the occasion to meet us, and was waiting. One of his caregivers, Pat Bruno, was also there. Inside on his low table, Stanley had prepared the piles of paper to go over with me. Pat set out the cups of tea and left us alone. Stanley was immensely tired. He missed Elise, who had died a few years before, though this was something he did not speak about much. No matter how kind his helpers, they were not his true companions.

But when Joe came up the walk, Stanley straightened and hobbled outside down the steps to meet him. He showed us the garden, regretted that he could no longer work in it, and then he showed us his birthday gifts. They were, of course, all garden plants. Extraordinarily beautiful plants in pots, enormous! Just ready for planting. Exotic red maples, their roots still in burlap. So many spectacular plants! We gazed, and Stanley seemed completely overwhelmed. We were too. All these huge, shiny, new plants and trees — there were so many. It was overwhelming. Some were tall and needed special conditions.

Stanley sighed, his fatigue increasing as he tried to stand outside with us. He could not envision their place in his garden design. In his one hundred year and one day–old gaze, I watched him fade in and out, sometimes into what seemed a thought beyond absent space. He was in a way already done with his garden as he had known it. He didn't seem all that interested, actually. Bent like a question mark on his walker, Stanley maneuvered himself near the edge of the garden near the house. As Stanley pointed, Joe moved a heavy plant in its pot to Stanley's proposed space for it. Sometimes he liked that. More often Joe had to move a plant many times so Stanley could visualize how it would finally look.

Joe offered to dig and place some of the new shrubs and trees where Stanley wanted. But that day, Stanley didn't want to plant. Moving inside, he sat with me quietly, gazing where I could not go. We drank the tea. Occasionally he patted my arm. I had been famous for making Stanley laugh, which I still could do. His caregivers reported that he hadn't laughed like that since Elise had died — and I don't remember a word of what we said. Maybe we didn't talk much. He told me not to give up, that he had a second go-round at creativity and recognition after the age of seventy and that I would too. He said many interesting things about writing and poetry. This between long silences, while Stanley moved far beyond the present into somewhere else.

I had never sat with someone so old, I realized. Companionship was all that was needed, no words. He seemed to be already far away. I was afraid of tiring him, but he didn't want me to leave, and his caregivers didn't want me to either. At one hundred years old — and a day — Stanley was looking beyond the earthly things of which, so long, he had been a faithful custodian. In all he'd worked on, he had created beauty from the wilderness. His eyes were hooded and opaque. He seemed to be already looking through the portal into another world.

Lowell and Women
Students, Friends, and Wives!

Lowell had a complex attitude toward his women students. He played a supportive role for both Plath and Sexton. Sylvia was fairly recently married and was both straitlaced and unsure of herself. Anne was struggling with breakdowns and writing, children, and trying to get a sense of confidence about herself and her work. Lowell seemed, for a time, a father figure. Anne in her *Letters* conveys this feeling, though Sylvia's *Journals* are circumspect. She and Ted Hughes had dinner with Cal, and Anne, too, introduced her family to him. My impression is that Cal had a strong personal, as well as a professional, connection with these women, and also with Adrienne Rich and Elizabeth Bishop. But in public — after classes or meetings — the male poets buzzed around him and were more visible.

In the later workshops and office hours at Harvard, the women played a quiet role. Many of them felt too intimidated to speak, and when they did, it was so softly that they were soon overrun by the more confident men. Gail Mazur, subtle and nuanced, occasionally brushed aside a curtain of hair, venturing, with a graceful gesture, a gentle remark. Estelle Leontieff sat without moving, leonine. Lowell was quixotic in his encouragement of the women; he often acted as if they didn't count at all, but occasionally a poem would catch his eye. I remember Celia Gilbert submitting a most moving poem on a child's illness and death. Lowell's glasses misted over, his eyes gently diaphanous behind the thick lenses, as he bent forward, murmuring a few words, his expressive hands gesturing in Celia's direction. Celia hunched into herself and didn't speak, a small, dark bird.

But when the young British economist Emma Rothschild visited the office hours, Lowell suddenly claimed to have discovered a half-Jewish ancestor. Somewhere, way back. A prestigious ancestor, of course, for Lowell was a horrible snob! He looked at Emma intently, his eyes magnified and teasing behind thick lenses, leaning his deferential body toward her and gesturing with his expressive hands. Perhaps he thought in some desperate way that he was putting her at ease. Emma was beautiful, brilliant, composed. And said almost nothing.

For the most part, as writers, women didn't count much with Cal, except as decoration. He could be kind to the fragile female mental patient, and even gallant, but attractiveness in a woman was the essential quality; once that was established, intelligence and wit could shine. In fact — theoretically this would never be allowed to happen now — when selecting for his writing classes at Harvard, Lowell read the work of the male students when making his decisions, but invented a pretext for interviewing, and thereby looking at, the women who applied. He took very few women into the classes, and he told me quite openly that he selected primarily on looks.

This could, and did, boomerang on the young women selected, as the course progressed. Cal came down especially hard on the women he had chosen for their seductiveness. It was as if he let himself be tempted by them, then slapped them down. Having selected the most attractive of the young women, he was then perfectly capable of — and did — turn on them in class. "Don't ever write again," he told a lovely young woman, after he had decimated her poem in class. The woman burst into tears and left the room. Cal had been completely open about telling me his selection process, conveniently forgetting the fact that I was a woman also. He had looked shocked when I was not terribly supportive. Thereafter I became known as "the feminist," and he liked to tease me, inventing ways to get a rise out of me, especially if we were in a group with mostly male poets.

In terms of his love affairs, one had the sense that Cal operated in much the same way; first attracting, and then turning on the women who succumbed to him. It was a position one wanted to avoid. It had devastating effects on the women selected, rather than on Cal, who survived, wrote about them, and remained attached to Elizabeth Hardwick even throughout his marriage to Caroline Blackwood. When Lowell, married to Caroline, had breakdowns in England, it was Elizabeth Hardwick who flew there from New York to take charge. And when Lowell died, it was in a taxi returning to New York to visit Hardwick.

While Lowell supported the work of Sexton and Plath, he could be very hard on a poet who violated his canons of good taste. Denise Levertov was a poet he admired, but she fell from grace. Cal and I were walking toward the inevitable late-afternoon cup of tea at a café, and puzzled, he took my elbow. "You know," he said, in a strained, careful, musing way, "Denise used to be a very good poet. One of the best women writing in America today. But I just heard her read in New York. And she read her poems — some good ones — and then," here Cal paused, lowering his voice, with half-concealed mischief in his eyes, "she read a poem about her *cunt!* How she didn't like it, and oh, how horrible it was, she described it in detail . . ." His voice trailed off, only to resume in a musing way, "and then," long, wondering pause, "she decided she liked that cunt poem so much she read it to us a second time."[43] Cal was shocked, and Denise, alas, was relegated to the ranks below minor. Denise, with her usual courage, wrote on, whatever Cal or anybody else might think.

Lowell reserved his greatest ambivalence for Anne Sexton. While he was helpful to her in her work, continuing even after his first meeting with her at Boston University, a slight distance grew between them as Anne's illness continued to surface. Cal did not approve of the turn Anne's poetry had taken, a loose, unstructured expression. Perhaps her poetry was too close, or threatened his control. It was hard to tell. Also, the relationship had always been an uneasy one of teacher and student; Anne wanted to lean heavily on Cal for more support for the breakdown part of her life than he could give. Cal grew uncomfortable with Anne's personal expressiveness, particularly her anger. When Anne's play appeared at the American Place Theatre, a play that dealt mostly with an unstable female central character, Anne, in an interview with the press, made uncharitable remarks about her husband. This alienated Cal. Anne, as a person and poet, did not have enough restraint to put Cal at ease.

Later, when Cal returned to Boston in the late '70s to take up living there again with his new wife, Lady Caroline Blackwood, and a son, Sheridan, I got another sense of his domestic life. Sheridan was the same age as my youngest son, Marin. Cal, Caroline, and Sheridan came to my house often, and the children played together. The Lowells, now older parents, did not know many people with young children in Boston, and they were happy to find a household to which they could come after the Harvard classes, with their children. It was a relaxed, domestic friendship, and ordinary in that respect. Suddenly, we were running "play groups" at their house or mine. It was an odd feeling.

At any rate, I occupied many roles vis-à-vis Lowell: student; friend; "the feminist," as he teasingly called me; or "the psychologist," as he and Elizabeth Bishop would joke when they told me their troubles — they told everyone their troubles, I do believe — and additionally I became "the mother" and "playgroup/babysitter."

Caroline — billed as the "younger woman" — was older than myself.

She was very attractive, but what struck me most was her physical resemblance to Cal. Caroline had the same wide, high forehead; eyes straining to understand; the same way of staring without blinking while apparently formulating a thought; the same wit; and a wise, quick intelligence. Like Lowell's first and second wives, Jean Stafford and Elizabeth Hardwick, she was a writer of prose. She shambled and lurched, rather than walked: a long, hunched, stumbling stride, like Cal's. Whereas Elizabeth Hardwick had picked up after and taken care of Cal, Caroline needed taking care of.

Next to Elizabeth Hardwick's poise, Cal's repeated breakdowns had seemed undisciplined. It was humiliating for Cal to have to be rescued and/or committed again and again by his wife and friends. Elizabeth Hardwick was approved of — by the poetry and critical elite, and their friends — for her courage in sticking it out. This position was not easy, and to counteract it, Cal sought the approval of students and other younger writers.

Caroline was helpless about domestic details, Cal told me with great good cheer. She was at least twice as messy, and four times as screwed up, as he was. Why, she couldn't even pack and close her own suitcase, he told me happily. Upon meeting Caroline, one felt the depth of Lowell's conflict, for she was a woman of deep intelligence and sensitivity. Clearly there was a great bond, but it lacked the long history of his marriage to Elizabeth Hardwick. Hardwick, as a woman, thinker, and writer, was incomparable. She also had achieved a quasi-detachment in the face of Lowell's instabilities that had allowed her to endure. Friends had taken vehement sides during the Blackwood-Hardwick period, as Cal wavered between the two women. Many of his friends felt he had betrayed Elizabeth Hardwick, who had stuck by Cal so loyally during his many breakdowns. Lowell published some of Hardwick's letters, somewhat changed in the form of poems, and was severely criticized for doing so.

Adrienne Rich was particularly vocal about this, and published a severe criticism of Lowell's new poetry during that period in a literary review. Elizabeth Bishop was more discrete in her criticism of Lowell, but nevertheless reproved him in letters and in person. He obsessed about Adrienne's "betrayal," as he saw it — on and on, interminably in his Harvard class at the top of Holyoke Center. It was dismal, it was winter, and Lowell obsessed. Lowell writhed, publicly wounded and humiliated by Adrienne, whose work he had fostered and supported. He never repaired his friendship with her. His friendship and respect for Elizabeth Bishop survived. Although

Bishop had also reproved Cal for the same misuse of Hardwick's letters, she had done so privately. The pain of choosing between Elizabeth Hardwick and Caroline Blackwood — two wonderful women, and he loved them both — was compounded for Lowell by the fact that many of his other friends seemed to be taking sides. Cal never really made a decision between the two.

I had known Cal throughout some of his love affairs, well documented in Ian Hamilton's biography. Their tone had always seemed strained, desperate, and depressing; the women wrenched with Cal through an emotional ordeal neither they nor he could understand. These were not happy affairs. Cal seemed miserable when they were going on. And the women, some of whom I knew, were none too happy either. But Lowell's love for Caroline did not have the same quality. It rocked and threatened everything, precisely because it was so important to him. In it he felt torn in his love for Elizabeth and their child. The letters, the poems from that period, all document the agony he felt in trying to make a decision.

His connection with and love for Elizabeth Hardwick persisted. At the same time, his love for Caroline, especially at the beginning, seemed a rejuvenation. Friends took sides right and left, and it was generally felt that Elizabeth, who, after all, had braved those draining years of mental illness, had the greater claim by virtue of her kindness, patience, and willingness — repeatedly — to take Cal back. This was later emphasized in Ian Hamilton's biography, with its focus on Lowell's insanity and a willingness on the part of the Lowell entourage to denounce Caroline Blackwood.

A questionnaire circulated by a Harvard graduate student about poets and poetry asked, "Why haven't there been as many great American women poets in the past as men?" And of course, the logical answer is, "Few women poets have had wives." There is by this time, nothing original left to say on the subject. Hamilton's biography of Lowell, Paul Mariani's biography of Lowell, Eileen Simpson's biography of John Berryman and his friends, all answer the question for us. The martyrdom of the wives of these twentieth-century poets is evident. They endured humiliations and blame, and yet continued to type and revise manuscripts. They had, as Eileen Simpson put it, "agreed to marry the work," and were either fully or almost destroyed in the process. The only mercy the men showed them was, paradoxically, in leaving them, and that was accomplished with the utmost degradation of their dignity. And still the women persisted in taking them back. These "geniuses" treated their wives inhumanly. Wives of that era seemed to have a heroic tolerance.

Caroline Blackwood was light and loving and funny. She listened to Cal with an admiring gleam in her eyes. I had lunch with Cal the first time he introduced me to Caroline, and noted her appreciation for him. He wanted me to meet her, wanted her to have a friend. Cal was in rare form, and entertained us both. He did not seem manic, but sane and calm and happy. Caroline visited Cal's office hours and classes at Harvard. She seemed to genuinely like him. It was difficult for her to deal with the disapproval of his friends, and she confessed her terror to me of Elizabeth Bishop, among others.

A gentle woman, Caroline understood Cal's conflicts, even if they were too hard for her to handle. Years later, she spoke compassionately about this to me in an interview. "Cal loved his original family totally. It was incredibly difficult for him. He felt guilty about leaving them. He suffered a great deal." She added, "You know, he was conventional, really. A proper Bostonian." Caroline continued in our talk together, "He had a terrific sweetness to him. He wanted everyone to write like a dream. He wanted everyone to be happy."

Caroline had struggled with the fact of Lowell's illness. She had three, then four, children to take care of, and she was overwhelmed with the intensity of his bouts with mania. "They were like attacks, really. And then you wouldn't recognize the person you'd loved." Sometimes Cal would go for years without such an attack, but then the illness took over, totally. Caroline spoke of the difficulty of seeing someone you loved so transformed.

It was difficult for Caroline to know how to handle Lowell's breakdowns in England. Conflicted about his marriage to Caroline, Lowell broke down under this and other stresses. Elizabeth Hardwick, who had much more experience in being with Cal during these difficult periods of illness, came to England to rescue Cal, to visit him in the hospital, and to take him home. Caroline's fragility and sensitivity were overtaxed.

It is a tribute to Cal that he evoked from both these woman such beauty of character and a caring goodness. This, despite the difficulties of the situation. Lowell was a lightning rod for publicity, and his private life did not remain private. This must have been extremely painful for both Elizabeth Hardwick and Caroline Blackwood, yet they both talked to me about those times with dignity and compassion.

The last years of the Blackwood-Lowell marriage were turbulent. Caroline frequently visited me. Sheridan, her youngest child, was very popular with my children: a stouthearted little fellow, with a strong Devon accent. As time went on, Caroline aired her worries about Cal's breakdowns. And his drinking. Could I say something to him? she would ask. Caroline was increasingly afraid for Cal. I felt out of my depth. Then Cal, meeting me for coffee in Harvard Square, would talk to me about Caroline. She drank too much, had breakdowns. Could I say something to her? They were clearly both in a great deal of pain; the twinship so apparent to me when I met Caroline with Cal for the first time was now taking them toward separation.

"How did he feel about it?" I asked Elizabeth Hardwick later. "What were his attitudes to all these women?"

"He married three wives. And each of them was a writer. I call that rather heroic, don't you?" said Elizabeth Hardwick, leaning toward me, laughing.

Caroline, discussing the same point with me said, "He loved to joke." She remembered Cal. "Most male writers like to marry women who type their manuscripts and sew on their buttons." Cal preened about choosing women who were individuals rather than appendages.

He told me, "Nobody commends me for my bravery in marrying three writers!" He muttered softly to me with a sly sidewise smile, pleased with his own little joke; leaning down and pressing my arm for emphasis. A good line, I thought, I bet he uses it a lot!

Lowell and Elizabeth Hardwick shared wit, intellectualism, and fashionable domestic verve. Elizabeth Hardwick's courage and faith during so many difficult periods had been outstanding. It is heartbreaking to read, in Ian Hamilton's book, her letters to him. Later, after Cal's death, I asked Elizabeth Hardwick how she had managed to sustain her relationship with Robert Lowell throughout these difficult times. She spoke with honesty and understanding about the hardships and the pain involved. "And yet," she said, "I felt he was such a valuable person. And certainly valuable to me." Pensively, she added, moving into the present tense, "The oddity and brilliance of his mind still interests me . . ."

Cal was always teaching, in the schoolroom or wherever. I was happy to have the benefit of this relentless instruction in a large span of culture past and present. Had I not been happy, I would [have] received the flow just the same. What was almost always enjoyable was the exuberance, the casualness, the throw-away aspect of this learning — quite unlike the academic or the specialist. To have him fly off on poetry or history, for instance, was like having a cocktail — and of course there was the cocktail also.

⦿ ELIZABETH HARDWICK

Literature was his passion, his *real* passion. He thought to be a poet was the only thing on earth. Most people don't think that, do they?

. . . What he did all day was lie on a bed — he liked working on beds — revising his revisions. With a bottle of milk! He had a double bed in his study because he was such a large man he really needed to sprawl and see all the pages. . . .

. . . I don't think people generally realized the terror he was in that he might lose his mind minute by minute. In fact, his last lines were about that.

"Christ, may I die at night with a semblance of my senses . . ."

That was just a part of an idea. We were living in Ireland at that point and I went over to England to see my children who were in school. He stayed on an extra night before going on to the States. Where he died.

I found this note on our pillow when I returned to Ireland.

Although he lived with the threat always, he was incredibly funny. He wasn't somber, like the work. . . .

. . . He had that quality, that he could make the dullest thing, like going to pick up the laundry, seem exciting. Probably the same thing applied in class. He had such intensity that if he read something aloud you felt: you won't hear this again. You might never have it properly read again. . . .

⦿ CAROLINE BLACKWOOD

Hardwick: Note to Kathleen Spivack, 1986.
Blackwood: Conversation with Kathleen Spivack, 1988.

Young Marriage in Somerville

A Small Apartment, a Mad Inventor, Literary Visitors,
1960–1977

I got married in 1959. My husband and I moved in 1961 to an airy, one-room apartment in Somerville, not far from the Cambridge line. The neighborhood was full of trees, gardens, and small houses. Mayer was trying to make a living as a freelance inventor, and only his patent attorney was getting rich.

At one end of the large living room was his workbench, with power tools and bits of plastic and screws and all the materials that went into his proto-typic construction of gadgets. At the other end was a couch and my writing desk, on which also rested a sewing machine, for at that time I still had the intention to make my own clothes, as well as those for friends. My desk was ringed with large aquariums and terrariums, which accounts for the number of poems about reptiles and amphibians in my first book. We had numerous pets, among them a mynah bird that emitted piercing screams as it flapped around the room. It flew freely, as my husband did not believe in caging birds. He tried unsuccessfully to "house train" it to crap in a speci-fied place in the room by making a little nest of twigs in the center of the space. But the bird refused to be "twig trained" and flapped hugely, yelling. We learned that a mynah bird can deposit ten pounds of crap, randomly, a week. I would flail at it madly with the fireplace broom whenever it flew over my desk. I was trying to write, accompanied by the background noises of Bach on the record player, the bird's screeches, and the steady sound of my husband's machine tools.

At the other end of the room, Mayer was busy inventing a better vacuum cleaner. He had collected enormous bags of broken glass, which he poured on the floor to demonstrate the superior sucking power of his machine over any other on the market. My husband hoped to demonstrate to Laurence Marshall, the president of Raytheon, the superiority of his vacuum cleaner. He made an appointment with our friend John Marshall's father, and we appeared on their doorstep one evening. Mayer looked like Santa under the weight of his huge laundry bags of cinders and debris. "Come in, come in," called the Marshall parents, welcoming. It was their cocktail hour, and they were already well into it. Mayer entered and with a flourish, emptied all the bags onto their priceless Oriental carpets.

The contents, about forty pounds of broken glass and ashes, carefully collected from the Cambridge and Somerville city dumps, seeped into the rich crimson pile, a beautiful priceless Oriental carpet, stretching wall to wall. The elderly Marshalls stared in dismay. "Watch this," said Mayer, plugging in his prototype vacuum cleaner. There was an ear-splitting grinding noise as Mayer's vacuum cleaner began to spread the debris around, digging it deeper into the carpet. Cinders rose up, whooshed in the air and settled down again. Mrs. Marshall started to cough and had to leave the room. Mayer tried again and again, but the vacuum cleaner did not pick up a thing. I phoned their son John, who took his time getting over to his parents' house. Mr. Marshall poured himself a third (or was it the fourth?) stiff drink. We stood around staring at the mess, except for Mayer who was sweating and running about madly as he searched for one electrical outlet after another. "Wait, wait! It worked at home!" John Marshall eventually arrived and, taking pity on Mayer, helped him clean up, using the conventional vacuum cleaner the Marshalls kept by their kitchen door. Mr. Marshall did not invest in the project.

But Mayer persisted. He was bent on developing a better model. The efforts lasted a year. I became used to working through almost anything. Rrrr, rrrr, went the vacuum cleaner, attempting to eat the crushed glass. Eeek, eek, went the mynah bird. Our landlord and landlady lived upstairs from us, and occasionally they would bang on our door when the noise of power tools and vacuum cleaner threatened to dislodge the plaster. "You are hurting the house," they screamed. I did not know how to deal with this situation. "It's all right, Mrs. Correia," my husband would shout to reassure them, "I am only brushing my teeth."

We also had an emerald tree boa, which hung off the ceiling lamp fixture over the couch, in front of Cal's and other visitors' eyes. Although we had tried feeding it raw hamburger, as we did with our snapping turtle, the snake disdained this. Eventually we had to resort to live mice, acquired from a friend who was a grad student at the Harvard biology labs. "Here snakey, snakey," my husband would coax, trying to get the boa to open its jaws for a pinkish quivering victim. The mouse dangled by its tail, its red-rimmed eyes flashing with terror. The boa opened its jaws . . .

The chief attraction of our apartment in Somerville was the backyard: a vegetable garden, enormous flowers, a hedge of lilacs that bloomed under our bedroom window, and a grape arbor. We sat under the grape arbor all summer and ate our meals there. Our landlord made wine from these grapes, supplying our household as well as his with a thick, sweet brew that was a Portuguese version of Manischewitz. Once during a flood we had to go down into the cellar, where he kept the wine press, and float the huge casks and barrels of the year's wine out the cellar window into a driveway. I picked the grapes in autumn with our landlady, carefully cutting the bunches with their silvery purple sheen. We all had diarrhea during that season from eating grapes nonstop. Photographs taken by my husband at that time caught the translucence of the grapes, myself in a kerchief, young and happy and a cat — for we had numerous cats as well — perched in the arbor, looking through the leaves into the shadows below, where his green eyes were shining.

Among my husband's more successful inventions was a radio jammer that created horrible static whenever our next-door neighbor took the radio off his back porch and into his side yard, which was closer to our bedroom window. "Damn the thing, I just can't get proper reception," he complained, carrying the radio off the lawn and back up the steps into his house. My husband would lie in bed twiddling the dials of his device until our room achieved the proper level of quiet.

My favorite among his inventions was a diaper-changing machine, invented when I was pregnant with our first child. This machine was designed to be placed next to our bed to alleviate the necessity of getting up at night and changing diapers. It had a small platform upon which one plonked the soiled baby, and a series of levers and arms that came down. The device was intended to remove the dirty diaper, clean and oil the baby, throw the diaper into a pail, and whisk the contents of the diaper down a chute into the aforementioned neighbor's yard. We borrowed a friend's baby. With impressive clicking and huffing sounds, the machine went into overdrive and whisked the *baby* down the chute into the neighbor's yard instead. The diaper-changing machine was never put into practice.

More efficacious was a large string, put into use after our first child was actually born. Mayer tied one end to his big toe at night. The other end was hooked to the rocker of the cradle in which, only a foot and a half away from us, slept our beautiful baby. The idea was, if the baby fussed or slept fitfully, for Mayer to simply wiggle his toe. The heavy antique cradle would start to rock gently, as if of itself, and the soothed baby would fall back asleep. This invention worked pretty well, and two weeks after the baby's birth (whatever possessed us?) we went on an extended camping trip — it rained the whole time — taking with us the baby, the cradle, and the string.

I invited John Malcolm Brinnin, my thesis advisor, and a visiting writer at Boston University to our Somerville apartment one evening in the mid-'60s to meet Anne Sexton, about whom he was curious. We served dinner under the grape arbor outside. Brinnin, a well-known author, was a reserved and graceful literary figure. His book *Dylan Thomas in America* was a classic,[44] but he had also written on Gertrude Stein and others. Brinnin had never met Anne Sexton, and he looked forward, in his courteous and contained way, to this evening. Anne arrived late with her husband, Kayo, and a bottle of gin, which she consumed alone in a couple of hours under the arbor. We lit mosquito candles, served coffee, sat outside, and shifted nervously as Anne grew more and more maudlin. Brinnin, who had rather his fill of poetic histrionics during his long and documented friendship with Dylan Thomas, was polite. But a strained smile betrayed his suffering. Earlier, in a rare burst of confiding, Brinnin had told me how difficult it had been for him to accompany Dylan Thomas on his self-destructive journeys, as well as to write about it later. He described the writing of the book as a fearful obsession, from the grip of which he hardly felt released. Thomas had a lack of discipline in his life that both fascinated and repelled the self-controlled Brinnin. Anne that evening became tearful while Kayo sat there uncomfortably, trying to remain amiable and relaxed as Anne told us how no one — and most of all, Kayo — really understood her. The evening came to an end when Anne passed out on John Brinnin's lap.

The writer Kay Boyle had a fellowship at the Radcliffe Institute in Cambridge, and came for dinner fairly frequently, as well. She had lived an amazing life abroad, documenting in her stories the wartime climate of Europe. Married to a succession of apparently alcoholic writer-husbands who wrote and left Kay and their children, Kay Boyle raised her children mostly alone while quietly amassing her own literary work. Having returned from France, she now lived and worked in San Francisco. The Radcliffe fellowship was one of her few moments, late in life, to devote full time to her writing.

She was elegant, alert, with bright eyes and wild hair. She was the first adult I knew who casually walked around with a knapsack full of books and papers. What funny details stick with us. Other women still carried purses.

Mayer with baby and banjo. Photograph by Mayer Spivack.

I'd read all of Kay Boyle's work and loved it. At the moment she was out of fashion, but had been rescued by the grant from the Radcliffe Institute. But she was rather lonely in Cambridge and often walked over to see us, producing bottles of wine from her knapsack, and exotic breads. She had lived a wild, bohemian life in Paris and elsewhere, although she talked more about her daughters and her life in San Francisco. She introduced me to her editor, Ken McCormack at Doubleday.

Kay Boyle, though she talked of grandmotherly things, had broken ground for women writers. Her stories about prewar Vienna were little jewels. She reminded me of Jean Rhys and Djuna Barnes, but her prose style was akin to that of Katherine Anne Porter. I tried hard to create meals that would go with her bread and cheese and wine, produced with a flourish.

In our little apartment in Somerville, with its green, claw-footed stove, the green boa constrictor twining about the ceiling light for warmth, and the glossy mynah bird flying free, Robert Lowell was our most constant literary visitor. "Paroled" by McLean Hospital — that is, allowed to visit us — Cal sat on our blue couch drinking in the midst of chaos. He cradled a large milk bottle in a paper bag and sipped from it. I never really knew whether he mixed liquor in with the milk, or drank the milk to soothe his stomach between swigs of alcohol. While Cal sipped from his bottle, we tried to carry on a conversation. The mynah bird would become particularly excited by the pitch of Cal's voice, as well as by the steady drone of monologue. Hyped up, the bird flapped around the room, screeching in a manic rant, bumping into things and shitting copiously. Mayer thought it cruel to limit the bird's freedom. Occasionally Mayer would run after the bird, trying to train it to sit on his finger. But Cal, who seemed barely to notice, was in a heavy talking mood. In his manic state he discoursed upon Henry VIII. He occasionally interrupted his monologue to suggest that the mynah bird disturbed him. Mayer turned a deaf ear. The frenetic activity relieved me of having to contribute anything to mad discourses upon English history. I had nothing to say on the subject anyway. Like a good girl, in desperation I served tea, and for Cal, the "something stronger."

Cal seemed to enjoy these evenings, however — or perhaps they merely relieved the dreary dullness of drugged McLean. He visited repeatedly, often twice a week, obligingly chauffeured back and forth by my husband, who was glad to take a short break in between bouts of chasing the bird and running his prototype vacuum cleaner.

He Was Ancient! He Was Over Forty!
(After Office Hours at Harvard)

Lowell continued to commute from New York to his classes at Harvard, and it was mostly in Cambridge that I saw him. At the Iruna restaurant, scene of those famous Lowell lunches, and a favorite hangout in Cambridge, the interior was bright, but cold. There was one small radiator hissing near the coatrack, and an acrid smell of wet wool, grimy windowsills. An icy wind blew in off the Charles River during winter afternoons. Small white tablecloths, small dirty windows — but at least some light — and long, intense lunches during Cal's stays in Cambridge. Lunch started with a pitcher of sangria, and Cal's long, slender fingers balled up bits of bread. He most often ordered the Basque omelet, a crepe-like dish in a white sauce. Sometimes, the garlic soup before that, with an egg in it. Everything in the restaurant was slightly bland: the tablecloths, the bread, the omelets, and the flan. The food was washed down with sangria and coffee in small white cups. Cal talked and talked. The Iruna was a place for conversation and confessions.

I remember going to the Iruna with Grey Gowrie, at Bingo's instigation. Grey confessed that he was having trouble getting up in the morning. Since I had been designated the "psychologist" because of my work with writing and writing blocks, I was supposed, so Bingo thought, to say something constructive on the subject. I sensed Grey might be talking about something deeper than mere fatigue, perhaps his feelings about his writing at the moment. But Grey was a late-night person.

The waiters at the Iruna were discreet. Later, poet Nina Alonso married one of them. The restaurant was a comfortable and quiet place to linger over lunch. Although Cal suggested and often took me to more elegant places — the old Chez Dreyfus, for instance, with its French food — the Iruna usually won out. It was best, too, for the larger groups that often went to lunch after the office hours. The group luncheons were much more relaxed than the office hours: Cal was treated with deference and listened to respectfully. This was a time for him to relax and enjoy being with his students. People told jokes and talked more casually about their lives and work. Frank Bidart was often there, along with Grey Gowrie, Robert Pinsky (grave and gallant), Lloyd Schwartz, Paul Levy sometimes, and others. By that time, I had my own special jokey relationship with Cal and enjoyed provoking him, outrageously — a bit of loosening up. The group got more stiff, however, when Cal would revert once again to the classification of poets into major and minor. As if by agreement, people tried to divert him from this topic, although Frank, kind and patient, would usually succumb, nodding. However, Cal was interested in people generally, in the backgrounds of his students, and a student writer who came from South America, for instance, could engage everyone's interest.

After these lunches, the group would break up, heading in different directions on the cold and windy sidewalk outside the restaurant. "Which way are you going?" people would ask, not wanting to brave the cold Cambridge wind alone. Too-thin coats flapped, a muffling with scarves and gloves. "Goodbye, dear," and a courteous kiss from Cal, who was going back to Harvard to teach his afternoon seminar on the Bible. I was going back to work, and presumably the graduate students would go back to their carrels in the library. Occasionally Cal might have more conferences with his students. He would make another plan to meet me in the late afternoon when he was done teaching and when I had finished my work in the counseling center at Brandeis University. He sprawled in his room and rambled in his soft, Southern-ish accent about poetry and poets, although we were both tired.

His temporary rooms at the Harvard houses were always dark and unkempt. I found myself sinking into familiar melancholy as I sat in a black "Veritas" chair at dusk, listening to Cal, who was exhausted but still wanted to talk. "I'll just change my shirt and then we'll go out for coffee," he said in his stammer. I became alarmed, wondering if this was a preamble to seduction, and looked stonily out the window. I knew friends who had had affairs with Cal, and it had turned out badly in every case, although in theory, that sounded glamorous. I prayed Cal wouldn't reveal his bare chest. I loved him, couldn't imagine "making love" with him; was both attracted and afraid.

Lowell played on his physicality, yet there was an overbearing quality to it that made me shrink from succumbing totally. Settling back down, sprawled across a sofa, Cal regarded me with bemusement. He'd take my hand, put an arm about my shoulder, and watched from a nearsighted vantage point to see how I'd react. He'd push it a bit, then, abashed, start talking about my father, Peter Drucker. Then he'd seem to forget about seduction. But of course he never forgot about anything he wanted.

A familiar literary frown would appear on his face as he launched into a discourse about the class, or the lines of a poem he was working on. But somehow he'd get back to the suggestion that he might have had a half-Jewish ancestor "way back when." Oh, nothing too overt; someone discreet and aristocratic. Not exactly like the Druckers, of course, he would say, looking at me pityingly. More like a Rothschild, perhaps! He put his arm around me again, patting me consolingly. He moved in closer. Behind his spectacles, his eyes watched me slyly. They glinted with curiosity and triumph and something like hopefulness.

I picture him at Harvard slouched in a leather chair, a penny loafer dangling from one foot, shoulders scrunched up toward his massive head — his hands framing a point in the air, held up before his face as though to protect it from attack, now and then righting the black-rimmed glasses that kept sliding down the bridge of his thick nose, one of many True cigarettes between his fingers. With his broad face and "oval Lowell smile," he bore an uncanny resemblance to the pictures of Amy Lowell and James Russell.

RICHARD TILLINGHAST

Tillinghast: "Robert Lowell in the Sixties," *Harvard Advocate*, November 1979.

The Underside

"Madness" and the Culture
of Nervous Breakdowns

To Boston's upper classes, "nervous breakdowns" were a large part of the Boston Brahmin social picture. The upper classes even had their own hospital, McLean, where they could be "put away" for a bit at a cost of $1,000 to $1,500 a week, a huge sum in those days. The lower and middle classes had Boston State Hospital, complete with strait-jackets and one-flew-over-the-cuckoo's-nest horror stories. Anyone who was *anyone* had been in McLean, as we know. It seemed almost a literary badge, the way "foot traveler" had been the badge in my Girl Scout days. And even if they weren't in McLean, or, as in the case of Anne Sexton, *wanting* to be there, it was normal in those conversational circles for poet friends to say, behind each other's backs of course, that he she or whoever was having a nervous breakdown, often when they couldn't cope. Thus Caroline Blackwood, after marrying Lowell and being confronted with the extent of his manic-depression, fell apart under the strain. She had married Lowell without really knowing him that well, was an alcoholic, and was also raising three small daughters and going through messy separations from other men. Well, she had a nervous breakdown. Not only did Lowell and Bishop have nervous breakdowns; most people who had to cope with them did too. Or perhaps they were attracted to people who were vulnerable in the same way. Only Elizabeth Hardwick showed amazing fortitude.

So after I first arrived in Boston, and Lowell was suddenly inexplicably absent, it was a while before I learned that he was off having a nervous breakdown. What did that mean? Was he coming back? Personally, as his student I felt bereft, cut off, and slowly I began to realize that I was going to have to be my own teacher. The Grolier Poetry Bookshop saved my life. Gordon Cairnie, then the owner, took me under his wing, and I read, both at the shop and at home.

But those empty winter days, back in my rooming house, I stared at my poems, which were yellowing on their pads of lined already yellow paper, and worried that Oberlin would not give me credit for my senior year if I didn't have an advisor to vouch for me. What had happened? What a mistake. I lived on instant coffee and the ever-present "bouillon cubes," heated on my one-burner hotplate, while the first months of 1959 went from snow to slush to mud. I had made a few friends, and occasionally visited with them. Everyone's apartment was dark and cold and smelled of gas from the gas space heaters that made the looming three-decker houses of Cambridge and Somerville halfway bearable. Everyone wore multiple sweaters and couldn't or didn't wash them, so the odor of sweat mingled with the strong gas fumes in poorly heated, poorly ventilated rooms. Life enclosed itself into the kitchen, the only room that people could warm up. I drank lots of tea in those years, and huddled, not able to express my despair.

I tried to follow Lowell's dictates for revision, which always seemed to boil down to "Put the beginning at the end and the end at the beginning." I made my poems worse. Then I tried reversing the axiom, back to the same old form. The poems seemed just as hopeless either way. A crisis of doubt overcame me; I walked the slushy streets and felt totally lost. Why had I come to Boston, and where was my teacher? To my parents of course I pretended that everything was fine, great, that Lowell was helping me. To myself it was another story. After a while Robert Lowell came back to class, and we proceeded as if nothing had happened. My famous classmates were watchful, tentative — and he seemed quieter and more reduced.

Later I started to see the pattern in Lowell's breakdowns, and to recognize the period when one was looming. There was a transformation in the man, and it was frightening to see. At that point, I distanced myself, unable to deal with the situation. So I never actually saw Robert Lowell in his most difficult moments. To me he was always the soul of kindness and courtesy and generosity. Bill Alfred, Elizabeth Hardwick, and later Frank Bidart often came to Lowell's rescue, and I heard from Bill and Elizabeth — secondhand — about Lowell during his manic pre-breakdown phase.

During the course of our lives, Lowell noticed that I would suddenly draw away during his bad periods, and he teased me about it later as we became more intimate. With Lowell, as with the other poets I knew, any signs of a pending breakdown were so threatening that I would go to great lengths to avoid being around. Lowell's breakdowns were so painful that I have avoided all interviews for books on the subject. For me, although his illness was there, it did not diminish his greatness as a poet, nor his kindness to me and to his friends. It stands next to, is a part of the picture, but not the whole one by any means.

There was something terrifying in Cal's unpredictable pre-breakdown lapses. Most of the time he was mild and kind, but he could, during these manic episodes, lash out in class, or at his friends. Often this was done in an amusing way; a kind of aggressive intelligence that made one shiver. Meanwhile, he tried to draw one in, a co-conspirator. His face swelled, and his eyes became small and raging, pinpointed with intention and a strange gleam; his forehead strained, grew more protuberant. I think he was somehow aware of exactly what was happening to him but that this was somewhat cloaked by the label "manic-depressive." The usual controls were deliberately let go while Lowell pushed and prodded and watched for a hoped-for reaction.

Directly before and during the manic phase, Cal turned into someone almost unrecognizable, but later, this would be followed by the opposite, the depressive side. He was unusually quiet, depressed, sunk inward into himself. He seemed diminished, unable to move or think or write. Later in his life the advent of medications for bipolar conditions alleviated the mood swings somewhat. He complained that they flattened him out, all his moods; there was a creative price to pay for medicines. His illness caused him much suffering and uncertainty. He spoke quite openly about that, both to me and others. In July 1959, he wrote to his great friend Elizabeth Bishop, "Five attacks in ten years make you feel rather a basket-case and it's excruciating. . . ."[45] There are many other sad references in his letters.

I was afraid that Cal, so unpredictable, might turn on me as he did on everyone else. Eileen Simpson wrote about Lowell and his first marriage, to the writer Jean Stafford, in *Poets in Their Youth*. The book describes the friendships of her husband, the poet John Berryman, with Lowell, Stafford, and others. In it she depicts the manic side of Lowell, his competitive meanness that surfaced during these periods toward his peers, whom he also admired and championed in other moments. The Stafford-Lowell marriage was unraveling: Lowell, intelligent and cruel, does not emerge as an admirable character in that book.

Before manic phases Lowell talked outrageously, praising, for example, Adolf Hitler. James Atlas writes from the student point of view: "In the seminar room on the top floor of Holyoke Center we waited nervously — perhaps even expectantly, given the status accorded anyone who had been present at one of these celebrated episodes — for it to happen before our eyes, watching eagerly for any manic soliloquies, references to Hitler or outbursts of unnatural gaiety. These were the signs that Lowell had 'gone off' and would have to be 'put away.' "[46]

Cal's pre-breakdown periods over the years were mainly signaled by an increased and obsessive classification of other poets. The classroom got more and more gloomy as Cal spent the endless hours in examination of his peers. His body hunched as he obsessed over a poem or a line repeatedly, or an author. The classification persisted, was unrelenting. "John Berryman. Major or minor, would you say?" There were long pauses. "*The Dream Songs* are brilliant,"[47] Lowell mused. "But what about some of the other work?" The male graduate students made subdued murmuring noises. Lowell ignored them. "Well, it's not clear . . ." he would offer, as if laying a clue. "He doesn't have the depth of, say, Randall Jarrell." More silence. Perhaps Lowell might turn his attention to the poetry of another writer. "Now Emily Brontë, that's clearer. Major or minor? What would you say of her?" This was not clear to anyone. Cal turned to a poem of hers. He read it aloud, musing upon it.

Then again, "But Berryman? Major? Or minor?" After an hour and a half of this, eventually some sucker would lean forward, clear his throat, and speak loudly enough to penetrate the Lowell fog. "I think Berryman is a major poet. I mean, look at his achievement . . ." "Wrong!" Lowell visibly swelled, looked as if about to crow. His eyes glazed, seemed almost to cross. With a pitying smile he leaned forward, addressing the poor misguided student who had dared to hazard a guess. "Wrong. He's minor. Definitely minor!" Triumphantly, he untwisted himself, regarding the group with expansive pleasure. The issue was settled. "Now, what about Frost?" Chastened, the graduate student settled back into silence, as did the rest of the class. These sessions seemed endless. It was insufferable to be forced to sit through this, but we were so afraid he would completely "crack up" that no one dared leave. Embarrassed for him, we could hardly look at each other as we left the room.

Visiting Cal at McLean Hospital after his breakdowns, I was shocked to see how damped down and depressed he was. The hospital itself was depressing. The setting was gray, the amounts of drugs used on patients excessive. Cal's expressive hands lay quietly; he seemed so hopeless. "People think my mania is necessary for writing," he told me during one of these visits, "but in fact it isn't so at all. It's so boring, and I don't write when

I'm ill, and it is all a fantastic waste of time." Lowell's despair at his illness, his always-present fear of recurring episodes, has been well documented. There was a sense of helpless terror about them that cast a shadow.

After Lowell had been in McLean for a while, depression would set in, and persist afterward; that was the state I knew best in him. During one of those many McLean visits, when the afternoon seemed endless and outside it was raining, we sat in a grim mental-patient lounge drinking Coca-Cola. Lowell showed me a draft of a poem he was reworking.

> Remember standing with me in the dark,
> Ann Adden? In the mad house? Everything — [48]

I felt it was one of the most beautiful poems of his I had seen. The music, the bold use of the woman's name "Ann Adden," and the final image of salmon struggling illuminated that gray institutional afternoon. Lowell would revise that poem — it appears in various versions throughout his books — but that first draft continues to have, for me, a passionate lyricism. Later, in *Near the Ocean*, Cal changed the first lines of the poem and moved the significance and position of the central image and then changed the first lines back again in *History*.

Much has been made of the mental illnesses of the poets who were around Robert Lowell, as well as Lowell's own manic-depression. Their illness and their genius appeared intertwined, but not necessarily in genius-serving ways. Perhaps it is in the nature of writers to have an absence of boundaries. This allows them to enter fully into the states of imagination and empathy. But the despair, depression, the unbounded endlessly gray and boring mental states experienced by writers during their illnesses sapped their time and energy. Huge amounts of creative time were wasted because of the exhaustion involved in harnessing the illness. Any of the writers who suffered so, when asked, would have preferred not to be mentally ill, emotionally disturbed, or whatever; they would have preferred stable marriages and relationships with others, as well as freedom from alcoholism and other addictions.

Lowell, Bishop, and Sexton spoke about this issue frequently. None of them equated the price of their mental illness with their creative gift or output. While the reading public has found a relationship, to the poets themselves, these periods of darkness, confusion, and despair did not seem to relate to the job and focus of the creative act.

I had a number of jobs during my time with Robert Lowell, but increasingly turned to the field of psychology. I came to respect the unknown in some of the illness I saw. While Lowell, Bishop, Sexton, and Plath saw psychiatrists and desperately sought solutions to their pain through this "talking cure," they did not actually seem to benefit markedly from these psychoanalytic and therapeutic forays. Psychiatry could offer them support, but it could not touch the basic cyclical nature of the illnesses. Otherwise, these poets would have been long cured. The more we look at this situation, the more complex it is.

Lowell was keen-eyed, soft-spoken, and totally aware. I never saw the other part of him. Everything I know about teaching I learned from his class. In the deepest sense, he changed my life. The first class I took from him I was at the time in a Protestant seminary and came to the class in total depression, expecting nothing. I would leave class feeling whole. It happened every week. It wasn't mystical. It was human. Lowell was the most completely intelligent person I ever knew.

✐ DONALD JUNKINS

Junkins: "Robert Lowell," from a letter to Kathleen Spivack, 1992.

Alcohol and Drugs

Psychopharmacology, in the late fifties and sixties, was at a beginning stage in understanding the brain chemistry of mental illness. Lowell decided to try lithium. Lithium affected him adversely, slowed him down, he felt, and it was difficult to control the proper levels and dosages. Anne Sexton had been taking Thorazine off and on for a long time. But since her psychiatrist had seduced her, and then abandoned her to an even darker despair afterward, it was hard to tell from where her terror and fears came. In any case, medication helped for a time, although the death wish was ultimately stronger.

Alcoholism was an integral part of New England — well, U.S. — life at that time. Alcohol, of course, figured heavily in American writing and movies, but it wreaked havoc with the personal lives of poets like Bishop and Lowell. When I look back, nearly everything was accompanied by the clink of ice cubes falling into amber liquid. What made the fact that those poets all drank heavily worse were the anti-psychotic drugs that they were taking simultaneously — the drugs do not go with alcohol; the combination creates an internal poison. Lowell took lithium and other pills; Anne Sexton took Thorazine; Bishop — I don't know what she took, and she was a quiet drunk. In fact, I hardly knew what that was, having seen her pass out in my presence just once — after Lowell's death. It was as if she had already died of shock.

For a while it seemed that the prerequisite to being a poet was to be alcoholic and/or suicidal. Dylan Thomas had been a great example of this. His voice and poetry had a large sweep to it, and he was alcoholic on a grand scale. This "poetic tradition" was to continue in its glorified way, culminating in the kind of agony we saw in Lowell. For women and later followers, who idealized the deaths of Sexton and Plath, it seemed that suicide and greatness were somehow linked, and if only one could go to the edge of madness as these poets had, perhaps one could go to the edge of greatness as well.

Lowell did not glorify his illness; he felt that it got in the way of his poetic output; it embarrassed and humiliated him. Many of the poets of Lowell's time died tragically, many of them emotionally ill as well as alcoholic, and there were a large number of suicides. Delmore Schwartz, Randall Jarrell,

Anne Sexton, Sylvia Plath, John Berryman, Theodore Roethke: one wonders why such a high proportion of them shared this pattern. At the same time that Elizabeth Bishop and Robert Lowell wrestled with their demons, Stanley Kunitz, James Wright, Muriel Rukeyser, Marianne Moore, William Carlos Williams, Robert Frost, and others of the same or ancillary generations also documented periods of despair. But they lived to achieve the full fruition of their writing and lives. And among other poets — Robert Bly, Robert Peters, William Stafford, Allen Ginsberg, Gwendolyn Brooks, Adrienne Rich, Maxine Kumin — suicide did not seem to be the only option. So what explains these differing life patterns?

Certainly these poets who were mentally ill were no more or less gifted, historically, than those who were not. But they do seem to have had to struggle harder against the odds their illnesses posed. But the despair inherent in the work of being a poet has not changed. The constant rejections, the problems of making a living, and so forth, are always present. This could drive anybody mad. Mental illness, suicide: how little we really know. People often try to equate mental illness with the mark of a truly creative person, but there are plenty of people around who are suffering from illness, yet are not especially creative. Rather the opposite! Interestingly, the glorification, particularly of Sexton and Plath, took place after their deaths, irrespective of the quality of the poetic work. Each became the poetic version of the glamorous, doomed heroine, a poetic Marilyn Monroe representing something larger than the actual fact of death. Sexton and Plath seemed to stand as emblems of desperation, abandonment, and rage, carried to its absolute end. They were the representations of what many people, but especially women, felt.

The poets of Lowell's circle felt cursed, and spoke of the waste of time and energy involved in illness. And for the reader, the force of feeling sometimes flawed the work itself. Sylvia Plath and Anne Sexton, although both recognized in their lifetimes, attained their full stardom only after their suicides. This would seem to indicate that the fact of suicide itself might give a poet a special stature not otherwise attained by their merely writing good poems. But then, as a younger contemporary, I felt deprived of the poems each woman might have written in her maturity.

Gender and Suicide

The women poets in Lowell's circle, as well as their male contemporaries, were all shaped by World War II and the subsequent postwar period. The 1940s and '50s were their formative climate. By all the standards of that time, they couldn't measure up. The oppressive restrictions of that period, the insistent drive for conformity, crushed them all, and very clearly drawn gender roles and definitions may also have contributed to the pressure these poets felt. Not only women poets committed suicide; so did many of the men. Randall Jarrell, John Berryman, and others were killing themselves at an alarming rate. Why?

Perhaps the men and women writers who committed suicide were mirror images of each other, of the pressures that each faced. Many of the male poets seemed to come from a milieu where masculine roles were strictly defined. Hunting, shooting, fishing, fighting, and most of all, drinking, were seen as essential to the stereotype of the red-blooded American man. If we look at the histories of the male poets of the late '50s and early '60s, as documented in their own work, we can see that most of them came from families in which their fathers had been alcoholic and abusive. The mothers could not protect their sons. And the male poets, by the fact of being poets, could not fit themselves into this seemingly orthodox masculine role. They were resented and belittled by their fathers, but also by the outside society at that time. They could not meet the "masculine" standard — except for the drinking part. This they managed quite well.

Delmore Schwartz, John Berryman, Theodore Roethke: all of Lowell's contemporaries seemed to came from a similar family pattern. Later, the poet Robert Bly would document this more fully and address the subject in his work on what he termed the "wounded" male. But at the time of Lowell's breakdowns, and the various suicides of both men and women poets, men had to be "real men," and women had to be "real women": and there were strict definitions of what each term meant, and how to live it out correctly.

If we adopt a Jungian interpretation of creativity — and this is not antithetical to a Freudian interpretation, but seems more applicable here — we might frame these '50s poets' conflicts in a larger context. Jung wrote of the animus and anima, meaning the masculine or feminine spirit that infuses all human beings and endeavors. A full human being had to harness both, in Jung's terms. As I observed the poets around me in the period following the '50s, this seemed a useful way to look at creativity.

Male artists always referred to their "muse," that is, the inspiration for their creative selves, as feminine. Robert Graves, particularly, named this "the White Goddess." The male poets craved being "immortal"; but women, the men pointed out, were able to give birth to children. The male poets had to assert their egos to appear important. Otherwise, how would they know they existed? Often in their poetry readings it seemed the male poets bred in the '50s tried — too hard — to appear as "real men" in their public personas. They drank heavily and bragged about that; they fought, they swaggered; and they boasted about their sexual conquests and potency. All this to camouflage their tender and receptive feminine side — the inner self that feels things, writes poetry, creates.

Some poets, such as Robert Lowell, Richard Wilbur, and Stanley Kunitz, did not seem to feel the need to posture about. They did not need to hide their education nor their nobility of bearing with pseudomacho displays. Products of the "East Coast establishment," they had been able to integrate their poetry-making "feminine/anima" side. Somehow, in their work and being, they allowed themselves to be whole.

But for many other of the male poets of the macho/masculine '50s, and the generation just after, to fully admit the "feminine" in their nature was perhaps unbearable. A part of them was tempted to destroy, to silence forever that essential core of poetic being, or they tried to dull it to death with drink or maybe drugs. Society, as exemplified in their fathers, could not accept the feminine/creative/artistic/poetry-making side in its men; so neither could they. But being artists, they could not deny this part of themselves: they had to create. Their inner core cried out to be expressed. Later, poets like Robert Creeley, Galway Kinnell, and others were able to reconcile different sides of themselves. The poet Robert Bly has been most important in bringing about changing attitudes and understanding also.

In what looks like opposition, Plath, Sexton, and other women writers from that time were shaped by the "female" gender expectations of the '50s, in which women were "good" or "bad" girls, whores or good housewives, or all of the above. The end of World War II and the return of veterans needing jobs had bounced women out of the workforce. Now they were expected to get married, stay home, follow recipes, and take care of their families. They were being told — from an early age — not to be too smart, or no man would want them.

Women's ambition was seen, critically, as "male" or "masculine." If a woman tried to achieve, she had "penis envy," according to the Freudians. (Men never seemed to have "vagina envy.") A woman could be seen as "castrating"; she could be accused of wanting to cut off/steal a man's sexuality. A strong streak of misogyny ran through American pioneer/masculine culture: Puritanism and Freudianism combined both gleefully and conveniently to keep women "in their place." Add a bit of Blame-the-Mother for any possible societal and psychological ill, and every homespun expert conspired to make sure that women stayed in their allotted places: stupid, pleasant, and compliant. For a woman to achieve, even to think, was to trespass on "masculinity," that is, "the animus." Television shows of the time celebrated the "dumb broad": men could relate to that, they were not threatened. (Definition of the word *threaten*? The worst thing that a woman could do to a man!) Marilyn Monroe was an American icon. She was beautiful and smart, but knew enough to play dumb.

Both Anne Sexton and Sylvia Plath, in their work and lives, reflected that duality of expectation. In Sylvia's *Journals* we see the conflict between the needs of the writer and of the dutiful housewife. Passages that discuss the process of writing her poems, and her attempts to find a good last line, are interrupted suddenly by the need to make dinner for Ted, to prepare the roast beef, to be a model mother. In her letters she talks chattily, her mother's (perceived) "good girl." Her writing achievements are offered up to her mother, but then quickly buttressed by an account of Sylvia as the conventional good housewife of the '50s. When you read Sylvia's *Letters* and *Journals*, there seems something inherently false about them. You have to put them down; they "protest too much," there is something airless, often claustrophobically saccharine or corrosive about them. They are exhausting in their emotional exaggerations. Of course, Sylvia regarded them as private communications, personal rants that she did not intend for publication. She couldn't know that her family would share those private, mortifyingly melodramatic writings. She was above all an artist who painstakingly crafted her poems.

While Sylvia tried to live the life she thought her mother wanted her to, the self-disappointment was too great. It's only in her later (too late) poems that Sylvia Plath allows herself full expression. She had a lifetime of training in form and discipline, learning to shape a poem to get the meaning right.

For Anne, as for Sylvia, the drive to create and be successful was seen as a "masculine" one, at odds with what her mother, mother-in-law, and husband expected. Anne tried to be a good woman/housewife too, but she couldn't seem to get that role right. She thought too much. She was too overtly sexy. She lived in direct conflict, so she felt, with traditional women's roles of the time. She couldn't conform to the expectations of her mother, mother-in-law, and husband.

Anger, helplessness, and a sense of not fulfilling societal gender expectations were overwhelming to these gifted and sensitive poets. And, most forbidden to women, especially during that postwar period, was the expression of rage. Rage was a man's prerogative. But these women poets, forced to pretend to suppress the masculine/achieving part of themselves to please others, were full of rage. We hear it in the suppressed teeth-clenching anger even in Sylvia's early poems. We see it in all the Anne-as-beautiful-victim poems. In all of these women poets, and also in earlier ones such as Louise Bogan and Edna St. Vincent Millay, the expression of rage was forbidden. Rage had to be disguised.

Yet, if we look carefully, we see that rage drives their poetry. The suppression of that rage; all those forbidden emotions fuel what we now see as their strength.

Some women poets killed themselves as a way of getting rid of the "animus," the "forbidden masculine" inside them, that part they could not reconcile with their feminine role. In this way they resembled the male poets of their period, but in reverse. Same pressures on each, same inability to reconcile the two parts of themselves. "I saw the best minds of my generation destroyed by madness," Allen Ginsberg wrote in *Howl*. And he was right. He fought against the death of his core self.

The women's movement in the '60s and '70s came too late for some of the female poets whom I knew and also for the male poets, as well; it opened the floodgates to the expression in life, accepted now, of "forbidden" emotions such as rage and helplessness. It also paradoxically opened the way for men to express more of their "feminine" tenderness in their poems. Male poets do not write today the way they did then: it is accepted to write of love for their children, for instance, subjects that poets like James Wright or Randall Jarrell never approached. The women's movement, with its emphasis on expressiveness, also opened the way for the gay liberation movement that followed. John Malcolm Brinnin spoke to me in private conversation most movingly on this subject.

The women's movement gave women permission to openly express their anger rather than choke on it and kill themselves. And, as a side effect, it permitted men poets to write from their non-macho/feminine/anima side: to explore in their poems their relationships with parents, women, men, and children. This was not possible before. Look at the guardedness of T. S. Eliot, for instance, or of Ezra Pound or Wallace Stevens, the earlier poets who had such an influence. They kept their personal emotions out of their poetry; their mission was to write about history, philosophy — the more abstract and larger themes. Theirs was a different kind of poetry with different aims and concerns. They wanted to preserve a dying culture, to make sure we remembered. Their personal lives seemed absent, or at least carefully concealed.

Now, after the upheaval of two world wars, this could no longer be so for poetry. The wars had left behind them terrible memories and fear. There was the ever-present threat of the atomic bomb and radiation fallout, bomb shelters, the Cold War. Society, culture, and countries could be obliterated in a moment. People wanted desperately to return to some semblance of peace and domestic stability. They wanted certainty. They wanted their personal lives to matter!

Lowell and his circle were right on the cusp of this change. They were trying to bridge the gap between the political/historical/societal and the individual life. From Snodgrass to Berryman and Jarrell to Lowell and Adrienne Rich, American poets were trying to find the link between the meaning of history and the meaning of their own private lives. Emotions of rage or of tenderness were now no longer to be designated the exclusive prerogative of either the "masculine" or the "feminine" in American society.

A Gifted Young Student
Peter Kaplan, 1963–1977

There were a requisite number of people who came to Lowell's classes from mental hospitals, to which they returned afterward. Some of the writers were unintelligible, but one happened to be a young genius, Peter Kaplan, who, at age seventeen, was already as large as a grown man. Peter eventually left McLean Hospital, where, he later insisted, his family had incarcerated him for suspected homosexuality. He moved to Woods Hole and founded a small literary press, the Pourboire Press, and worked as a waiter to support that enterprise. He killed himself at age nineteen, jumping off the Bourne Bridge into the Cape Cod Canal one frozen winter day.

One morning in Lowell's "office hours" I found myself sitting next to a very large, bearded man. He had an earnest look, short stubby hands, and a strong, unwashed odor. The hours went on, and during them I felt a large leg brushing mine under the table. I moved away as much as I could, but the leg followed me. So, too, did the odor. This was Peter Kaplan at first meeting. At the end of the session, as Lowell was packing up and putting away books and papers, Peter handed forward a poem he had written. "It's late," Lowell protested. "Perhaps we can look at it next time." But something in Peter's persistence made Lowell agree finally to read that poem, and the group stayed past the allotted time to do it. The poem was a dreary sestina, or so it seemed at the end of a long session, about a man in a mental hospital. But it was well written and fulfilled the requirements of the form. It expressed the boredom a hospital patient feels, as well as a muffled despair. Lowell made some quick, kind comment. Writing about mental hospitals was only too fashionable in those days, and poets as well as mentally ill patients were always pressing such subjects forward. No one wanted to get into critiquing the poem. Then Lowell mercifully ended the class. "Who was that irritating man?" he asked me later.

At the end of class, that "irritating man" introduced himself. "I'm Peter Kaplan." He alluded to having wanted to sit on my lap, which he had almost managed to do during the class. Peter was vague about his being and whereabouts. He invited me to have coffee, and we went out and talked a bit. I was wary at first; "another poetry nut," I thought. In our first conversation, Peter told me his age. He didn't tell me much more, but he was, I learned later, staying at McLean Hospital. He was in conflict with his parents, who were divorced. He was close to his grandmother. And — he was vague about this — he had come to Boston because he wanted to be more in touch with the world of poetry. Upon learning my name, Peter began to recite my poems. He had read some in *Poetry Magazine,* and had memorized them. Needless to say, this was extremely flattering, and immediately my feelings softened toward Peter Kaplan!

One of the most striking things about Peter, which no doubt contributed to his difficulties, was the fact that this adolescent looked like a forty-year-old man. Photographs of him show a man of heft, with a full beard, and an outgoing, well-developed, fleshy face. But emotionally, he had the maturity of an adolescent. He felt unequipped to cope with the world, particularly the homosexual world, which he felt doomed to be a part of. He longed to be mothered, and he sought out women like myself, who became second mothers to him and would include Peter in their families. The poet Blossom Kirschenbaum was one; Meredith Luyten another. Peter claimed he had been sent to McLean Hospital because his parents felt he was a "bad influence" on his younger sister, of whom he spoke tenderly. Later still, we were all to realize the degree of Peter's suicidal impulses.

Peter had been, in his home city of Providence, an admirer of Edwin Honig, and Honig had taken Peter under his wing when Peter was still in high school. Peter had total recall, a photographic memory that allowed him to remember verbatim every work of poetry he read. He was able to befriend many poets with this ability, for he would show up on their doorstep having read and memorized everything the poets had ever written. The sight of a large, furry, friendly smiling man on one's doorstep, in a leather vest, a big wide-brimmed hat, with a bouquet of roses thrust forth, one's books presented to be autographed, and an accurate admiring recital of those poems was a phenomenon no poet in his right mind would turn away from. Peter carried his belongings in his knapsack, always ready to be adopted. His energy for poetry was outstanding, and he toured Europe, appearing unannounced on the doorsteps of his idols: Basil Bunting, Hugh MacDiarmid, and Robert Graves, a bottle of wine and a bunch of flowers in his hands, and on his lips, the memorized *Collected Works* of each.

Peter knew how to make himself welcome. He could cook, was a raconteur, loved poetry with a passion, and made himself an indispensable fixture in one's house. But he was also a troubled kid, and this, too, made itself felt in one's household rather quickly. Even his irritating qualities were large-scale. When Peter arrived at our house, we immediately handed him a large towel and directed him to the shower. Meekly, he would go and wash. His grandmother remarked to me on Peter's absence of personal hygiene: apparently I was the only person who could get him cleaned up. Then, clothes into the washing machine, and Peter, wrapped in a large towel, would sit down at the kitchen table and start talking. He was funny, with an irrepressible manic energy that never seemed to stop. "Down, Peter, down, boy . . ." He delighted in scandal, racy allusions, the forbidden, the secret, the shocking, and would get carried away by his smart-alecky verbal pyrotechnics.

He occupied our living room couch for weeks at a time, an amusing and irritating whirlwind. "Oh no," my husband groaned, as we would hear Peter outside our bedroom door at 7 a.m., stumbling about, then banging on our door. Mayer pretended to be asleep, but finally I would capitulate, and Peter entered, plopping a large breakfast tray down upon us, and then, beaming, flopping his large self at the end of the bed. He was like a huge eager puppy, and given the slightest encouragement would begin to entertain us; we would start laughing in spite of ourselves. We, who felt already overstretched with two small children only a year apart in age, had suddenly found ourselves the foster parents of a large, troubled, funny teenager with the brain of a full-grown genius. It was exhausting. My husband left it to me to deal with Peter. Peter loved to talk, and could go on and on.

Peter entertained my children. He knew the A. A. Milne books by heart, as well as Beatrix Potter, Ogden Nash, and Edward Lear. Peter knew all of Gilbert and Sullivan by heart too, and I remember with pleasure his singing of *The Mikado* while he cooked spaghetti in my kitchen. The kitchen was a red-stained mess when he finished, but he meekly cleaned up, flourishing large spoons.

Peter was an amazing poetic companion. And if he met a poet he didn't know, he would manage to read everything that person had written. He had a strong critical intellect, and was an acute and careful reader, not just an enthusiastic one. He had read all of Lowell, Bishop, Sexton, and everyone else, it seemed. An ardent fan, Peter came to all the poetry readings, and read new poems carefully and critically. He wanted to be a poet, but also a critic. His critical essays were original.

During his long stays, Peter did not talk about his emotional problems, but suddenly one day, I got a desperate phone call from him. He had tried to kill himself, a "silly mistake," he said. He had put his head in a gas oven, but then had felt so sick he had turned off the gas. He wondered if he could come to my house for a few days. He was at the Grolier Bookshop, and a friend and I went and picked him up, but he refused any further help. We tried to get him to see a psychiatrist, but Peter insisted he was all right. Estranged from his family, he refused to call them, and my attempts to reach Peter's father did not get through. This was the first time I had any inkling of his suicidal tendencies, so adept had he been at concealing them from us all. Louisa Solano, the owner of the Grolier Bookshop, also tried to get Peter to accept help. But, frightened off by our efforts, he suddenly left town.

He went to Woods Hole, a small village on Cape Cod, where he got a job at the Fishmonger Café, and lived at the Woods Hole Inn. I visited several times; he was in a small dark room there. Soon he made friends in the Woods Hole community. He had found families that adopted him: the Luytens, Cristina Rawley and Ron Zweig, and others. He was active in the Woods Hole Theatre Group. I went down to see a production of *Under Milk Wood*. By then Peter was renting a house with some other young people. Woods Hole struck me as the appropriate setting for Thomas's play, so like the Welsh seaside community did it seem. Peter founded the Pourboire Press, and I became an advisor. Peter "discovered" the Australian poet Judith Wright, and published her work first in this country. He published Hilda Morley, Denise Levertov, Michael Hamburger, and others.

On my visits to Woods Hole, Peter seemed in his element. He had friends, a job with people who liked him, and several families whose lives he could share. But there was unhappiness still. Peter had known his sexual preference from a very early age, but he despaired of finding the love he craved. At one point he told me that if he thought he would be condemned for the rest of his life to be looking for love from the homosexuals he had met, he would prefer to die. He felt rebuffed, frightened, unloved, and unlovable.

Peter telephoned me one night in Watertown. It was after midnight. "Oh no," my husband said, "It must be Peter. You get it." When I picked up the phone, Peter, in a fair imitation of Anne Sexton's husky voice, recited to me her "Ballad of the Lonely Masturbator": "At night, alone, I marry the bed."[49] He added his own unprintable lines.

Peter was wild about the poetry of Elizabeth Bishop long before many others knew about her work. He had, during one of his stays at McLean Hospital, telephoned her compulsively, sometimes two and three times a day, reciting her poetry to her, hoping to wangle an invitation to tea. It turned out he had been telephoning the wrong Elizabeth Bishop all along — a real estate agent. "Our" Elizabeth Bishop had an unlisted telephone number, but Peter determined to find his way to her through Robert Lowell, as he knew they were friends. Miss Bishop, when she did finally meet Peter, was impatient, wary, as was Lowell. The intensity of his admiration alarmed them.

I was on Cape Cod that summer, and my marriage was disintegrating. Peter came to visit us almost every week. We would swim, play with the children, talk. Mayer's parents were also visiting us. I sat on the beach flanked by my husband's parents and Peter. The combination did not work at all. Peter sweated beside me on the blanket, wearing a tweed jacket and a large leather wide-brimmed hat. He had a full beard, hadn't shaved or bathed, and refused to go in the water, although the sun was glaring on the sand. He talked to my mother-in-law like an old queen. "Love your shoes!" he told her, flapping his wrists. "Why thank you," she responded, surprised. She was barefoot. Peter cast about unsuccessfully for another female topic. He tentatively proffered a comment about hysterectomies. Finally, discouraged, he went off down the beach and played with my children.

After Peter's death, it turned out that he had made numerous suicide attempts during his young life, each time pledging his friends to secrecy. Later, after his death, we shared the individual pieces of this puzzle. Each of us had known only a part of the story, perhaps known of one suicide attempt, which Peter had presented as an aberration. As we sat in a circle together at a memorial ceremony in Woods Hole, we finally understood that this had been going on since a very young age.

Peter had wanted me to scatter his ashes in Vineyard Sound. After the memorial service his friends all went out on the ferry from Woods Hole to do so. The Sound had been completely frozen, and the ferry to the Vineyard was unable to run until an icebreaker from the Coast Guard freed a passage. But much of the surface was still thick with gray ice. I threw Peter's ashes overboard, and they sat on the ice, a bleak heap. They did not sink. They hardly stirred in the bitter wind.

The "Po Biz"

Submission, Rejection, Money

Cal's approach to student work was inconsistent, often more a gauge of his mood at the moment than of the poem presented in his class. But if Robert Lowell liked a poem, he would go to great lengths for the writer. He took some of my early poems to magazines and showed them to his friends, and it was owing to Cal's efforts that the editor John Crowe Ransom, who had been Cal's former college English teacher, published me in the old *Kenyon Review*. Lowell was generous in promoting his students and friends. But this could backfire.

Once Lowell advised me to send my poems to Judson Jerome, an editor of a prestigious poetry magazine. Jerome wrote back that anyone whom Lowell recommended must be a terrible writer, a member of the loathsome East Coast literary establishment, and that there was no way on earth he would even read or consider my work. There seemed to be extra amounts of coffee staining that rejected group of poems.

Another time Lowell telephoned me from New York to tell me that he had taken a poem of mine to the *New York Review of Books* but — this was a typical Lowell put-down — "they were only interested in publishing our crowd." He had a strong sense of who constituted "our crowd": Hannah Arendt, Mary McCarthy, and other literary heavies. Ah yes, the East Coast literary establishment.

Lowell knew about publishing and rejection. There was a certain law of averages. I had coffee with Robert Lowell and Anne Sexton when they discussed this. They decided that a 3 percent return on submissions was the best one could expect. Anne had kept careful track: "A 3 percent return on the investment." It was slightly better than the return on "direct mail" or "cold calls." When one looks at Lowell's books, one can note how few of the really good poems ever got into magazines before Robert Giroux published them as a collection.

Anne Sexton kept all her rejections in a stack of file drawers. God, she claimed, would know when she had accumulated enough. Then He'd send word: "Take her. She's got a file cabinet full of rejections. Time for a little mercy." Her file drawers bulged. The rejections seemed to get more insulting as poets became more famous. Writers sometimes papered their bathrooms with rejection slips.

It was considered a breach of etiquette to send copies of poems. Each submission had to be freshly typed, no carbon paper. This included completed manuscripts also: no multiple submissions allowed. Prospective publishers could hold the work for years. I handed over the business of sending out poems to my husband's aunt, Pauline "Polly" Spivack. A former executive secretary, a stroke had left her housebound. She enjoyed getting mail, and rejection of my poems would neither devastate nor stop her. I gave her a list of magazines, authorized her to sign my name on the cover letters, and soon she was accumulating a shoebox of rejection slips. Before long Polly was corresponding with editors, signing my name. She wrote supportive notes to conservative columnists, decrying irresponsible youth. She quarreled with liberal political magazines. Soon she was getting chatty letters back. She was also getting a 3 percent return on the poetry submissions. "Polly" got published! And she threw away the rejections before I saw them!

Years later I sat next to Howard Moss at a Poetry Society of America awards dinner. Then the poetry editor of the *New Yorker*, he told me how much he hated to send out his poems, and how he feared rejection. I did not point out that he was able to get round that problem by publishing himself. But I told him about Polly, who had decided to send his magazine a poem of mine every ten days until he finally relented and took one. He enjoyed her lively letters, he said. He wished he had an Aunt Polly too.

Robert Lowell, Elizabeth Bishop, Anne Sexton, encouraging by their example, were helpful. When I was sending round the manuscript of my first book, these poets read and made suggestions. Elizabeth Bishop made extensive notes in her tiny unreadable handwriting throughout the typescript. The older poets encouraged me with stories of their own first attempts to get books published. A poet-editor who rejected your work might later apply for a prize or to a foundation, and *you* might be the judge. Careers came round in circles. Today's golden young writer might be trashed tomorrow. If your book was praised, it was almost certain your next one would not be. Doing the work, sharpening the craft, accumulating the rejections, the acceptances, these were important. The "famous" poets had been us not so long ago. Patience, patience. What was important was the quality of the poem itself. Lowell himself wrote hundreds of drafts trying to get each line just right.

Cal was supportive of my work. However, after the first few years when I was his student, I showed him less and less. This was partly out of growth, rebellion, fear of his too-great influence, fear of his madness, fear of his criticism if I tried new things — I wanted to be a poet on my own, not "Lowell's student" — and partly because, as time went on, I did not want to impose on the friendship. My poems seemed such paltry efforts next to his greatness. Nevertheless, I worked on a first manuscript under his tutelage.

My advisor was John Malcolm Brinnin at Boston University. John Brinnin had a distance that was useful; one's work existed independently of his personality. Stanley Kunitz, too, had detachment that made it possible for one to "see" the work. Despite his own talent, Kunitz had the ability to tune into another poet's intention. Lowell's reading of poems was quite different. One's poem was somehow tied in with Lowell's work; it might at any moment be linked with "the greats," or somehow permeated with Lowell's process. He might see a student's poem, and then turn to a draft of one of his, as an example. While this might be construed as flattering, it was also alarming to see boundaries blur. While Brinnin scrutinized line breaks, punctuation, prepositions, and the transitions from one image to another, Lowell might use one's talent as a springboard for the workings of his own mind, giving rise to a brilliant and illuminating discussion.

I had written an earlier book, based on Mahler's song cycle *Kindertotenlieder*. These poems dealt with the loss of a child and the relationship of women to children. My editor, Ken McCormack, read it. It was "too sad," he said; no one would buy it. I kept the "Women and Children" poems, the best ones, and, after many tries, wove them into *Flying Inland*. The original *Flying Inland* poems were comfortable for my older poet friends. They dealt with mythology, nature, and other less-charged subjects; Lowell and Bishop had overseen the revisions.

Ken McCormack advised me to change the name on my book to a man's name. Perhaps I could be K. Spivack, or Karl! Definitely not "Kathleen." Women, and women's writings were the subjects of ridicule. Also, a woman was resented if she appeared to have a brain: she had to be beautiful as well. *Flying Inland* was finally published and reviewed. I had not disgraced my teachers or myself. Just before its publication I won the *Nation*/Discovery Prize.

I still did not dare show Lowell *The Jane Poems* in its completed form. I wanted to wait until the book was published. I didn't think he would like it. It was too different from my earlier work, which he had liked a lot. Finally Cal read the advance publication copy of *The Jane Poems*. His eyes misted when he spoke to me about it. He hated to think of me ever being unhappy, he said.

He saw the review in the *New York Times Sunday Book Review* before the paper was on the stands. I was having lunch with Caroline Blackwood that Thursday, and Cal came into the restaurant and found us. The same reviewer had once panned both himself and Berryman, he said. Cal invited me to come to visit him and Caroline at their house in Brookline the following Sunday morning. We would have a fine time. And, most important, he said, I would avoid the telephone. "You have no idea," he said, "how many of your so-called friends will call you up, pretending to sympathize but, in fact, gloating." Cal imitated them, "Oh Kathleen, have you read that terrible review? Isn't it awful?" Cal snuffled. He suggested I not read the review, which, by this time, I was convinced must be unspeakably awful. "Just remember, it's column inches," he said. He was right. I received masses of "sympathetic" phone calls, even after that fateful Sunday. But I was not home. Just as Cal predicted, many helpful souls volunteered to press that review into my hands. My editor at Doubleday claimed it helped sales, however. "Just so they spell your name correctly . . ."

That Sunday turned out to be blue and clear. I spent most of the day sprawled on the double bed between Cal and Caroline. It felt rather like being a favorite child — dreamy, protected. We had lots of cups of tea and toast. Outside the sky changed color and the clouds moved and light came into the room, and then went again. On the bed, Cal read Coleridge aloud to Caroline and me. We laughed, we ate, dozed. Cal drank a lot of milk, and Caroline smoked and commented in her husky Lauren Bacall voice. Lying on the bed between them I joked about how wonderfully Oedipal — rather, "Electral" — this was, after all these years. Cal's amused eyes glinted behind his glasses.

Cal had memorized every word of his own reviews and could repeat them as if the sting never left. "Never read a review," Stanley Kunitz advised me, "unless it begins by declaring, in the very first sentence, that you are one of the 'greatest living American poets.'" Part of the endless Roethke-Lowell-Berryman-Schwartz-and-Jarrell "rating and dating" of poets stemmed from an uneasy realization that there were so few opportunities and places for poetry, that unless one were designated either "major" or "minor," there was no hope at all, either of an audience or, especially, of making a living.

Perhaps this is why Lowell so assiduously cultivated the "great poet" mystique. He delighted in repeating stories of elegant lunches with "Jackie" and with "Bobby" — as in "Kennedy." He enjoyed being publicly political; he marched with Norman Mailer at the White House, and accompanied Eugene McCarthy on the campaign trail. Stuck in stuffy Cambridge, we heard all about it. The extreme vulnerability, and its other side, relentless all-devouring ambition, affected the male writers of Lowell's generation more than the women. The women didn't seem to concern themselves too much with whether they were "major" or "minor."

Money played an enormous role, and still does, in how poets spend their time. Robert Lowell had a trust fund, and supplemented that by occasional teaching. Making a living, for most poets, remains the central preoccupation. Although I had come to Boston to study with Lowell on a fellowship, that soon ran out. Lowell found other funds for me, off and on, but rather speedily I needed a job.

I had taken the job at the Whitty Boiler Factory. I had other jobs as well. One was at a magazine, *Business Scope,* where I was soon fired for economic ineptitude. Jerome Bruner at Harvard hired me to work in his cognitive psychology group. He had written that one can "teach anything to anyone at any age," and he wished to see if a poet could learn "new math." This new math was in vogue and was supposed to be the solution to American children's perceived lack of mathematical ability in comparison to the Soviets, who had produced Sputnik. I was the exception to Bruner's optimistic theory.

I worked for Baba Ram Dass in his "Richard Alpert" days, evaluating teachers and math curricula. Timothy Leary was also involved in this project, but we didn't see much of him. He was too busy threatening graduate students with expulsion if they didn't participate in his LSD experiments. I had jobs in the area of language development and learning, and some of them even worked out. I was everyone's favorite research assistant. I had also always had a vocation for teaching, and even at Oberlin had taught creative writing classes as part of the terms of my financial aid. Out in the world there were few creative writing positions. Being a woman was also a distinct disadvantage. But I found teaching jobs.

In the early '60s, I did my thesis at B.U. under the supervision of John Malcolm Brinnin. I chose Doris Lessing's *The Golden Notebook* as a topic.[50] I wanted to explore this novel, and I looked to Virginia Woolf as a source. It was before these writers became popular. "Oh, Kathleen," sighed fastidious Brinnin. I was testing his patience. "Must you be so" — he hesitated delicately, looking for just the right word. "Must you be so *clinical*?"

Wellesley College offered me a teaching position, with the stipulation that I would be earning a thousand dollars less than a man in my equivalent position because "men had families to support." Although equal opportunity employment was supposedly a reality, the U.S. Senate had amended the act to exclude the teaching profession. Women who tried to buck this system were labeled "castrating," the pejorative word of the day. Even in the early '80s, Harvard, Tufts, and the bigger universities were able to avoid hiring women. They had so much money, the heads of departments boasted, that lawsuits by women did not bother them. It was easy to make a woman unemployable just by slander.

I was invited to a dinner during which the heads of the English departments of four Boston-area universities conveniently forgot I was present. They talked among themselves and compared notes on the numbers of lawsuits filed against their universities by "pathetic" women. Harvard and Boston University shared an illustrious female professor, Helen Vendler, so that, they said, took care of their "affirmative action" problem. (Later they were to share the poet Derek Walcott.) Otherwise, the universities at that time, mid-'60s to early '70s, made sure to hire what they termed "inadequate" junior women, whom they could then with good conscience let go after a couple of years. Earlier, Theodore Morrison, a professor at Harvard, had interviewed women for adjunct teaching jobs there to balance Frost's occasional appearances. The female counterparts were to do four-fifths of the work, and receive a fraction of the salary. Tufts had the same arrangement later, their male star being Philip Levine. When women candidates questioned this arrangement there was always the same response: "There are plenty of desperate faculty wives around here who would be grateful for this opportunity!" Unfortunately, this was true.

One summer I was asked to fill in for the *Atlantic Monthly* editor, Phoebe Lou Adams, who was going on vacation. The *Atlantic* seemed a most glamorous magazine. Even the name signified commitment to intellect: Boston and the Transcendentalists, frustrated Emily Dickinson, and high literary standards. I was terrified when I entered its rooms, the parquet floors and high windows overlooking the Public Garden, and quaked through my interview with Miss Adams. I was hired at a salary of $40 a week, and told to start the following Monday. To support my glamorous job at the *Atlantic*, I kept my other job as well: I worked after hours in the child psychiatry unit of Boston University Hospital in a unit for autistic children. I spent my late afternoons and evenings being clawed, spit upon, thrown up on, and bitten. But in the mornings I hastily changed into my one black dress and arrived pristine and ready for heavy literary considerations.

I had read that Coco Chanel said every woman should have at least one "basic little black dress," and Filene's Basement had provided me with one. I wore heels, resisting the impulse to shout "Timber!" as I tottered on the curved staircase to the large room where I sat with the other junior editors, trying to clear the shelves of manuscripts. I felt much like the miller's daughter in the fairy tale "Rumpelstiltskin"; each day the piles of manuscripts grew higher, and there was more pressure on us to "spin them into gold." Manuscripts poured into the office along with clever supplicating letters begging for publication. There were a couple of Harvard students, summer interns who paid the magazine for the privilege, working with me, also toiling over the piles of print.

Michael Janeway, Richard Todd, Michael Curtis, Whitney Ellsworth, and poet Peter Davison at one time or another coincided in middle editorial positions on the *Atlantic*, and I supposed they would one day inherit, one of them, the job of Edward Weeks, that legendary, erect, fastidious editor who appeared once a week at our meetings. Peter Davison was intelligent and critical. He wrote poetry, yet seemed to keep that part of his life outside the office. The atmosphere was self-consciously literary, as the younger editors felt themselves under constant competitive scrutiny.

I tried to appear anorexic and invisible, one of the glamorous young things who, perhaps, still grace the magazine today. The volume of reading material made one tremble for the authors; it was more than possible to miss or reject good work, and there were no controls on what was sent back. We rejected out of hand, and no one watched what we did. A Harvard undergraduate, paying the magazine for his summer internship, had total power of rejection, as did anyone else who could be pressed into service. In our desks were several printed forms for various levels of rejection, along with templates for letters we were to type out — by ourselves! —

delineating various grades of more encouraging rejections. Sometimes we were allowed to write personal notes. A small handwritten "Sorry" on a rejection form was meant to be high praise indeed. Since we were reading so much and so quickly, our judgment faltered by the end of the day.

Only if we liked something inordinately were we supposed to send it round to the others for further critical appraisal. This meant we could open ourselves to ridicule on behalf of the authors we championed. We were supposed to write our reasons for selection on large pink "Crit. Sheets" which were appraised by the more senior editors. We used lots of qualifying words to cover our backsides: words like "rather" and "somewhat." One didn't want to be caught recommending something that Mr. Weeks would later reject. Mr. Weeks made the final decisions.

What I remember best about [Lowell] was his habit of rating every writer. I can still hear him drawl over dinner at the Athens Olympia, "Don't you think Trotsky is one of the three best journalists of the twentieth century?" Being timid, I agreed.

   Ⓦ BILL CORBETT

Corbett: Note written for Kathleen Spivack, 1990.

"Genius at Work"
Revision, Presentation, Contribution

Drafts of Lowell's poems appeared again and again in subsequent volumes of his poetry. In his study at Marlborough Street, I saw drafts of some of his best poems for *Life Studies*. I remember the window open, the scent of magnolia rising, and Cal showing me drafts of "To Speak of Woe That Is in Marriage." He read the lines aloud in a soft and halting way, murmuring right through to the end.

> Gored by the climacteric of his want,
> he stalls above me like an elephant.

Oh my! I shivered, delighted, only half-understanding the poem itself. I could never think of Lowell's household in Back Bay Boston without thinking of that poem: was I seeing the "truth" of his marriage? It was a hidden thing, slightly pleasurable and not — like biting one's nails. I also saw a lot of drafts of the poem "For the Union Dead," in which the "Mosler safe" was worked and reworked.

Elizabeth Hardwick, Stanley Kunitz, and other friends of Lowell's sometimes were fed up with his constant questioning and revision of each line. He was obsessed with a poem while working on it and demanded the same attention, or obsession, from others. Lowell flattered me, as he did later Bidart and others, by asking my opinion of the versions. But I did not feel in a position to give an opinion, nor, I suspect, did he want an opinion as much as a sounding board to test out various alternatives. So the poems got changed, and changed again. "Skunk Hour," a beautiful and complex poem, got clearer in subsequent drafts. "Near the Ocean" emerged fully lyrical and formed, it seemed.

When Lowell started working in sonnet form, he wrote and rewrote, and the original drafts were clotted in parts, and more clear in others. Grey Gowrie saw a lot of them as well. Sometimes the poems got clearer as subsequent drafts helped Lowell rethink the poems. But a lot of them could not be called "clear," even when they were finished.

I had come to study with Lowell, but I did not understand a word of his early work, *Lord Weary's Castle*. It still seems a difficult book. But the "Jonathan Edwards" poem and the "Quaker Graveyard" were masterpieces.

Lowell sought to achieve the same quality in free verse, and later, in the sonnets. In his later work, he becomes more accessible, less mannered, less privately a "Lowell of Boston."

Endless revision could be a limitation. Sometimes it was an extension of Cal's madness, as he would become ever more obsessive about the drafts, reading and rereading them to me and my husband — but really to himself — in our living room, carrying them around with him, and asking everyone what they thought. He stared at them endlessly, and a lot of nervous obsessive energy focused on the revision process. "I don't know which is better," I would say lamely, miserably, looking at the same very slightly altered Lowell last line for perhaps the twentieth time. "They all seem good." I hoped that would mollify him, at least for a time.

In a personal conversation Elizabeth Hardwick remembered that, even in the mental hospitals, Lowell read aloud to his fellow inmates. " 'Listen to this,' he would say. 'Let me read you this.' He was teaching, so to speak, these mixed-up people. It was really kind of touching." Hardwick continued, "He was constantly reading his poems. He would come into the kitchen. 'Oh, listen to this,' Cal would say. He was constantly revising. 'What are you doing?' 'Can't you see I'm cooking dinner?' Then I would say 'I don't like this, I don't like this ending.' And sometimes he would change it."

It was almost impossible to say whether a poem was indeed better in a later version in one of Lowell's books, or whether one preferred the earlier version. Since Cal was not only writing for posterity, but also for Allen Tate and Edmund Wilson, he could never give up. "Even God rested on the seventh day. And called it good." But God was not creating for John Crowe Ransom, Richard Blackmur, Mary McCarthy ("our crowd"), Eliot, Yeats, and Milton. Cal was. He never rested.

Lowell wrote about the revision process:

> I am not an authoritative critic of my own poems, except in the most pressing and urgent way. I have spent hundreds and hundreds of hours shaping, extending and changing hopeless or defective work. I lie on a bed staring, crossing out, writing in, crossing out what was written in, again and again, through days and weeks. Heavenly hours of absorption and idleness . . . intuition, intelligence, pursuing my ear that knows not what it says. In time, the fragmentary and scattered limbs become by a wild extended figure of speech, something living . . . a person.

I know roughly what I think are my better poems, and more roughly and imperfectly why I think they are; and roughly too, which are my worst and where they fail. I have an idea how my best fall short. To have to state all this systematically, and perhaps with controversial argument, would be a prison sentence to me. It would be an exposure. But which is one's good poem? Is it a translation? Can one write something that will sing on for years like the sirens, and not know it?[51]

Reading aloud was not a thing poets were expected to be good at, with the exception of Dylan Thomas, who read like a dream. Allen Ginsberg was a phenomenal reader, and had very much his own style, somewhere between chanting and incantation. Anne Sexton read beautifully, like a stage actress, projecting a wistful vulnerable quality, even when she read with her backup rock band made up of Weston High School teachers and students. But Anne reading alone could magnetize an audience.

Among the academic set, and I include Lowell in that, it was considered slightly vulgar to be good at reading poetry aloud, and most poetry readings were, and still are, agonies of boredom. Although the competitive demands of performance have ensured that poets now read their work aloud more convincingly than they did then, there was not yet much money around for readings.

That situation was altered due to what was vaguely referred to in the academic world as "the economy." As poetry became more popular, as more colleges and universities added creative writing programs, some audiences were willing to pay to hear poets read their work. Also, rock, rap, and hip-hop altered the way poets presented their poems. Performance looked back to the tradition of the Beat poets and to earlier groups like the Fugs. The Fugs had presented their own works as well as the works of visionary poets, Blake especially, like intimate theater pieces. Poets began to perform their work slightly more enthusiastically. Currently the interest in Performance Poetry, coming out of the Poetry Slam, has made listening to poetry more vivid.

But Robert Lowell as well as Elizabeth Bishop were matter-of-fact readers of their own poems. Elizabeth Bishop could put you to sleep, her readings were so dull. Cal mumbled, and his obscure poems became even more obscure in his soft voice. Even his most rapt students had trouble not falling asleep at his early B.U. poetry readings. The last reading that Robert Lowell gave at Harvard was different, however. In the gloomy lecture hall, Lowell unbent; explaining his poems in a clear, gentle way before reading them. The student audience was with him, leaning forward, listening and appreciative. During his time of being a poet, he had become, in his presentation of his work as well as in the work itself, less obscure, more clear and direct, accessible and at ease.

The most amazing and painful reading I heard at Harvard was that of Theodore Roethke, the American poet whose work I felt closest to. I had looked forward to his reading for weeks. I loved his nature and greenhouse poems, his poem to his student "Thrown by a Horse," and others. He had spent time at Bennington College, along with Kunitz. I had grown up there as a faculty child and identified with the view of nature in both men's poems. When Roethke came onstage, he swayed with nerves: he was uneasy and already quite drunk. The Harvard English Department was as stuffy as it could possibly be. Roethke was a large, flabby man. Terrified and insecure, he hardly read at all. As he jigged to a tune in his head, he mumbled, was incoherent, and made little jokes concerning the incongruity of his being at Harvard. Then he gave up reading poems and sang improvised anti-Nixon political ditties until Professor Harry Levin firmly removed him from the stage.

"Here I am," Marianne Moore beamed at us all at another Harvard reading, from under her tri-cornered hat and large cape. "A real toad in an imaginary garden!," quoting her poem "Poetry." This after a particularly flowery introduction by Harry Levin. Then she read her poems in a businesslike, get-it-over-with way. That was definitely Harvard, I thought: an "imaginary garden."

But poetry readings went on nevertheless: Auden, Spender, Frost, Gwendolyn Brooks — all were available to be heard. Just being in their presence was enough. Looking at Auden's hands, that papery skin, the pouched eyes, I felt that I had never seen a face as wrinkled and used-up as that of Auden's.

What Lowell had to teach his students was not something to which critics would have paid particular attention. Lowell's contribution, as far as his students were concerned, was to search for his own individual American voice, and to foster the discovery of voice in those with whom he worked. He struggled throughout his writing to synthesize his personal experience with the historical and political realities that were the environment for writing. In Lowell, the personal and political were fused: the poet existed in a context. That context expanded from the directly personal — his birth family, the family of marriages and children — to the immediate historical and political realities that were a part of the American scene. His poems encompassed the civil rights struggles of the '70s, the protest against the Vietnam War, the assassinations of President Kennedy and Robert Kennedy, the loss of greatness that characterized the United States. He was always "relevant," it seemed. Lowell chronicled his personal life against a larger historical tapestry.

Few poets had the scope and breadth to tackle such a background. But there was a felt need for this, coalescing earlier in the response to Allen Ginsberg's *Howl*. Lowell's great contribution was to never deny his American roots; indeed, he celebrated them. Lowell's poetry had the scope of Whitman, the compression of Dickinson. He drew on these two American poetry traditions; you might say he was a twentieth-century American Transcendentalist. He was a philosophical poet of our time, our place.

Additionally, his classical education imposed strong technical expectations upon everything he wrote. He had a prodigious mind, and read widely through many cultures. His own language became clearer, his intentions more direct, as his work progressed. The clotted difficulty of the earlier work gave way to an ease in sonnet form in his final books of poems. After the arcane poetry of his first two books, especially *Lord Weary's Castle,* Robert Lowell set about finding simplicity of language that, combined with a tightness and discipline of form, could adequately convey the real experiences he was having. *Life Studies* was just that: a book of poems that were studies from life. He wrote of being in mental institutions, in bed with his wife, in jail as a conscientious objector, and about experiences with his family. It revolutionized the concept of poetry, or rather, what could be written about. For everything in life was allowed to be a poet's material, not only exalted stuff of history and fiction. In *For the Union Dead* Lowell combined, almost casually, his sense of Boston and history along with personal life.

Lowell lived as much in his education as in the present. In *Imitations* he explored his debt to other writers. The *Imitations* were not meant to be exact translations; they were meant to be approximations to the poetry of the original authors, transformed by Lowell into heightened English.

Notebook 1967–68 took the ease of *Life Studies* one step further. Here personal and historic events were recorded and written about in loose fourteen-line sonnets, largely unrhymed, but faithful to the underlying force of iambic pentameter. *Notebook 1967–68,* which covered a period of the Vietnam War, Robert Kennedy's death, and the 1968 Democratic Convention in Chicago, was later revised and expanded in the volume *History.*

Here are a series of beginning lines from *Notebook 1967–68.* They show the range and ease of the poetic line, and the everyday quality of the topics Lowell chose and later transformed:

The black hardrubber bathtub stoppers at the Parker House
(from "The Spock etc. Sentences")[52]
Our '*New York Times Cookbook*' looks like '*Leaves of Grass*'
(from "The Vogue, the Vague")[53]
Election Night, the last Election Night
(from "November 6")[54]
The slick bare tar, the same suburban station
(from "November 7: From the Painter's Loft")[55]

The poems start quietly, matter-of-factly. Then they take off, leaping into a final sense of the brevity and preciousness of life. But what Lowell showed was that everything was material, a fit subject for poetry. There was no distinction between what was "poetic," and what was merely one's life.

Lowell wrote poems for and about his friends, his wives, his children, for Ovid and Horace and Rimbaud and Boston, for history and John Berryman, and the cities and houses he lived in. He made poems out of his breakdowns, his difficulties with alcohol, his love affairs and embarrassments, self-doubts, teaching, and travels. His later books, *The Dolphin, History, For Lizzie and Harriet,* and the later *Day by Day,* were published close together. In them he documented three areas of interest, as far as he could divide them.

History dealt with the poet and public life. *The Dolphin* dealt with Lowell's love affair with Caroline Blackwood, a breakdown, and his sense of regret and guilt toward Elizabeth Hardwick. In poems like "Records," he tried to understand Hardwick's feelings, and paraphrased some of her letters into sonnet form. And *Day by Day* expressed Lowell's joy at his new love, and the birth of his and Caroline's baby, Robert Sheridan Lowell. In both *The Dolphin* and *Day by Day,* Lowell struggled with his ambivalence toward his marriages, caught between two women who loved him and whom he loved. In his books, the same poems often reappear in slightly different forms. On returning to Boston, Lowell mused again on his past: "Alas, I can only tell my own story..."[56]

Lowell's life, his thoughts, books, friends, and political and social milieu were his poetic material. He approached this more and more directly, and the progression of his work and life shows a paring away of pretense and artifice. Lowell expanded the sense of what was *possible* in poetry. It was possible to write about Greek urns and nymphs and history. But it was also possible to write about the commonplaces of our lives, and the junctures where the personal and political became one.

Watching his commitment to voice, and his ambitious demands upon himself as he strove to combine personal and historical, one felt the possibilities in one's own writing. By example, and by direct encouragement, Lowell inspired us to write from our own experience. He validated our lives as well. For his American students were not meant to write as Europeans, nor as people who did not live in a contemporary context.

Of the writers who studied and developed with Robert Lowell, not one came out sounding like a carbon copy of Lowell in his or her own work. Lowell directly encouraged the use of individual geography and experience. I can remember the delight in his eyes as he would lean forward, incline his head toward a young writer, his fingers pointed together almost prayerfully. "Now *that's* the genuine article!" he would offer, smiling gently at the writer. He would lean back; the air shimmered with pronouncement: "to be old, do nothing, type and think."[57] Lowell had written for all of us.

As I go through my papers, I find and re-read with delight the many notes and letters I had from Elizabeth Bishop, Stanley Kunitz, Elizabeth Hardwick, Anne Sexton, and others of the time. There are more than I had thought; some I had even forgotten receiving. Of course I kept all my letters and notes from Mayer. But my letters from Robert Lowell were more carefully put aside. They went with care to a "special place" — you know: that special hiding place where one keeps most cherished things — only to never find them again! Perhaps after my death, when they clean out the upper closets, the back attic, the cobwebbed hidey-holes, too far too reach without a ladder... I can see the crumpled paper, some with the words "Milgate Park," where he lived with Caroline Blackwood, on the elegant letterhead.

I kept most of the letters from my parents. We were of the generation of letter writing, and they wrote me at least once or twice a week. I wrote them too, once or twice a week, no matter where I was: long, chatty letters. This seemed to be usual among friends and relatives. We all wrote letters to each other. Then e-mail took over for all of us. Lively and funny, but not the same. A whole literary form vanished.

Peter Drucker continued to write and teach until his death. At this writing, Doris Drucker is one hundred, and still playing tennis. At their fiftieth wedding anniversary, I wrote a poem for them which celebrated their lives, put them in context with every one of my father's books, and rhymed them in quatrains. I read — performed, rather — this poem at their anniversary party. Suddenly my father perked up and with great enthusiasm exclaimed, "Now *that* poem, Kathleen, should win the Pulitzer Prize!"

The poem was a masterpiece of doggerel, my private specialty for family occasions. "Please Fa, don't write any more books. I don't think I can rhyme one more!" I begged. He had written so many. But he wrote a few more and — I wrote for his ninetieth birthday. And for my mother's one hundredth as well. I won't impose that utterly *brilliant!* fiftieth anniversary poem for Peter and Doris Drucker on this Serious Literary Book, but should you happen to be interested in how a poet manages to rhyme thirty-five heavy political and economic book titles while telling the history and journey of two European refugee intellectuals and their life together — and make it funny too! — just let me know.

Of course my parents were my literary champions! Even today, Rejection makes me go to bed and moan. And even today I phone my mother to share news (how lucky is that!), exactly as I did all through school; and she understands, cheers — and sympathizes.

A creative original person looks at literature in an off-hand way, so different from an academic. Cal's prose has that wonderful off-hand quality. Everything is at the moment, not prepared. There is a quality of engagement like conversation. His choice of words is so casual, yet very unusual and to the point.

⊘ ELIZABETH HARDWICK

Hardwick: Conversation with Kathleen Spivack, 1988.

Allen Ginsberg and Robert Lowell
Two Branches of American Poetry

"Modern" American poetry owed much to its forebears, and to two distinct branches, that of Emily Dickinson, on the one hand, and on the other, Walt Whitman. Lowell and Ginsberg might be said to have embodied the two sides of American literary output: that tension between the sides of poetry and of personality. The Apollonian and the Dionysian heritages were often the inspiration for of New England authors. Hawthorne, for instance, and later Henry James, Edith Wharton, and others wrote of the tension between formality and the transgression of passionate abandon and the price to be paid for that: punishment, shunning, or death. Puritanism and its other face, abandon, made for exciting literature.

Beneath the formality of Emily Dickinson's poems was a breathless tension that made her poetry so elliptical and so intriguing. Dickinson combined formal expression of controlled emotion with religion and delight in the natural world. Her work hinted at great love as well as delicate perceptions of nature and the world around her, held in with precise verse. Passion was suggested, unrequited, hinted at, and lay just underneath; scholars have written reams while trying to figure it out. The formal poetry of Archibald MacLeish and Richard Wilbur, for instance, perhaps even that of Robert Frost, relate to the Dickinson branch of the literary family.

Whitman, on the other hand, celebrated the body, "forbidden" love, and the larger (masculine) scope of war, history, and passion. There was not another poet like him, although Carl Sandburg, James Agee in some of his work, perhaps Vachel Lindsay, Stephen Crane, Jack Kerouac, and others owed a debt to the freedom and scope of Whitman's writing. Allen Ginsberg seemed a direct descendant, in his poetic aesthetic, of Walt Whitman. He saw himself that way, and in *Howl* tried to achieve a modern epic poem with a Whitmanesque sweep.[58]

While Elizabeth Bishop with her formality and reticence might be seen as directly related to the Emily Dickinson approach, Robert Lowell spanned both traditions in the progression of his work. From his early formal work, to *History* and including *Life Studies,* he strained against the bounds of either branch of American poetry and tried to transcend them.

Allen Ginsberg and Robert Lowell at St. Mark's Church, New York City, 1977.

Lowell and Ginsberg were polar opposites, but each was a scholar as well as a poet. There was an inventiveness in each, a willingness to push the boundaries of what was and could be written about. In personal style they had little to do with one another; Lowell was and presented himself as an Anglophile High Church (sometimes Catholic) Boston Brahmin whose references were British history and literature. Allen Ginsberg looked to Judaism, Far Eastern tradition, ecstatic poetry, chant and trance states, and mysticism. Yet Ginsberg, in poems like "Sunflower Sutra," was close to the sensibility of poet William Blake in the romantic/mystical infinity-in-a-grain-of sand viewpoint. Blake was a touchstone.

Ginsberg identified in many ways with Walt Whitman. He embodied the expansiveness of the American imagination, the "dare-to-write," "dare-to-be" poet from Paterson, New Jersey. He came from the side of American poetry that included Hart Crane, William Carlos Williams, and later, Kerouac, William Burroughs, Lawrence Ferlinghetti, Gregory Corso, and Gary Snyder. Ginsberg became a household word, anathema in the late fifties. He was an antidote to Puritanism. He wrote freely about forbidden things: drugs, alcohol, madness, homosexuality. Like Whitman, his poetic voice was open, singing, and his poetic lines long and meditative as the landscape itself. In poems like "My Sad Self" and "Sunflower Sutra," ugly, hopeless, ordinary life became transformed into a transcendent experience. He celebrated loneliness and love and friendship and cities and nature and the tumult of destruction: in the wildness of his poetry was a sense of the oneness of the universe, of multiple human experience. Like Whitman, he let his lines go free, but he managed to contain his universal vision at the same time. He was our bard.

Allen Ginsberg believed in the presentation of poetry, and reading poetry aloud became a dramatic event. Where before it was enough for a mousy tweed-suited poet to look down at the page and mutter along to himself for an hour or so, this was no longer acceptable. Poetry readings became less "academic" and less boring. Ginsberg had shaken us awake. Poets perked up in later generations as the emphasis on oral presentation led to the Poetry Slam, and the academic poets felt themselves challenged by the emphasis on performance of poetry aloud. They had to get better at reading their poems aloud to an audience.

Ginsberg educated America to his unique reading-aloud style. He had an eccentric, somewhat crotchety reading style with or without music. As Ginsberg chanted, sang, and conducted the air as he read his poetry, there was always a didactic quality about him, even in his most "beat" days. He could not escape the appearance of a small Jewish Talmudic scholar, even when clad in Buddha-like white swirling robes. He hunched over the audience, looking gnomishly professorial with his thick glasses and bushy hair, high domed forehead, beating out the sound of the lines with one hand incessantly. He got his father, friends, and lovers to come up on stage with him sometimes. The audiences put up with all that — Peter Orlovsky and the rest of the show. It was always a circus and celebration. Ginsberg never varied his reading style. Lots of poets tried to imitate him.

I remember going to hear Ginsberg read translations of Russian poets at Boston University, in the late sixties and early seventies. It was very exciting: some Russian poets were being "let out" and they were trooping about the country giving readings. The Russians were impressive; they had high cheekbones, lots of hair, large tossing heads. Poets Yevgeny Yevtushenko, who had read at Boston University earlier, and Andrei Voznesensky put on a marvelous show. As we had hoped, they read their poetry in a grand theatrical manner, with surging voices and gestures, even in little Hayden Audi-

torium, packed to the gills at Boston University. They were used to projecting in Red Square, we thought, feeling guilty that we were so few in number.
Then Ginsberg came in after each of their poems with a translation. He did
not try to imitate the Russians: not at all; he read as always, carefully, in
his professorial manner, chanting rather quietly, beating the rhythm of the
English translations.

Ginsberg's earlier readings in the Village in New York City, with Ed
Sanders and a musical/poetic group, the Fugs, were legendary. Ginsberg
with the Fugs declaimed the poems of Blake in dingy bars in New York, ac-
companying himself with finger cymbals or harmonium. These readings —
sung, chanted, backed by eerie music in small smoky cafés where all the
performers wore colorful outfits that shouted at the audience "I'm weird as
hell and proud of it!" — were cloaked in the excitement of something new,
something truly "American," a validation in poetry and jazz about what was
happening to us right now.

During those years, I used to go from Boston to New York to visit my
friend Gerard Malanga. We read our poems together in the little smoky
dives that opened their doors to aspiring writers. Even though our only lis-
teners were mostly drunk, sat at the bar, and smoked and talked through
our entire readings, we felt we were part of everything that was happening
in an exciting and evolving world. Gerard was in fact part of the sophisticated world of "happening" in New York. A talented poet and a beautiful
young man, he worked for Andy Warhol and starred in many of Warhol's
films. He was also a photographer, and his photographs and poems record
the times and the sense of beginnings then.

I thought of Gerard as the most glamorous of my friends. When I went
to visit him, I was always surprised to see the small apartment from which
this matinee idol emerged. He invited me to Warhol parties with him.
But first, we had to sit somewhere and wait until midnight so the Warhol
crowd would not think that Gerard had nothing to do beforehand. We sat
out many a night in Gerard's local laundromat, watching his laundry whirl
round in a dryer, until he determined that it was time to make an appearance at "The Kitchen," or some such place. Gerard always made a fantastic
entrance, fashionably late, dressed in a long outrageous sweeping coat. He
was extremely handsome and mysterious, and everyone was sure he had
come from other parties earlier in the evening. I, the girl from Boston, was
amazed at the scene once we entered the crowded, smoky rooms. The girls

were so thin! Lovely bone structure, Edie Sedgwick and others. I tried not to stare too obviously. "But, Gerard," I pulled him aside, "she has *green hair!*" "Shh," said Gerard, trying to appear cool, as if used to all sorts of displays of sophistication. Years later I was amazed to see Gerard's work in the Pompidou Center in Paris: the times we lived through were now considered "historic," and Gerard had become an icon of "pop."

Meanwhile, Robert Lowell, the poetic descendant of Emily Dickinson, Emerson, Wallace Stevens, closely linked to Pound and Eliot, of the "we came over on the *Mayflower*" Boston Brahmin family, lived and worked in Boston, New York, and England. His poetry had High Church Christian religious allusions. It was formal and scholarly, and looked to Europe for its references.

Linked now to the West Coast, Ginsberg traveled to India, and incorporated Nepali and Tibetan Buddhism into his work and thought. He traveled to Japan, where they tried to throw him out for pissing on the street. He went often to Paris. He made outrageous statements to the French press. He was a close friend of George Whitman, the proprietor of Shakespeare and Company. Mr. Whitman, who claimed a somewhat mysterious relationship to "Walt," always hoped that one day Ginsberg would come to live in an apartment at the bookstore, that bookstore which has extended so much generosity over the years to American writers.

Ginsberg became part of the Naropa Institute in Boulder, Colorado, where poetry, esoteric poetics, and Buddhism found their particular mix. Sitting on a rock in white robes, chanting "Om" against a background of snowy peaks, he was a media star. He was part of another poetic aesthetic entirely than that of East Coast Robert Lowell. Ginsberg's poetic discoveries looked to the Far East for inspiration.

Freedom of expression, the free speech movement, the sexual revolution, the overt celebration of homosexuality, Tibetan Buddhism, all these Ginsberg sponsored and embraced with enthusiasm. The distance from California to staid East Coast Boston, it turned out, was not so great. Both Timothy Leary and Richard Alpert, who later transformed himself into "Ram Dass," had set their roots in Boston. With Ginsberg and the subsequent social revolution, the U.S. East and West Coasts were no longer so isolated by a vast geography.

I had occasions to meet and spend time with Ginsberg, sometimes in the company of Lowell. And others: Robert Creeley, Lawrence Ferlinghetti, and so forth. Later, I got a teaching job in Paris. Ferlinghetti, the owner of City Lights, the famous literary bookstore in San Francisco, came often to Paris. I was teaching there. George Whitman, his friend, shouted to me out of a top floor window of Shakespeare and Company as I passed his book shop one day, and commanded me to dinner that night in the little book-treasure-lined rooms on an upper floor of Shakespeare and Co. George wanted me to pose as his "young" girlfriend because Ferlinghetti was apparently showing up with one. That "girlfriend" turned out to be my age, and we ate George Whitman's rice and beans and used old newspaper pages to dry the dishes. Later, George Whitman dried the pages and used them for toilet paper.

But as I witnessed, in the later years when he visited or read in Paris, Ginsberg's eyes were often focused just beyond, searching the room, as he had told us all, for some beautiful young man. After a while I realized that Ginsberg, who had been my first choice of a poet to study with, those many years ago, had almost never helped the career of a woman poet in his life, with one or two exceptions. Come to think of it, he hadn't been too helpful to young men poets either, except for his lover.

I thought of the many women poets whom Robert Lowell had helped: Elizabeth Bishop, Anne Sexton, Sylvia Plath, Adrienne Rich, and others. And the men: Snodgrass, Hugh Seidman, Frank Bidart, his friends Kunitz and Peter Taylor, and other writers. For many reasons Lowell would always be for me the poet's poet — maybe I was just more familiar with his work — and the most generous of teachers and friends.

As Ginsberg's scholarly contribution to the poetic scene continued to grow, he became less a prankster, more a literary institution. I remember his beautiful presentations on the poets Walt Whitman and William Carlos Williams for our educational television series *Voices and Visions*. Ginsberg read the poetry of these poets as if he himself were the creator. He went from margin to mainstream; he became included in anthologies, and his poetry, formerly indignantly banned, is now taught in schools.

Honored at a meeting of the Associated Writing Programs at Temple University in Philadelphia, the hall was filled with writers from all over the country who rose to their feet in homage. Ginsberg came on stage accompanied again by Ed Sanders and the Fugs, a "blast from the past," wearing the same ponytails and leather and tie-dyed outfits that they had sported some twenty-five or more years ago. They recreated past glories, reciting

Blake's poetry to hypnotic drones and drums. Their penetrating reading of Blake's poetry thrilled us.

Ginsberg then read his newer poems, played the finger cymbals in accompaniment, but looked far beyond the crowd impatiently as if this agglomeration of poets was far too "square" ("academic") to be of interest now. There was a flat feeling in the room; everyone, including Ginsberg, seemed to be waiting for something to happen, some transcendent poetic moment to lift us all — where? It was Rip Van Winkle; it was déja vu. Ginsberg was a bit tired of being a self-promoter, perhaps. He was restless to move on; he wanted some new poetic inspiration. He had already, at that time, passed into the Pantheon.

Lowell's presence and being had a peculiar *density*. He seemed to carry around within his body the whole of his past life, past art — both as grace and as burden. Valéry's words about Mallarmé irresistibly come to mind: "Near him while he was still alive, I thought of his destiny as already realized." Several months before he died, he said to me with an air of resignation, despair, and pride: "I don't know the value of what I've written, but I know that I changed the game."

② FRANK BIDART

Bidart: "Robert Lowell," *Harvard Advocate*, November 1979.

The "Romantics" Seminar, Harvard University, Spring 1977

*O*ne of the last seminars that Robert Lowell taught at Harvard before his death was concerned with what he termed the late "Romantics" of the nineteenth and twentieth centuries, and featured Blake and Whitman. I sat in whenever I could.

In his usual rhetorical style of inquiry, Lowell would read one line, "Oh Rose, thou art sick" and then pause. He took off his thick spectacles and rubbed his eyes; his fingers squirmed around the book. He asked, "What does Blake mean? What is the rose?" A long silence, as Lowell frowned downward at the page, and at the same time, into his own thoughts. Sometimes the silence became unbearable, and a student would offer a tentative morsel of interpretation. Lowell acted as if he hadn't heard the comment. There would be an even longer, more awkward silence. "Maybe he means love?" someone would venture, his voice rising uncontrollably into a question, rather than a statement. Another long silence. Finally, slowly, as if the thought were being pulled out of him, Lowell would give his own tentative interpretation. "Well, perhaps he means love. Or is he referring to Christ?" His words fell and rested in front of us. Lowell seemed to strain onto the page, as if he were writing Blake's poem at that very moment. Lowell's explorations into poetry were more than exegesis. They were reflection, meditation, a deep fusion with Blake or whichever poet was being discussed. It was in these meditative silences that one seemed to merge with Blake, or Whitman, penetrating to the heart of the poet and his creation.

Wings of greatness, pure poetry, beat about our heads. The class ended, and it was as if we were coming out of a deep trance, waking up. There was a white silence in the air, deeper than any rational explanation of the poems we had just read together. "It's strange," I said to Cal as we walked together after class across the leaf-strewn quadrangle, past Harvard's great Widener Library, "It's as if we *become* Blake, or Whitman, in the class." "I have the same sense this term," he said. "I have the sense that I am reading poetry as never before."

The long silences, during which one strained to understand a word, or a passage, the pauses, the rhetorical grasping for some rational explanation that final teaching term, all seemed to reflect the unexplainable center: the mystery that is poetry.

Helen Vendler, the prominent literary critic and professor, was occasionally present in the class, amid the group of more or less silent students. I had never met Helen Vendler before this, and I was struck by the alive quality of her responses. Her coloring and bearing were vivid, as if she had stepped directly out of Irish mythology into Emerson Hall. She listened intently, yet with a misty engaged look, a seemingly dreamy state in which everything was recorded in some inner journal. Her face was thoughtful, expressive. Occasionally she spoke, one of the few who did. There would be a feeling of sleep in the room; Lowell would have become almost inaudible, muttering mostly to himself. Suddenly, a tingle charged the air as Helen leaned forward.

"But don't you think . . . ?" she would begin. This was, in part, rhetorical. Her eyes sparkled. She spoke with conviction, scholarship. She had a scintillating mind. Everyone came awake when Helen spoke. There was electricity between Lowell and Vendler as they came at a poem from different sides. Helen brought to bear her background on the poets discussed, and a textual analysis, which included vast critical scholarship. Lowell loved this, of course. Suddenly he would speak a bit more clearly, interrupting Helen, who somehow managed to finish her sentences anyway. No one else could have dared enter this, but Helen fearlessly put forth her point of view. She had a warmth, a degree of commitment to poetry, which made you not want to miss a word she said. Her delight was contagious: there was such tangible happiness in her enthusiasm that one leaned forward, smiled. Her logic, her brilliance, were gifts: Lowell appreciated these at the same time that he tried to press on, interrupting her; still impatiently caught in his own poetic monologue.

Helen began to lay out what she thought about the poems, an erudite but utterly contradictory take on the poet Keats, for instance. She was clearly an expert and very sure of herself, but came at poetry from a different point of view: that of a critic, not a creative poet. No one else in the class would have dared to have the chutzpah to venture a word of contradiction: they would not have had the courage, first of all, to even hint at contradicting Robert Lowell in a class. But it was far, far worse to be seen as contradicting Helen Vendler! She had a very strong presence. So it was shivery; it was exciting to watch the two, Lowell and Vendler, in battle — the Battle of the Titans. (Well, it wasn't exactly a *battle*, more like a *skirmish*.)

Helen spoke in long convoluted sentences, nuanced and deep and difficult to follow. As she spoke, I sometimes tried to replay her sentences in my mind to get their full meaning. I wished I could read them to myself. Her approach was abstract, intellectual. Lowell came at poetic work from a process-oriented, poetry-creation point of view. He was interested in how Blake, for instance, chose a specific word. How the poem took its rhythm and rhyme scheme, how Blake chose the precise ending among alternative ones. He discussed a poem from the vantage point of a working poet, made you see Blake actually writing the poem, the decisions Blake must have made, and the reasons why. He could spend an entire class period on the words "O Rose, Thou art sick . . ." What was the meaning of the "invisible worm?" The many meanings?

Helen saw a different process. She was a meticulous scholar. These different ways of seeing — and of course there were some crossovers and shared points of view, between that of a working poet and that of a working literary critic — enhanced and enriched this seminar.

Lowell began his classes on each successive poet with an apparently indolent, speculative, and altogether selective set of remarks on the poet's life and writing; the poet appeared as a man with a temperament, a set of difficulties, a way of responding, a vocation, prejudices. The remarks were indistinguishable from those Lowell might have made about a friend or an acquaintance; the poets *were* friends or acquaintances; he knew them from their writing better than most of us know others from life. This, in the end, seems to me the best thing Lowell did for his students; he gave them the sense, so absent from textbook headnotes, of a life, a spirit, a mind, and a set of occasions from which writing issues — a real life, a real mind, fixed in historical circumstance and quotidian abrasions. . . .

What his privileged students heard was original discourse; what they experienced was the amplitude of response stirred by past poetry — which, in Lowell's hands, always seemed poetry of the present — in a poet who had earned his place "on the slopes of Parnassus." It was a response in which familiarity and reverence went hand in hand, in which technique and vision were indissoluble; it made the appearance of poetry in life seem as natural as any other action. I felt, always, that a scanning faculty quite unlike anything I could describe was reviewing and judging and annotating the lines or stanzas he took up; it made one feel like a rather backward evolutionary form confronted by an unknown but superior species. And when one asked what the name of the species was, the answer came unbidden: Poet. Lowell's classes were a demonstration in the critical order of what those mysterious beings in the anthologies had in common — a relation to words beyond our ordinary powers. In that sense, his classes were as inimitable as his poems.

⊘ HELEN VENDLER

Vendler: "Lowell in the Classroom," *Harvard Advocate*, November 1979.

Final Spring, 1977

Lowell had returned from England for his last term at Harvard without Caroline Blackwood. He looked suddenly so much older, tired, beaten. The marriage was starting to unravel. My marriage was also starting to disintegrate, and we talked openly about our various problems and questions. We had been associated, as teacher and student, as friends, for nearly twenty years. The veils, fears, hesitations, pretenses, and differences were gone.

Cal had been so much a part of my courtship and marriage, as well as of my poetry, the thing we both shared. There was a tenderness to him, outspoken, that had not always been there before. We had a pure and very quiet friendship, somehow independent of all the turmoil that had surrounded his, and my, private life. The instinct that had kept me away during the worst of his illness, that had kept me from ever getting too involved, had served me in good stead. I was able to be a listener and a friend to Cal in ways that did not compromise either him or myself. He was transparent those last few months, and my heart ached to see him so troubled and tired.

We walked out of class together into the spring air and spent the afternoons together. Cal was openly tender and loving to me, which I thought a bad sign. No longer the sidewise malicious teasing: he was too tired for that. I knew he was going to die — and I would worry — his character was too transformed. His classes felt like a religious experience. Poetry communicated directly. It was only a question of getting out of Blake or Whitman's way; these visionaries opened doors into our own hearts.

Now, eighteen years later, we had achieved a comfortable understanding. I had probably, according to Cal's standards, never written "one good line," or if I had, I had learned how difficult it was to sustain an entire poem. We talked of Anne Sexton, of Sylvia Plath and Ted Hughes, their poetry, their marriages. Speaking of my own marriage, its unbearable breakup, I said, "Well, at least I didn't marry another poet." Looking for small comfort. "Oh, but my dear," Cal reproved me gently, "that's the trouble. You did."

Nevertheless, despite our own differences, my husband was surprisingly at ease with Cal, especially toward the last years of his life, when there was a gentleness and simplicity about his presentation that had not been there during the middle years at Harvard. He was formally addressed as

"Robert" by my children, since Cal felt "Mr. Lowell" was, after all, too formal. "Are you a famous poet?" one of the children asked. And then, "My
mother is a really famous poet. Do you know her work?" Cal was graceful.
For this he was allowed to shoot my children's bow and suction arrows —
endlessly — against the door of the garage. He enjoyed this, his eyes glinting with sly enjoyment. He stayed often for dinner; he was sane and gentle.

His erratic aloofness was gone. I was suspicious about this accessibil-
ity and gentleness. He was *too* open and tender. One evening, after supper,
while my husband put the children to bed, I sat downstairs with Lowell
and talked a bit, and then I played some of my favorite records for him,
among them Brahms's "Songs for Women's Voices." We held hands as we
listened. As so often between us, we didn't need to speak. The music was
tender, coaxing, and expressive; the voices soared with longing and loss.
So much beauty and sadness: the poignancy of suppressed/expressed love.
It was almost unbearable; a moment when one's humanity and senses are
so sharply keyed together, listening to, penetrating to the core of Brahms's
passionate human outcry: a prescience. That poignant evening was documented in my journals. It was the last time I would be with Robert Lowell
in an intimate setting.

Cal had been my "in loco parentis" when I first came to Boston. He
had stood up for me to my parents, approved my marriage, comforted me
when I lost my first child, taken my poems to magazines for publication.
Throughout, there was an attraction acknowledged yet managed somehow.
There was above all a deep and intimate friendship.

A few days later, sitting over coffee in one of Harvard Square's stale,
dingy cafés, he kidded me that finally, he and I should marry. A spark of
the old malicious gleam came back into his eye. He sat back, waiting to see
what I would say. "No, no, this is best," I said, and then added impetuously,
without thinking, "and besides, I hate mental illness!" Cal appreciated this
with a quick smile. Throughout the years he had teasingly referred to me
as "the psychologist," whenever he wanted to discuss some weighty issue,
but my absences around Cal's breakdowns had been noted. "But we know
each other so well," he pressed. "We've had the best of each other," I parried,
happy to let the matter drop.

I had often felt very much the observer. During the times when I did not
see him, we wrote a few letters and postcards. Lowell's notes to me from
England were chatty, boringly domestic, brief. He wrote me about missing

his American life, Elizabeth Hardwick, Harriet. He wrote me when Caroline's beloved youngest daughter, Ivana, spilled boiling water over herself. I wrote him too, little letters, nothing special. I thanked him for all he had given me.

I still thought of myself as Cordelia in relation to Cal: one who loved, but did not speak of it. He lived on a grand poetic stage. In the blinding glare of that noon brilliance our friendship was steady and quiet. It belonged to private life. The sometimes unspoken yet always realized feeling between us did not fall easily into a defined category. Cal, in his gifts and his self-destructive torment, was certainly the closest to a Lear that I was likely to see walking about this earth.

After Lowell's death everyone converged in Boston. Caroline arrived from England late at night; the Gowries brought her round to my house, and then Grey went out in search of her favorite whiskey. He found it, she drank, we stayed together a while, and then they all went back to their hotel. The next day Grey arrived with a few bottles for my cupboard, a limited supply that he intended to monitor without depriving Caroline during this time. The following day the Gowries managed to get Caroline through the service, and to Dunbarton, New Hampshire, Lowell's gravesite, and back. Afterward, everyone got together in Boston, a dark evening indeed. Anguish, loss, and desolation were palpable.

At his funeral at the Church of the Advent in Boston, with its austere, Church of England atmosphere, I raged inwardly at the hypocrisy and coldness of the service. Hardly anything was said about Cal as a poet. "They might as well have been burying a banker," I whispered to my husband. He knew how I felt. I was so angry I was unable to cry. Afterward there was a flurry of visiting as the mourners reassembled at the home of Robert Gardner. Elizabeth Bishop, Caroline Blackwood, and others fell apart. Elizabeth Hardwick did not.

Some of the funeral party drove behind Robert Lowell's coffin to Dunbarton Oaks, in New Hampshire. I cared for Caroline's children in my home while the rest went to New Hampshire. The night of the funeral we all convened again. While everyone, including gallant Elizabeth Hardwick, worried about Caroline, no one thought to monitor Elizabeth Bishop in a custodial, don't-let-her-out-of-our-sight way during the long, sad aftermath of Lowell's funeral. Elizabeth Bishop grew more and more restrained and austere as the night grew long, and finally she passed out. She was such a quiet drunk that no one noticed how much she had taken in. I feared she had undergone a fatal heart attack. Her friend Alice managed to get her out of there, but I thought then that Lowell's death, for Bishop, had been a mortal blow, in the real sense of those words. The next few days were a blur, held mainly together by Elizabeth Hardwick's courage and by the Gowries' kindness and patience.

It was not until later that I was able to feel the full implication of Cal's death. It was not until the final breakup of my marriage of nineteen years, that following spring, that I was able to also mourn the death of my friendship with Lowell. In one instant, the passionate love of my young life, my husband, and the intimate guide and companion of my life's work, Cal, were gone. In both cases there had been recognition, almost from the first moment of meeting, of the bond. And, perhaps, a precognition of its inevitable end.

Robert Lowell had been my teacher, mentor, intimate friend — and these words weren't sufficient to express our relation. Throughout ran the vein of deepest respect, reticence, acceptance, and appreciation. What can explain the correspondence that draws two people together? It supersedes words like "attraction," for instance. It was love, of course, a many-sided thing. But in fact we never sought words, no articulation of this rather quiet intimacy. It created no conflict, no melodrama. It was a lifelong sympathy between us, a source of acceptance and support: an intense conversation sparkling with humor and understanding, always ready to be picked up.

It was a historic moment lived, a turning point in contemporary American poetry in a historic place, Boston, which nourished this. It melded historic and personal considerations. Yet it was only a brief time in a particular place that would in retrospect have such an impact on the work of poets who followed.

What I have tried to record in this description of Robert Lowell and his circle were some aspects of the journey as I lived it. Lowell and his contemporaries traveled into the heart of poetry. Although younger, I happened to be of like mind and spirit. To be honest, I brought my own zest and enthusiasm, generosity, inquiry, and delight to all these relationships. I also shared an aesthetic sensibility. It was not only time and place, but also an adventurousness of spirit that united us. These poets enjoyed sharing life and work with me and their other colleagues as much as I did with them. It was fun!

The achievements of some of these writers influenced the century and the many writers after them. We were aware of living a great moment together: no one more than Robert Lowell, in his persistent investigation into literature and its relation to one's life. The prismatic dust-mote moment I spent with Lowell gleamed with poetic/intellectual/human attraction, but refracted separate lives and a strong sense of equality and boundaries. It resonated with light, a faceted crystal I would turn over and over, pondering its many-sided reflections, the heart of a shape-shifting ruby.

Language only gives us a certain palette of word-colors with which to paint complex emotions. In our lives the colors blended, overlapped, segued into each other, edge-tinged, swathed across the wide page of our almost two decades together. Give this experience the many shades of multicolored closeness: *is* and *was*, those variegated words. Try to name it if you can. *Friendship. Mission. Obsession. Fascination. Eros. Agape.* We lived it, but it was always too complex to define.

The gods reached down and touched us all: we shimmered, sprang alive in puritanical/free-thinking/transcendental New England. Here once again poetry flared up surprisingly, two-thirds of the way through the twentieth century. Now the poems, like memories, remain, banked embers, waiting to leap alive again at a reader's glance. Reader, open the page. Let the poems whisper their music.

Robert Lowell died on 12 September, right at the end of a journey between his home in Ireland and his home in New York. The death shocked his friends and readers but not, one may guess, himself. He was 60, the age both his parents also died of heart attacks, and he had always doubted that he would, in this sense, survive them. No other 20th-century poet has integrated us so fully with the people he knew. Father and Mother, as they appear in the poems, join friends and lovers, writers and historical figures, his children, wife and ex-wives in the long drama of self-depiction, the life studies. A measure of his achievement is that all these people step out of the poems into the reality we associate with great novels and seem no less clear than the figure of the "confessional" poet himself. How you win and lose love, how it both defines and boxes you in, what it has to do with language and so with history: such is Lowell's theme. It is unbearable therefore that this story and these characters are finished.

⊘ GREY GOWRIE

Gowrie: "Robert Lowell, 1917–1977," obituary, *New Statesman* (1977).

Looking for Robert Lowell's Grave,
October 1977

The telephone rang. I was at home on a lovely October weekend, nursing a sick child. The rest of Boston, it seemed, was outside having fun, enjoying one of the last warm days of the year. "Hello," a deep voice said. "Katya? This is Andrei Voznesensky. I am here to visit Robert's grave. Robert spoke so often of you when he visited me in the Soviet Union. I come to Boston to visit his grave with you." It took more than a moment for me to switch realities. "Robert has spoken so fondly, so often, of you," Voznesensky persisted. It was this comment that made me suspicious. Was this some sort of joke? I could not imagine Cal *ever* talking about me on a state visit to the Soviet Union, where he had spent time during the summer before his death. What did this Russian poet really want? "I visit Robert's grave." Yet I did not know where "Robert's grave" was.

I had heard the Soviet poet Andrei Voznesensky read his poetry at Boston University a few years before. Allen Ginsberg had read with him. Voznesensky read grandly, his leonine head thrown back, declaiming as if in Red Square. Then Ginsberg had read his translations of Voznesensky's poems, "*dovening*" like a scholarly rabbi as he beat out the rhythm with one hand. Nearsighted, he adjusted his spectacles as he squinted owlishly at both the page and at the audience, slightly sidewise, wanting us to love him. (Ginsberg, always our Gifted Clever Child.) It had been a mandarin moment for Boston University.

Voznesensky was one of only two officially sanctioned Soviet poets who occasionally were allowed to turn up in the United States, the other being Yevtushenko. Stepping momentarily through a crack in the Iron Curtain, bowing to us briefly before that curtain closed on them again, these men had suffered when they criticized their regime in a fairly scripted fashion. The State Department and universities (officially) loved them, whatever else may have been going on behind the scenes. We were being given a glimpse at something otherwise forbidden to our view: Communism!

Now "adventure" was calling me on the telephone. How I longed to go. But upstairs, my oldest child was sick. "I take plane," announced Voznesensky, "I meet you in Boston in two hours. We go." I heard someone take the phone out of his hand. A few muttered words, hand over the apparatus.

The connection was broken. I made a few telephone calls to in-laws and to friends to see if they could come over and babysit. No one was home. It was a peak tourist weekend. Everyone in the entire city was enjoying themselves on the Esplanade. I felt more and more discouraged. Meanwhile, I got another telephone call from Washington, this time directly from the poet William Jay Smith, who as the "official" host of Voznesensky, informed me of the airline and time that Voznesensky would be arriving at Logan Airport. "Be there," he commanded. This was not up for negotiation.

This Soviet poet was a valuable item. Voznesensky had flown to the United States bearing a wreath woven from twigs of a tree that grew on the dead Soviet writer Boris Pasternak's estate. In homage, he planned to put it on Robert Lowell's grave. And I had been selected to accompany him. In a stroke of panic, I telephoned William Alfred. Could he go in my stead? But Alfred did not drive, and he was, for a number of perfectly sensible reasons, reluctant to go. He agreed to ask Frank Bidart.

Frank was a wonderful poet, a great person, and, most important, he had a working car, a new Porsche! My rusting thirteen-year-old Toyota would have had some difficulty bearing Voznesensky to New Hampshire. Frank agreed to drive the Soviet poet northward. He went to meet "Andrei," as we were beginning to call him between ourselves. At the airport, Frank and Andrei telephoned me. "I must see you," Voznesensky murmured again. "Robert spoke so much of you." I thought of all the legendary beakers of vodka that Russians seemed to put back in large quantities. But, let's face it; I was also eating this up. I was ready to go. ("Just call my Naaayaymmmme . . .")

It was decided — by Andrei — that after their little trip to Dunbarton the two poets would come for dinner that evening. I would solace myself by dreaming enviously all day, preparing a wonderful meal. The Julia Child cookbook was all the rage, and I was determined to use it. I prepared myself to meet Andrei's gaze without having to tell him that he had been chatting up the wrong girl. I was pretty sure that Lowell would never have spoken of me to this Soviet poet; it would not have served any purpose whatsoever. Also, I had never met William Jay Smith, who had arranged for the Soviet poet to visit. How had Voznesensky gotten my phone number?

The beautiful fall afternoon and evening stretched on and the needs of my two children occupied the time. I set the table, cooked a beautiful supper, out-did myself. I even made Julia's "Chocolate Cake." But the dinner sat uneaten, waiting, grew blackened and dried. Throughout that evening, and into the following day I got several phone calls from Frank and also — muffled thickly, dark and furious with vowels — from Andrei. The two poets did not return to Boston that evening as planned. It would be more than just a little pleasure jaunt: they ended up having to stay overnight and did not return until late the following afternoon.

Dunbarton, New Hampshire, was hardly the center of the universe. More significant, a headstone had not yet been placed on the grave. No one seemed to know exactly where Lowell's grave was located. There was no way to find it. Andrei was bearing his wreath. In Russia, visiting the graves of poets was a national pastime. The two poets drove round and round in the vicinity of Dunbarton, inquiring occasionally of townspeople who didn't have a clue. Frank seemed to remember that the grave was in a cow pasture somewhere. But New Hampshire is full of cow pastures. It was growing dark.

When it was too dark to distinguish one field from another, they decided to stay overnight in a motel and try again in the first morning light. Andrei retreated into his room, intending to stay up all night working on a poem "for Robert." He would finish his poem by 4 a.m. and then wake Frank to go and look again for the grave.

I was beginning to feel relieved that it was not I, a nervous driver under the best of conditions, who had not been able to find the Lowell family plot and grave in Dunbarton, but rather, kind Frank. I had a slight pang about missing "my night with Andrei" in a New Hampshire motel, which I envisioned as potentially quite romantic. But perhaps staying home with a sick child had been a stroke of good luck.

Voznesensky described this experience from his point of view in an interview with Linda Charlton in the *New York Times*: " 'It was dark, dark, dark,' the poet Andrei Voznesensky said. . . . 'It was about 7 o'clock. It was impossible to find him. I began to write.' "[59] The next morning Voznesensky had written the poem and woke Frank early. After a while, driving around a bit more, somehow they found the Lowell plot. In the midst of farmland, Cal's resting place was undistinguished. There was of course no marker. Andrei was horrified, but nevertheless placed his wreath near or on the freshest mound of earth.

Relieved, the two poets set out to return to Boston. Andrei was scheduled to fly from Boston to Washington that noon, and if they drove quickly they might still make the flight. After a series of wrong turns and wrong directions, somehow they drove toward Canada instead of Boston. Then the engine of the Porsche failed. The poets had to abandon the car and walk to a nearby farmhouse. By now it was past noon. The phone rang again. It was Frank informing me of the situation. Frank had plans for that day; everything had to be cancelled.

All morning I had been getting increasingly more urgent calls from the State Department, demanding to know where Andrei Voznesensky was. What had I done with him? Didn't I realize that *he was an important personage*? If I lost him, didn't I understand what trouble that would cause? They hinted darkly at international espionage.

By the end of the afternoon, Frank's Porsche had been towed to a garage in northern New Hampshire; the two poets had rented a car, and finally reached Boston. Frank put Andrei safely on a plane to Washington, back to what must have been his own immensely complicated political theater. I never heard another word from Andrei Voznesensky. How Robert Lowell would have laughed, loving this story of misadventure! I imagined his sideways glinting gleam of ironic appreciation, the held-breath slightly snorty laugh. And all that commotion, about *him*, how great!

Andrei's poem in translation appeared on a page of the *New York Times*. A lovely poem, it suggests the greatness of Cal as a poet, and the treatment of his grave. Robert Lowell would have loved a poem of *his* to be in the *New York Times*. But alas, Philistine America, his poems never made it. It took his death to put him there: an American poet, immortalized by a Soviet writer in a polite poem that served official purposes. But how had his poem made the *Times*? I wondered.

[From] Family Graveyard (To Robert Lowell)

The family graves lie deep within the wood:
Your parents both are there, but where in the dark are you?

    ⊘ ANDREI VOZNESENSKY,
        translated by William Jay Smith and Fred Starr

Voznesensky: From *An Arrow in the Wall: Selected Poetry and Prose by Andrei Voznesensky,*
ed. William Jay Smith and F. D. Reeve (New York: Henry Holt, 1988).

Notes of a Witness

As one relives these times with Robert Lowell, and with the poets that he trained, the experience becomes present again. Boston and Cambridge link with this and the even more distant past; the rainy glistening streets, the bookstores, the people shuttling through them emerge from ghostly presence into actuality. Those darkening classrooms, with their views of Commonwealth Avenue or the rooftops of the red Harvard Houses, superimpose themselves over the more urban skylines of the present.

The air smells of the slightly vomitous odor of books. Gentle pages are turned. Focusing on a page, one moves into it, and it becomes the entire framed picture, much as a scene on a movie screen shuts out all other surrounds in a theater. A poem becomes larger than the world.

In a classroom, Robert Lowell hunches over a page, reading aloud in a high, questioning drawl. He is forever wondering what a poem "means," inquiring into the heart of it, prying it open with tapered fingers, as if taking apart an artichoke. He will be peeling back a real artichoke in only a few hours, dipping the leaves in butter with much less interest, seated at the Iruna restaurant among his students, still discoursing upon poetry and poets of the past. The Iruna has pushed four tables together to seat us all; we look among us, down the row of snowy linen tablecloths. Allen Tate, Randall Jarrell, John Berryman, W. H. Auden, and others are as real and present to Lowell, in his discourses and memories, as Anne Sexton, Sylvia Plath, Elizabeth Bishop, and Robert Lowell himself have become to me.

I am forever walking up the steps to Lowell's Marlborough Street house, waiting nervously until he should open the door and lead me up three steep flights to the top of the house where his study waits. The books, the papers, are as before. Lowell frowns at his revisions of poems in *For the Union Dead*. He is still revising, always revising. He reads to me in a tentative, soft voice. It is going to be dark when I go back to my rooming house.

In Lowell's class at Boston University, Sylvia Plath waits, with neat page-boy hair, sitting ramrod stiff and attentive, for her poem to be passed out and discussed. Anne Sexton rustles her chiffon dress and her bracelets. They watch each other. Lowell hunches near the window at the head of the table, and transforms, brilliant and incoherent, into someone we do not understand.

Out in the green suburb of Weston, Anne feeds her Dalmatian dogs and puts on her bathing suit. She shifts in a swivel chair in her small study and looks up from reading poems, mine and hers, to smile at me. She puts the sheaf of papers down on her desk. "Oh God, the sun. I love the sun!" she exclaims, stretching out in a chaise lounge next to the swimming pool in the backyard. There is a bottle of Champale by her side; her backyard is a country club for Anne and her friends.

Lowell takes my elbow as we cross Mount Auburn Street toward Quincy House. He leans toward my listening ear, gossiping softly, playful, letting his fingers trail, as if abstracted, up my arm. Sylvia and Ted Hughes make dinner in their small flat and settle down to read each other's poems and revisions. Adrienne Rich works on her poetry after dinner, limping with dark, hunched determination into her study after struggling to get three children into bed. They keep interrupting her with calls for drinks of water, but she pretends not to hear them.

Anne writes a love poem for her psychiatrist. She picks up the telephone, lights another cigarette, calls Maxine Kumin, and reads the poem aloud to her. And everywhere, in all the small student apartments, poets Frank Bidart, Robert Pinsky, and others, work on their poems they hope Lowell might read in class.

Elizabeth Hardwick reads a draft of her essay to her husband, who listens. William Alfred, after a light supper, and his fourth tutorial student of the day, goes back into his dark high-ceilinged study and tries to hear the Irish dialogue of his youth.

And Elizabeth Bishop watches the Ping-Pong table in her foyer darken as evening comes. She takes up a book, puts it down again. She winds paper into her small typewriter once more, and tries to read her own writing, her own crossings-out. She is exasperated with herself. The phone rings.

Outside, a light spring fingers the air. Dusk is falling. The energy of poems, of poets, rises over the roofs. A flock of swallows wheels, dives, rises. They are like punctuation marks on a sky. The real Cambridge, the Cambridge of today, recedes. "I think continually of those who were truly great," the poet Stephen Spender wrote. And so do I.

Even while I write, new poetic history is being made. The prow of a boat cuts the water. But the sun reflects off the wake on an ocean behind me: it is too dazzling to see ahead. We, as poets, "rowing toward God,"[60] are all part of a historic tradition, and always, in our reading and writing, we are made aware of that. Poetry, coming as it does from a common language, has its origins in speech, in the development of rhythms and insights.

Lowell knew he was a part of a great poetic tradition. He lived it, read it, and the dead poets that he read were tangible, alive to him. His insistence and persistence in bringing them alive for us were unrelenting, as if, by focusing on their writing, he could once again will them into being. I didn't understand that then. I understand it now.

I realize that I have been privileged, through a series of fortunate coincidences, to witness firsthand how poets were trained. I was forced to look directly into the heart of the poetic process. Obsessive reading of texts, the revisions, the exactitude of this scrutiny that Lowell insisted upon made possible the deepest revelation of the meaning of poetry itself. I hadn't started out with a deep understanding of poetry; I was fired by the passion of sound: lush rhyme and rhythm and flashy metaphor. Robert Lowell trained me, painstakingly, exactingly, as he did with everyone who worked with him, until the heart of poetry, the tender white heart, peeled, stood open before us, gleaming, patient, yet even more mysterious. The poem became a flashing aureole of light.

This ability: to look at, or to listen to a poem, and to be able to penetrate that mystical heart, to be able to comprehend the surface, and the depth at the same instant (the form and texture, the underlying structure, the meaning, and the resonant overtones of a poem) were things I absorbed from Robert Lowell.

After such sessions, standing up and stretching, one would be aware of having been cramped, since during the focused hours, leaning inward into poetry, one wouldn't have moved. The Being poured into, merged with poetry; the Body was left behind. Then, with surprise, one reentered one's body, went downstairs, had a cup of tea on a tray, and made real conversation.

This merging with the poem, with the poetic process, and with the other people studying the poem was an extraordinary experience. It is hard to describe the closeness felt after sharing such experiences with Lowell and other colleagues. Somewhere our souls hovered above the actual bodies sitting in the classrooms, merging with the souls of John Donne, Milton, and Yeats, as well as with Robert Lowell.

After such mystical intimacy, real intimacy was possible, shared. It made possible and actual my friendships with other poets, although they were older and more established than I was. Lowell bridged the distance for me, and so did the city of Boston, which is most conducive to the fellowship of writers.

It was possible to enjoy time with Sexton, Bishop, Rich, Kunitz, and other poets. Not quite a generation younger than Sexton and Plath, I was both of, and apart from, the cultural context that had shaped their values. During the period of my study with Lowell, possibilities arose for women that had not been there before. The split between being a woman and being a writer was healed and bridged. It became possible, even valued, to express both parts of oneself. The slightly older women poets had helped to heal that split for those who followed them. But they paid a huge price for their integration of self as woman, mother, lover, writer. It was acceptable, later, to write about mothering and bodies and rage and need for love, and not to have to make a choice.

It was easy for Plath and Sexton to think of death as a way out of their dilemmas: the swirl of forbidden emotions, unshared and unsupported, exhausted them. Sylvia's betrayal by her husband, Anne's seduction by her psychiatrist — these events seem to have left both women defenseless. They thought of suicide reflexively as a solution, in the same way that other women poets, not as mentally unbalanced, might think of going to bed for a few days, or getting away to the country. I don't think either of them realized the finality of suicide; they talked of it, played with it in their minds, and attempted it, as we see, in the hopes of getting a Rest, not a Death, out of it.

I had grown up during World War II in a German-speaking household in rural Vermont. Already isolated from the culture around me, my models were the alienated European writers that I had grown up reading. *Tonio Kröger,* by Thomas Mann, was emblematic of my adolescent state. I too, stood small, dark, Jewish-looking, outside the circle of the tall, blond, and carefree Aryan-seeming culture of my new and very foreign country. Later, reading more, I found other models for the life I thought I might one day lead. Whereas the poet Rilke, in the purity of his dedication, had been the model of an artist-poet I had imagined my life would emulate, this model, the male Rilke, had become irrelevant to what my life was actually turning out to be. The "otherness" that drives one to be a writer, the standing outside that characterizes a writer's stance; this only comes from pain. And the unbounded flowing into life that is the other part of the creative personality takes a lifetime to harness and control.

Issues of violation, betrayal, and abuse remained at the heart of Sylvia Plath's and Anne Sexton's feelings of helplessness and rage. Plath and Sexton died in the emotional outpouring of raw pain most rawly felt and uttered. We feel the power of their cry. But Adrienne Rich, Elizabeth Bishop, Stanley Kunitz, and Robert Lowell lived to learn to master pain, to progress beyond the raw outcry into integration and forgiveness, both of themselves, and of others. And Maxine Kumin, one of the best poets of her generation, continued to grow and develop in her art, quietly.

We must celebrate the survivors among our poets. For the pain of an artist, processed through the clarity of vision, allows us to understand more deeply how to deal with life's adversities. It took a lifetime of loss to learn this, distill it, and express it ironically. To progress through all the stages of life, to tell us what it's like, to report back to us from the outposts of wisdom; that is what we need from our poets.

When I first came to Boston on a reckless adventure, I didn't expect it to become the cornerstone of a constructed life. I didn't know or understand Robert Lowell's poetry. Nor did I realize that, sitting in Lowell's classes among these poets, I would become a survivor, a witness to their journeys. But after Lowell's death I realized this was meant to be, had to be. I didn't realize then that, so many years later, and at the midpoint of my own writing career, I would be paying tribute to my older brothers and sisters; that I would be led to tell, from one point of view, what it had been like to have been there, and to have shared in that luminous moment.

Other writers who were present during that period of Robert Lowell's teaching have their own memories, their own particular journeys. One of the pleasures for me, in putting together this memoir, has been the chance to relive the atmosphere then: the happiness, the shared delight in poetry, the engagement with poems. This was universal. In their own writing about Lowell's classes, writers speak again and again about the quality of concentration and encouragement. Robert Lowell changed all of our lives irrevo-cably. We knew, even then, how privileged we all were to be part of these classes. But all around us, real life was happening. When one reads these writers' works, one is struck by the unique talent of each. Lowell encour-aged each one of us to find our own voice. He had a clear sense of "the genuine article," as he called it. We were encouraged to be true to ourselves, and to claim who we were in a larger political and historical context. Lowell could be gentle but uncompromising. We existed within a cultural reality. Always aware of the larger viewpoint, he set us this example in his being as well as in his poetry.

Even now, as I write this, somewhere, out in the country or in an isolated city room, while everyone else is asleep, a young poet raises his or her head from a page. Outside, the crickets are sawing into the night. Or street noises are cutting the air with clangor. This young person is sure that he or she is the only person in the world who has ever felt so passionately, hurt so much, cared so deeply, loved so intensely, and drunk so thirstily from the draught of feeling and language. Words, glorious exultant words, swirl from the night sky. Young writer, wherever you are, come out of your blue-black loneliness, your cloak of pain and joy, into a meadow of poetry. There have been poets before you; there will be writers after you. Your personal life, your song, is the life of all of us. We exist for each other. As I finish this writ-ing, the gentle ghosts of Robert Lowell, beloved friend and greatest teacher, and Anne and Sylvia and Elizabeth are blessing our efforts, sprinkling their words on us all like snow, like sparks, like fire-embers, like flowers.

Notes

1   Robert Lowell, "To Speak of Woe That Is in Marriage," in *Life Studies* (New York: Farrar, Straus and Cudahy, 1959), 88.

2   Doris Drucker, *Invent Radium or I'll Pull Your Hair* (Chicago: University of Chicago Press, 2004).

3   Andrew Marvell, *Thoughts in a Garden: A Golden Treasury of English Verse* (New York: Hartsdale House, 1935), 127.

4   Ibid.

5   Anne Sexton, "Elegy in a Classroom," in *To Bedlam and Part Way Back* (Boston: Houghton Mifflin, 1960), 45.

6   Anne Sexton, "The Double Image," in *To Bedlam and Part Way Back* (Boston: Houghton Mifflin, 1960), 53.

7   Ibid.

8   Lowell quoted in Ian Hamilton, "Interview: Lowell in England," *Review* (London) 26 (1971): 10–29.

9   Sylvia Plath, *The Collected Poems,* ed. Ted Hughes (New York: Harper and Row, 1981).

10   Sylvia Plath, "Doomsday," Juvenilia in *The Collected Poems* ed. Ted Hughes, 316.

11   Sylvia Plath, "The Manor Garden," in *The Colossus and Other Poems* (New York: Knopf, 1967), 3.

12   Sylvia Plath, February 25, 1959, *The Unabridged Journals of Sylvia Plath*, ed. Karen V. Kukil (New York: Anchor Books, 2000), 471.

13   A. Alvarez, "Sylvia Plath," in *The Art of Sylvia Plath*, ed. Charles Newman (Bloomington: Indiana University Press, 1970), 56.

14   Plath quoted in ibid., 301.

15   Ibid., 302.

16   Sylvia Plath, *Ariel: The Restored Text*, ed. and with a foreword by Frieda Hughes (London: Faber and Faber, 2004).

17   Robert Lowell, "Ford Maddox Ford," in *Life Studies* (New York: Farrar, Straus and Cudahy, 1959), 49.

18   Kathleen Spivack, *Flying Inland* (New York: Doubleday, 1973).

19   Elizabeth Bishop, "The Man-Moth," in *The Complete Poems* (New York: Farrar, Straus and Giroux, 1969), 16.

20   Elizabeth Hardwick, conversation with Kathleen Spivack, 1990.

21   Anne Sexton, "The Fury of Sunrises," in *The Death Notebooks* (Boston: Houghton Mifflin, 1974), 50.

22   Anne Sexton, "Her Kind," in *To Bedlam and Part Way Back* (Boston: Houghton Mifflin, 1960), 21.

23 Robert Lowell, *For the Union Dead* (New York: Farrar, Straus and Giroux, 1964), 317.

24 Rainer Maria Rilke, *The Notebooks of Malte Laurids Brigge* (New York: Capricorn Books, 1958), 377.

25 Kathleen Spivack, "Straining," in *Flying Inland* (New York: Doubleday, 1973), 14.

26 Peter Davison, *The Fading Smile* (New York: Knopf, 1994).

27 Elizabeth Bishop, "In the Village," in *Elizabeth Bishop: The Collected Prose* (New York: Farrar, Straus and Giroux, 1984), 251.

28 Elizabeth Bishop, "In the Waiting Room," in *Geography III: The Complete Poems, 1927–78* (New York: Farrar, Straus and Giroux, 1976), 159.

29 Elizabeth Bishop, "Elizabeth Bishop Speaks about Her Poetry," interview with Eileen MacMahon, 1978, in *Conversations with Elizabeth Bishop*, ed. George Montiero (Jackson: University Press of Mississippi, 1996), 108.

30 Brett Millier, "Elusive Mastery: The Drafts of Elizabeth Bishop's 'One Art.'" The complete essay is available in *New England Review* (Winter 1990) and in *Elizabeth Bishop: The Geography of Gender*, ed. Marilyn May Lombardi (Charlottesville: University Press of Virginia, 1993).

31 Elizabeth Bishop, "One Art," in *Geography III: The Complete Poems, 1927–78* (New York: Farrar, Straus and Giroux, 1976), 40.

32 Elizabeth Bishop, "Breakfast Song," in *Edgar Allan Poe & The Juke-Box: Uncollected Poems, Drafts, and Fragments*, ed. Alice Quinn (New York: Farrar, Straus and Giroux, 2006), 158.

33 Robert Lowell, "Red and Black Brick Boston," in *History* (New York: Farrar, Straus and Giroux, 1973), 205.

34 Paul Elman, "Robert Lowell, Death of an Elfking," *Christian Century*, November 16, 1977.

35 Cheryl Walker, *God and Elizabeth Bishop: Meditations on Religion and Poetry* (New York: Palgrave Macmillan, 2001).

36 Kathleen Spivack, "Short Stories," in *Swimmer in the Spreading Dawn* (Boston: Applewood Books, 1981), 21.

37 Frank Bidart, "California Plush," in *Golden State* (New York: Doubleday, 1973), 11.

38 Robert Lowell, *Robert Lowell: Collected Poems*, ed. Frank Bidart and David Gewanter (New York: Farrar, Straus and Giroux, 2003).

39 Lowell quoted in Hamilton, "Interview."

40 Theodore Roethke, "The Weed Puller," in *The Lost Son and Other Poems* (New York: Doubleday, 1966), 39.

41 Kathleen Spivack, "Paraphrase."

42 Stanley Kunitz, "My Mother's Pears," in *Stanley Kunitz: The Collected Poems* (New York: W. W. Norton, 2000), 249.

43 Denise Levertov, "Hypocrite Women," in *Poems 1960–1967* (New York: New Directions, 1966).

44 John Malcolm Brinnin, *Dylan Thomas in America: An Intimate Journal* (Boston: Little Brown, 1955).

45 Thomas Travisano, *Words in Air* (New York: Farrar, Straus and Giroux, 2008), 303.

46 James Atlas, "Robert Lowell in Cambridge: Lord Weary," *Atlantic Monthly* 250 (July 1982), 56.

47 John Berryman, *The Dream Songs* (New York: Farrar, Straus and Giroux, 1969).

48 Robert Lowell, "For Ann Adden I. 1958," in *Robert Lowell: Collected Poems,* ed. Frank Bidart and David Gewanter (New York: Farrar, Straus and Giroux, 2003), 535.

49 Anne Sexton, "Ballad of the Lonely Masturbator," in *Love Poems* (Boston: Houghton Mifflin, 1969), 33.

50 Doris Lessing, *The Golden Notebook* (London: Michael Joseph, 1962).

51 Robert Lowell, "After Enjoying Six or Seven Essays on Me," special Robert Lowell issue, *Salmagundi* 37 (Spring 1977): 112.

52 Robert Lowell, *Notebook 1967–68* (New York: Farrar, Straus and Giroux, 1969), 132.

53 Ibid., 133.

54 Ibid., 140.

55 Ibid., 140.

56 Robert Lowell, "Unwanted," in *Day by Day* (New York: Farrar, Straus and Giroux, 1977), 121–24.

57 Robert Lowell, "Elizabeth," in *For Lizzie and Harriet* (New York: Farrar, Straus and Giroux, 1973), 14.

58 Allen Ginsberg, *Howl and Other Poems* (San Francisco: City Lights Books, 1956).

59 Linda Charlton, "Voznesensky's Elegy at Lowell's Grave," *New York Times,* October 15, 1977.

60 Anne Sexton, *The Awful Rowing toward God* (Boston: Houghton Mifflin, 1975).

Selected Bibliography

Ackerman, Diane, and Enid Mark. *About Sylvia.* Wallingford, PA: ELM Press, 1996.

Alexander, Paul. *Ariel Ascending: Writings about Sylvia Plath.* New York: Harper and Row, 1985.

———. *Rough Magic: A Biography of Sylvia Plath.* Cambridge, MA: Da Capo Press, 2003.

Alvarez, A[lfred]. *The Savage God: A Study of Suicide.* New York: Random House, 1972.

Atlas, James. *Delmore Schwartz: The Life of an American Poet.* New York: Farrar, Straus and Giroux, 1977.

———. *How They See Us: Meditations on America.* New York: Atlas and Co., 2009.

———. *My Life in the Middle Ages: A Survivor's Tale.* New York: HarperCollins, 2005.

Axelrod, Steven Gould, ed. *The Critical Response to Robert Lowell.* Westport, CT: Greenwood Press, 1999.

———. *Robert Lowell: Life and Art.* Princeton, NJ: Princeton University Press, 1978.

———. *Sylvia Plath: The Wound and the Cure of Words.* Baltimore: Johns Hopkins University Press, 1990.

Axelrod, Steven Gould, and Helen Deese. *Robert Lowell: Essays on the Poetry.* Cambridge: Cambridge University Press, 1986.

———. *Robert Lowell: A Reference Guide.* Boston: G. K. Hall, 1982.

Barry, Sandra. *Elizabeth Bishop: An Archival Guide to Her Life in Nova Scotia.* Hantsport, Nova Scotia: Lancelot Press, 1996.

Baumel, Judith. *The Kangaroo Girl.* New York: GenPop Books, 2011.

Beam, Alex. "Mad Poets Society." *Atlantic Monthly* 288, no. 1 (July–August 2001).

Bidart, Frank. *Watching the Spring Festival.* New York: Farrar, Straus and Giroux, 2008.

Bingley, Xandra Bertie. *May and Mrs. Fish: Country Memories of Wartime.* New York: Harper Perennial, 2007.

Birkerts, Sven, and Askold Melnyczuk, eds. Issue titled "Mentors and Tormentors." *AGNI* (Boston) 26 (1988).

Bishop, Elizabeth. *The Collected Prose.* New York: Farrar, Straus and Giroux, 1984.

———. *The Complete Poems 1927–1979.* New York: Farrar, Straus and Giroux, 1983.

———. *Poems, Prose and Letters.* Edited by Robert Giroux and Lloyd Schwartz. New York: Library of America, 2008.

———. *Prose.* Edited by Lloyd Schwartz. New York: Farrar, Straus and Giroux, 2011.

Blackwood, Caroline. *The Last of the Duchess.* London: Macmillan, 1995.

Bloom, Harold, ed. *Elizabeth Bishop: Modern Critical Views.* New York: Chelsea House, 1985.

Boyers, Robert, ed. *Contemporary Poetry in America*. New York: Schocken, 1974.

Brower, Reuben A. *Twentieth-Century Literature in Retrospect*. Cambridge, MA: Harvard University Press, 1971.

Butscher, Edward. *Sylvia Plath: Method and Madness*. New York: Seabury Press, 1976.

———. *Sylvia Plath: The Woman and the Work*. New York: Dodd, Mead, 1977.

Colburn, Steven E. *No Evil Star: Selected Essays, Interviews and Prose*. Ann Arbor: University of Michigan Press, 1985.

Corbett, William. *Literary New England: A History and Guide*. London: Faber and Faber, 1993.

———. *The Whalen Poem*. Brooklyn, NY: Hanging Loose Press, 2011.

Costello, Bonnie. *Elizabeth Bishop: Questions of Mastery*. Cambridge, MA: Harvard University Press, 1991.

Davison, Peter. *The Fading Smile: Poets in Boston, from Robert Frost to Robert Lowell to Sylvia Plath, 1955–1960*. New York: Knopf, 1994.

Dictionary of Literary Biography. Vol. 5: *American Poets since World War II*. Detroit: Gale, 1980.

Doreski, William. *Robert Lowell's Shifting Colors: The Poetics of the Public and the Personal*. Athens: Ohio University Press, 1999.

Drucker, Doris. *Invent Radium or I'll Pull Your Hair: A Memoir*. Chicago: University of Chicago Press, 2004.

Drucker, Peter. *Adventures of a Bystander* (autobiography). New York: Harper and Row, 1979.

Elman, Paul. "Robert Lowell: Death of an Elfking." *Christian Century*, November 16, 1977.

Engle, Paul, and Joseph Langland. *Poet's Choice*. New York: Dial, 1962.

Ferguson, Suzanne, ed. *Jarrell, Bishop, Lowell, and Co.: Middle-Generation Poets in Context*. Knoxville: University of Tennessee Press, 2003.

Fountain, Gary, and Peter Brazeau. *Remembering Elizabeth Bishop: An Oral Biography*. Amherst: University of Massachusetts Press, 1994.

Galassi, Jonathan. *Left-Handed*. New York: Alfred A. Knopf, 2012.

———. *North Street: Poems*. New York: HarperCollins, 2000.

George, Diana Hume. *Oedipus Anne: The Poetry of Anne Sexton*. Urbana: University of Illinois Press, 1987.

———, ed. *Sexton: Selected Criticism*. Urbana: University of Illinois Press, 1988.

Gilbert, Sandra, and Susan Gubar. *A Guide to "The Norton Anthology of Literature by Women": The Tradition in English*. New York: W. W. Norton, 1985; rev. 2nd ed., 1996.

———. *No Man's Land: The Place of the Woman Writer in the Twentieth Century*. Volume 1, *The War of the Words*. New Haven, CT: Yale University Press, 1988.

———. *No Man's Land: The Place of the Woman Writer in the Twentieth Century.*
Volume 2, *Sexchanges.* New Haven, CT: Yale University Press, 1989.

Ginsberg, Allen. *Collected Poems 1947–1997.* Reprint. New York: HarperCollins,
2007.

Goldensohn, Lorrie. *Elizabeth Bishop: The Biography of a Poet.* New York: Columbia
University Press, 1991.

Gordon, Jaimy, and Ray Ragosta, eds. *Pourboire 16: Peter Kaplan's Book.* Providence,
RI: Pourboire Press, 1978.

Gowrie, Grey. *The Domino Hymn: Poems from Harefield.* Mayfield, UK: Agenda
Editions/Greville Press, 2006.

———. *Third Day: New and Selected Poems.* London: Carcanet, 2008.

Hall, Caroline King Barnard. *Sylvia Plath, Revised.* New York: Twayne, 1998.

Hamilton, Ian. *Keepers of the Flame: Literary Estates and the Rise of Biography from
Shakespeare to Plath.* Boston: Faber and Faber, 1994.

———. "Interview: Lowell in England." *Review* (London) 26 (1971): 10–29.

———. *Robert Lowell: A Biography.* New York: Random House, 1982.

Hardwick, Elizabeth. *The New York Stories of Elizabeth Hardwick.* New York: New
York Review of Books, 2010.

Hayes, Alice Judson Ryerson. *Journal of the Lake: Excerpts from a Seventieth Year.*
Cambridge, UK: Open Books, 1997.

———. *Sex in the Ancient World and Other Stories.* Lake Forest, IL: Privately
published, 2007.

Hayman, Ronald. *The Death and Life of Sylvia Plath.* Secaucus, NJ: Carol Publishing
Group, 1991.

Howe, Fanny. *Come and See: Poems.* Minneapolis: Graywolf Press, 2011.

Hughes, Ted. *Birthday Letters.* New York: Farrar, Straus and Giroux, 1998.

Junkins, Donald. *Crossing by Ferry.* Amherst: University of Massachusetts Press,
1978.

———. *Late at Night in the Rowboat.* Sandpoint, ID: Lost Horse Press, 2005.

Kalstone, David. *Becoming a Poet: Elizabeth Bishop with Marianne Moore and Robert
Lowell.* Edited, with a preface, by Robert Hemenway. New York: Farrar, Straus
and Giroux, 1989; London: Hogarth Press, 1989.

———. *Five Temperaments: Elizabeth Bishop, Robert Lowell, James Merrill, Adrienne
Rich, John Ashbery.* New York: Oxford University Press, 1977.

Kendall, Tim. *Sylvia Plath: A Critical Study.* London: Faber and Faber, 2001.

Kirsch, Adam. *The Wounded Surgeon: Confession and Transformation in Six American
Poets; Robert Lowell, Elizabeth Bishop, John Berryman, Randall Jarrell, Delmore
Schwartz, and Sylvia Plath.* New York: W. W. Norton, 2005.

Kroll, Judith. *Chapters in a Mythology: The Poetry of Sylvia Plath.* Stroud, UK:
Sutton, 2007.

Kunitz, Stanley. *The Collected Poems of Stanley Kunitz*. New York: W. W. Norton, 2000.

———. *The Wild Braid: A Poet Reflects on a Century in the Garden*. New York: W. W. Norton, 2005.

Lowell, Robert. "After Enjoying Six or Seven Essays on Me," special Robert Lowell issue, edited by Robert Boyers, *Salmagundi* 37 (Spring 1977).

———. *Collected Poems*. Edited by Frank Bidart and David Gewanter, New York: Farrar, Straus, and Giroux, 2003.

———. *Selected Poems*. New York: Farrar, Straus and Giroux, 1976.

MacMahon, Candace W. *Elizabeth Bishop: A Bibliography 1927–1979*. Charlottesville: University Press of Virginia, 1980.

Malcolm, Janet. *The Silent Woman: Sylvia Plath and Ted Hughes*. New York: Knopf, 1994.

Mariani, Paul. *Lost Puritan: A Life of Robert Lowell*. New York: W. W. Norton, 1994.

Mazzaro, Jerome. *The Poetic Themes of Robert Lowell*. Ann Arbor: University of Michigan Press, 1965.

McClatchy, J. D., ed. *Anne Sexton: The Artist and Her Critics*. Bloomington: Indiana University Press, 1978.

McGowan, Philip. *Anne Sexton and Middle Generation Poetry: The Geography of Grief*. Westport, CT: Praeger, 2004.

Menides, Laura Jehn. *The Use of the Past in Modern American Poetry: Eliot, Pound, Williams, Crane, Berryman, Olson, Lowell*. New York: New York University Press, 1978.

Menides, Laura Jehn, and Angela G. Dorenkamp, eds. *In Worcester, Massachusetts: Essays on Elizabeth Bishop, from the 1997 Elizabeth Bishop Conference at WPI*. New York: Peter Lang, 1999.

Menides, Laura Jehn, and Georgia Menides. *Of Daughters and Grasshoppers: Poems*. Kali Mera Press, 2011.

Merrin, Jeredith. *An Enabling Humility: Marianne Moore, Elizabeth Bishop, and the Uses of Tradition*. New Brunswick, NJ: Rutgers University Press, 1990.

Meyers, Jeffrey. *Manic Power: Robert Lowell and His Circle*. New York: Arbor House, 1987.

———, ed. *Robert Lowell: Interviews and Memoirs*. Ann Arbor: University of Michigan Press, 1988.

Middlebrook, Diane Wood. *Anne Sexton: A Biography*. Boston: Houghton Mifflin, 1991.

———. *Her Husband: Hughes and Plath—a Marriage*. New York: Viking, 2003.

Millier, Brett Candlish. *Elizabeth Bishop: Life and the Memory of It*. Berkeley: University of California Press, 1993.

———. "Elusive Mastery: The Drafts of Elizabeth Bishop's 'One Art.'" In

Elizabeth Bishop: The Geography of Gender, edited by Marilyn May Lombardi. Charlottesville: University Press of Virginia, 1993.

———. *Flawed Light: American Women Poets and Alcohol*. Urbana: University of Illinois Press, 2009.

Molesworth, Charles. *The Fierce Embrace: A Study of Contemporary American Poetry*. Columbia: University of Missouri Press, 1979.

Monteiro, George, ed. *Conversations with Elizabeth Bishop*. Literary Conversations Series. Jackson: University of Mississippi Press, 1996.

Moore, Harry T., ed. *Selected Letters of Rainer Maria Rilke*. Garden City, NY: Anchor Books, 1960.

Moses, Kate. *Wintering: A Novel of Sylvia Plath*. New York: St. Martin's Press, 2003.

Newman, Charles. *The Art of Sylvia Plath: A Symposium*. Bloomington: Indiana University Press, 1970.

Oberg, Arthur. *Modern American Lyric: Lowell, Berryman, Creeley, and Plath*. New Brunswick, NJ: Rutgers University Press, 1978.

Oliveira, Carmen L. *Flores raras e banalíssimas: A historia de Lota de Macedo Soares e Elizabeth Bishop*. Rio de Janeiro: Rocco, 1995.

Orr, Peter. *The Poet Speaks: Interviews with Contemporary Poets Conducted by Hilary Morrish, Peter Orr, John Press and Ian Scott-Kilvert*. London: Routledge and Kegan Paul, 1996.

Packard, William, ed. *The Craft of Poetry*. Garden City, NY: Doubleday, 1974.

Parini, Jay, and Brett Candlish Millier. *The Columbia History of American Poetry*. New York: Columbia University Press, 1993.

Perloff, Marjorie. *The Poetic Art of Robert Lowell*. Ithaca, NY: Cornell University Press, 1973.

Phillips, Robert S. *The Confessional Poets*. Carbondale: Southern Illinois University Press, 1973.

Pinsky, Robert. *Democracy, Culture, and the Voice of Poetry*. Princeton, NJ: Princeton University Press, 2002.

———. *Selected Poems*. New York: Macmillan, 2011.

———. *The Situation of Poetry: Contemporary Poetry and Its Traditions*. Princeton, NJ: Princeton University Press, 1977.

———. *The Sounds of Poetry: A Brief Guide*. New York: Farrar, Straus, 1998.

Plath, Sylvia. *The Collected Poems: Sylvia Plath*. New York: Harper and Row, 1981.

———. *Letters Home*. Selected and edited by Aurelia Plath. New York: Harper and Row, 1975.

———. *The Unabridged Journals of Sylvia Plath*. Edited by Karen V. Kukil. London: Faber and Faber, 2000.

Rich, Adrienne. *Dark Fields of the Republic, 1991–1995*. New York: W. W. Norton, 1995.

———. *On Lies, Secrets, and Silence: Selected Prose, 1966–1978*. New York, W. W. Norton, 1979.

———. *Tonight No Poetry Will Serve: Poems 2007–2010*. New York: W. W. Norton, 2011.

Roman, Camille. *Elizabeth Bishop and Her Art*. Ann Arbor: University of Michigan Press, 1983.

———. *Elizabeth Bishop's World War II–Cold War View*. New York: Palgrave/St. Martin's, 2001.

Rosenblatt, Roger. *Coming Apart: A Memoir of the Harvard Wars of 1969*. Boston: Little, Brown, 1997.

———. *Unless It Moves the Human Heart*. New York: HarperCollins, 2011.

Rosenthal, M. L., *The Modern Poets*. New York: Oxford University Press, 1960.

Rudman, Mark. *Robert Lowell, an Introduction to the Poetry*. New York: Columbia University Press, 1983.

Sandy, Stephen. *Weathers Permitting*. Baton Rouge: Louisiana State University Press, 2005.

Schwartz, Lloyd. *Elizabeth Bishop and Her Art*. Chicago: University of Chicago Press, 1983.

———, ed. *Elizabeth Bishop: Prose*. New York: Farrar, Straus and Giroux, 2011.

Schwartz, Lloyd, and Sybil P. Estess, eds. *Under Discussion: Elizabeth Bishop and Her Art*. Ann Arbor: University of Michigan Press, 1983.

Sexton, Anne. *Anne Sexton: A Self-Portrait in Letters*. Edited by Linda Gray Sexton and Lois Ames. Boston: Houghton Mifflin, 1977.

———. *The Complete Poems*. Boston: Houghton Mifflin, 1981.

———. *Words for Dr. Y.: Uncollected Poems with Three Stories*. Boston: Houghton Mifflin, 1978.

Spivack, Kathleen. "Anne Sexton." *American Poetry Review* (1975).

———. "Anne Sexton." *Croton Review* (1988).

———. "Anne Sexton." *Poets On* (1988).

———. "Anne Sexton." In *Critical Essays on Sylvia Plath*, edited by Linda Wagner-Martin. Boston: G. K. Hall, 1984.

———. "A. Sexton, S. Plath, A. Rich, E. Bishop." *Thirteenth Moon* (1989).

———. "Conceal/Reveal: The Poetry of Elizabeth Bishop." *Massachusetts Review* (2005).

———. "Elizabeth Bishop." *Worcester Review* (1999).

———. "Fusion and Loss in Elizabeth Bishop's Poetry." *Resonances* (2004).

———. "The Garden in the Life and Late Work of Stanley Kunitz." *Connecticut Review* (2012).

———. *A History of Yearning*. New York: Sow's Ear Chapbook Competition Winner, 2010.

———. "Journal Entries." In *Ariadne's Thread*, edited by Lynn Lifshin. New York: Harper and Row, 1982.

———. "Lear in Boston: Robert Lowell as Teacher and Friend." *Ironwood* (1985).

———. *Moments of Past Happiness*. Boston: Earthwinds Edition/Grolier Poetry Workshop, 2007.

———. "Notes of a Witness." *Worcester Review* (2010).

———. "Ping-Pong with Elizabeth Bishop." Poetry Society of America. *PSA Bulletin* (1979).

———. "Robert Lowell." *Antioch Review* (1985).

———. "Robert Lowell." *Agni* (Boston) 26 (1988).

———. "Robert Lowell: A Memoir." In *Robert Lowell: Interviews and Memoirs*, edited by Jeffrey Meyers. Ann Arbor: University of Michigan Press, 1988.

———. "Sharers of the Heart: Anne Sexton." *Boston Globe Magazine*, August 1981.

———. "Sylvia Plath." *Frank* (magazine, Paris), 1999.

———. "Sylvia Plath: Oh vase of acid, it is love you are full of . . ." *Virginia Quarterly* (2005).

———. "Talents in a Teapot: Robert Lowell, Elizabeth Bishop, and Boston." *Confrontation* 109 (Spring 2011).

———. "Tales of the Grolier Bookshop." Lamont Library, Harvard University, mid-'60s.

———. "Theodore Roethke." *New Letters* (1989).

Steinberg, Peter K. *Sylvia Plath*. New York: Chelsea House, 2004.

Steiner, Nancy Hunter. *A Closer Look at Ariel: A Memory of Sylvia Plath*. Introduction by George Stade. New York: Harper's Magazine Press, 1973.

Stevenson, Anne. *Bitter Fame: A Life of Sylvia Plath*. Boston: Houghton Mifflin, 1989.

———. *Elizabeth Bishop*. New York: Twayne, 1966.

———. *Five Looks at Elizabeth Bishop*. London: Bellew, 1998.

Tillinghast, Richard. "Robert Lowell in the Sixties." *Harvard Advocate*, 1979.

———. *Robert Lowell's Life and Work: Damaged Grandeur*. Ann Arbor: University of Michigan Press, 1995.

———. *Selected Poems*. Dublin: Dedalus Press, 2009.

Travisano, Thomas J. *Elizabeth Bishop: Her Artistic Development*. Charlottesville: University of Virginia Press, 1988.

———. *Midcentury Quartet: Bishop, Lowell, Jarrell, Berryman and the Making of a Postmodern Aesthetic*. Charlottesville: University of Virginia Press, 1999.

Travisano, Thomas, and Saskia Hamilton, eds. *Words in Air: The Complete Correspondence between Elizabeth Bishop and Robert Lowell*. New York: Farrar, Straus and Giroux, 2008.

Vendler, Helen Hennessy. *Anthology of Contemporary American Poetry*. New York: I. B. Tauris, 2003.

———. *Coming of Age as a Poet: Milton, Keats, Eliot, Plath.* Cambridge, MA: Harvard University Press, 2003.

———. *Last Looks, Last Books: Stevens, Plath, Lowell, Bishop, Merrill.* Princeton, NJ: Princeton University Press, 2010.

———. *Part of Nature, Part of Us: Modern American Poets.* Cambridge, MA: Harvard University Press, 1980.

Voznesensky, Andrei. *An Arrow in the Wall: Selected Poetry and Prose.* Edited by William Jay Smith and F. D. Reeve. Poems translated by W. H. Auden et al. Prose translated by Antonina W. Bouis. New York: Henry Holt, 1988.

Wagner, Erica. *Ariel's Gift: Ted Hughes, Sylvia Plath and the Story of the Birthday Letters.* New York: W. W. Norton, 2001.

Wagner-Martin, Linda. *The Bell Jar: A Novel of the Fifties.* Twayne's Masterwork Studies, no. 98. New York: Twayne, 1992.

———, ed. *Critical Essays on Sylvia Plath.* Critical Essays on American Literature. Boston: G. K. Hall, 1984.

———. *Sylvia Plath: A Biography.* New York: Simon and Schuster, 1987.

———. *Sylvia Plath: A Literary Life.* London: Macmillan, 1999. 2nd ed. Houndmills, Basingstoke, Hampshire: Palgrave Macmillan, 2003.

Whitman, Ruth. *Laughing Gas: Poems, New and Selected, 1963–1990.* Detroit: Wayne State University Press, 1990.

Williamson, Alan. *Almost a Girl: Male Writers and Female Identification.* Charlottesville: University of Virginia Press, 2001.

———. *Eloquence and Mere Life: Essays on the Art of Poetry.* Ann Arbor: University of Michigan Press, 1995.

———. *The Pattern More Complicated: New and Selected Poems.* Chicago: University of Chicago Press, 2004.

———. *Pity the Monsters: The Political Vision of Robert Lowell.* New Haven, CT: Yale University Press, 1974.

———. "Robert Lowell: A Reminiscence." *Harvard Advocate,* November 1979.

Wylie, Diana E. *Elizabeth Bishop and Howard Nemerov: A Reference Guide.* Boston: G. K. Hall, 1983.

Yenser, Stephen. *Circle to Circle: The Poetry of Robert Lowell.* Berkeley: University of California Press, 1975.

Credits

Parts of this work first appeared in the following publications,
all by Kathleen Spivack:

"Anne Sexton," *American Poetry Review* (1975).
"Ping Pong with Elizabeth Bishop." Memorial service, Poetry Society of
 America, New York, 1979.
"Sharers of the Heart: Anne Sexton," *Boston Globe Magazine*, August 1981.
"Journal Entries," in *Ariadne's Thread*, ed. Lynn Lifshin (New York: Harper
 and Row, 1982).
"Lear in Boston: Robert Lowell as Teacher and Friend," *Ironwood* (1985).
"Robert Lowell," *Antioch Review* (1985).
"Anne Sexton," *Croton Review* (1988).
"Robert Lowell," *Agni* (Boston) 26 (1988).
"Robert Lowell: A Memoir," in *Robert Lowell: Interviews and Memoirs*, ed.
 Jeffrey Meyers (Ann Arbor: University of Michigan Press, 1988).
"A. Sexton, S. Plath, A. Rich, E. Bishop," *Thirteenth Moon* (1989).
"Elizabeth Bishop," *Worcester Review* (1999).
"Sylva Plath," *Frank* (magazine, Paris), 1999.
"Fusion/Loss in Elizabeth Bishop's Poetry," *Resonances* (2004).
"Conceal/Reveal: Poetry of Elizabeth Bishop," *Massachusetts Review* (2005).
"Sylvia Plath," *Virginia Quarterly* (2005).
"Notes of a Witness," *Worcester Review* (2010).
"Talents in a Teapot: Robert Lowell, Elizabeth Bishop, and Boston,"
 Confrontation 109 (Spring 2011).
"Stanley Kunitz," *Connecticut Review* (2012).

All quotations in the text are used by kind permission of their authors
or fall under the auspices of fair use.

About the Author

Kathleen Spivack is the author of *Flying Inland,*
The Jane Poems, Swimmer in the Spreading Dawn,
The Honeymoon (short stories), *The Beds We*
Lie In (poems), *Moments of Past Happiness,*
and *A History of Yearning.* She received an
Allen Ginsberg Poetry Award in 2010, and
her work has been honored by Discover, the
National Endowment for the Arts, the Howard
Foundation, the Massachusetts Council for the
Arts, the Bunting Institute, Carpe Articulum,
and the Los Angeles, New York, and London
book festivals. Appearing in journals, magazines,
and anthologies, her work has received short-
story, American poetry, and best-essay awards.
She teaches in the French university system and
in the Boston area.